WxI

SWEET SONGS OF ZION

There, where no troubles distraction can bring,
We the sweet anthems of Zion sing.

John Mason Neale, p. 191

Songs of Zion to Cheer and Guide Pilgrims on
Their Way to the New Jerusalem.

Robert Murray McCheyne, p. 220

SWEET SONGS OF ZION

Selected Radio Talks

JOHN BETJEMAN

Edited and introduced by

STEPHEN GAMES

HODDER &
STOUGHTON

Acknowledgements, Introduction, Index and Selection
© Stephen Games 2007
Broadcasts © The Estate of John Betjeman 2007

First published in Great Britain in 2007

The rights of the author and editor have been asserted in accordance with the
Copyright, Designs and Patents Act 1988.

I

British Library Cataloguing in Publication Data
A record for this book is available from the British Library

ISBN 978 0340 943762

Typeset in Bembo and Perpetua by Avon DataSet Ltd,
Bidford on Avon, Warwickshire

Printed and bound in Great Britain by Clays Ltd, St Ives plc

The paper used in this book is a natural recyclable product made from wood grown
in sustainable forests. The hard-cover board is recycled.

Hodder & Stoughton
A Division of Hodder Headline Ltd
338 Euston Road
London NW1 3BH
www.madaboutbooks.com

CONTENTS

Preface   vii
Introduction   I

Isaac Watts   21
William Cowper and Augustus Toplady   31
The Wesleys   43
Reginald Heber and James Montgomery   57
Hymns of the Mission   67
Welsh Hymns   77
Hymns of the Oxford Movement   87
Mrs C. F. Alexander and Other Women   101
Keble and Other Tractarians   113
Victorians   123
More Victorians   137
Seventeenth-Century Hymn-Writers   147
Some Poets Laureate   159
The Yattendon Hymnal   169
American Hymn-Writers   179
More Translations   189
More Hymns of the Eighteenth Century   199
Four Rectors   211
Scottish Hymn-Writers   219
Some Bishops   229
From the Cathedral   239

Some Nonconformists   249
Songs of Old   257
From the Chief Musicians   267
From the Organ Loft   277
From Germany   289
From the Rev. J. B. Dykes   299
English Traditional Melodies   309

Index of Hymns   317
Index of Hymn-writers   322
Index of Composers   324
Index of Collections   325

PREFACE

There are vast numbers of alternative versions of hymns, with dozens of accreted verses and disparate punctuations. I do not claim that the versions quoted here are either definitive or historically accurate, but I have tried to help the reader by providing as comprehensive a view as possible of all the hymns that Betjeman mentions.

Several people and institutions have helped to make this book possible. The material itself came from the Special Collections Library of the University of Victoria in British Columbia, where Betjeman's archive resides. I have received endless help from the staff there, most notably Terry Tuey who has worked conscientiously and promptly, both at long distance and during my visit to the library during 2006. I am grateful too to Jeff Walden of the BBC Written Archives Centre in Caversham, Berkshire, who has assisted me with many inquiries. I should like to thank the staff of the British Library at the Newspaper Reading Rooms in Colindale, northwest London. I am indebted to John Heald and Peter Gammond of the John Betjeman Society, for their friendly encouragement and for their invaluable check-list of Betjeman's writings. My introduction would have been impoverished were it not for the fascinating contribution made to it by Rev. David Winter, the original BBC producer of *Sweet Songs of Zion*, with whom I have conversed by phone and email over the last two years and who allowed me to quote from his autobiography, *Winter's Tale* (Lion Publishing, 2001). I am also very grateful to Rev. Angela Tilby, his co-producer on the first series, who allowed me to quote from her correspondence about the series with Bracha Nemeth of the BBC.

As far as the production of this book is concerned, my thanks also go to: the executors of the Betjeman estate for approving the use of the material and specifically to Candida Lycett Green, Betjeman's daughter; to Clare Alexander of Gillon Aitken, who acts for the estate; to Judith Longman, my editor at Hodder & Stoughton, for commissioning the book and offering valuable guidance when I needed it; to the rest of the Hodder & Stoughton team including Amy Donovan, Jonathan Price and Cecilia Moore; to my beloved wife for her involvement behind the scenes and for providing me, during the editing of this book, with my first child; and to Sophie Georgette, for allowing me time to write in between feeding her, playing with her and changing her nappies.

Stephen Games
Muswell Hill
2007

INTRODUCTION

S*weet Songs of Zion* is the third of three Betjeman anthologies to appear around Betjeman's centenary year and in some ways the most mysterious. The first anthology, *Trains and Buttered Toast*, brought the public the best of Betjeman's forgotten radio talks from the 1930s to the 1950s – talks that, in the words of Geoffrey Grigson, had first established the cult of Betjemania in broadcasting. The second, *Tennis Whites and Teacakes*, looked at the status of Betjeman's prose in relation to his poetry and revealed his ambivalence about the England of his own age. Now comes *Sweet Songs of Zion* – a lost love-song to the Church and a valedictory as he approached the end of his extraordinary life.

Sweet Songs consists of twenty-eight radio broadcasts that Betjeman was involved with and that went out on Sunday evenings during the mid-1970s. Produced in what had been an unhappy period in his life, the programmes stand out as an ambitious and vigorous undertaking, in stark contrast to the listlessness of his late poetry. The first series in 1975 was so well received by listeners that the BBC eagerly commissioned a second series in 1976 and a third in 1978, yet the programmes seem to have gone unnoticed or uncommented on by contemporary and posthumous critics. There is no reference to them in any recent writings. No recordings appear to have survived. The BBC's card index system of his scripts does not include them. Even Betjeman seems to have said nothing about them. And yet they were perhaps the most important broadcasting project of his life.

Sweet Songs of Zion is a history of hymn-writers – that extra-ordinary army of priests, poets, missionaries and monks whose work once brought people together in thrilling choruses of shared worship. We take the hymns they wrote for granted today: three centuries ago they were a novel proposition; the best went on to challenge the life and times of the nation. In the seventeenth century, a time of widespread religious persecution, 'singing hymns was regarded as a popish aberration, putting "human words" on a par with Holy Writ', Betjeman explained in his introduction to the *Sweet Songs* series. The idea that a hymn was acceptable and necessary had to be invented and it was Isaac Watts – born in 1674 and the subject of the first programme – who invented it. 'Even the dissenters confined themselves strictly to the Psalter, albeit in a metrical version,' Betjeman continued,

> and heavy going it was, as young Watts himself is reported to have observed to his father on the way home one Sunday afternoon from the Southampton chapel where they worshipped. 'Then give us something better, young man!' said his father, and was probably shocked to discover the following Sunday that Isaac had brought to chapel with him a brand new hymn, not a paraphrase of a psalm but – horror of horrors! – a hymn of human composition.

Though hymns today can be little more than ritualised incantations, *Sweet Songs of Zion* showed that they were once at the forefront of popular literature and social engineering. In every programme Betjeman highlighted pioneering individualists who had responded creatively to the needs of the church and the community – and had done so persuasively. Isaac Watts's brand new hymn was

> Behold the glory of the Lamb
> Amidst the Father's throne;
> Prepare new honours for his name
> And songs before unknown.

'Very prophetic,' Betjeman had commented 'because the new honours and the songs before unknown poured from Watts's pen for the next fifty years and it is quite safe to assume that tens of millions of people this very day have been singing one or other of them.' Subsequent hymn-writers compounded that achievement.

The development of hymnody is a big subject and one that brings together different ages of the Church, different countries, different circumstances and different branches of the Christian faith. Betjeman seems to have taken part in the series because he wanted to rescue hymns and their culture from being forgotten, just as he had spent his life trying to rescue buildings and places that were at risk. He worked on it at a time when he was becoming physically frail and morbidly depressed (he had just been diagnosed with Parkinson's disease) and was turning down other invitations. He brought joy to the programmes and a profound commitment. Under such circumstances, his silence, and that of others, needs explaining.

To some extent, his own silence is unremarkable. He regarded all his journalistic work and prose as secondary to his poetry and spoke slightingly of commissions as a necessary evil. He also nursed a long-standing grievance with BBC Radio's Talks Department over what he regarded as its insultingly low pay rates and this turned him decisively against the medium that had first nurtured him. He found television, by contrast, ever more irresistible. He preferred watching it – in his later years he was a devotee of *Coronation Street* – and preferred working for it because it brought him bigger audiences, was more glamorous to appear on and enabled him to be less analytical and more poetic.

If the eclipsing of radio explains Betjeman's silence, the silence of others has more to do with the eclipsing of religion. The mainstream church is unpopular in Britain: it surfaces at moments of significance – births, marriages and deaths – but not otherwise. The fact that *Sweet Songs of Zion* was commissioned by the Religious Department of BBC Radio – the Cinderella of the Corporation – and that it was scheduled for Sunday evening's despised 'God slot' meant that it was consigned to a broadcasting black hole. Nor did the Corporation come to its rescue, failing either to preview it or follow it up in its own organs, the *Radio Times* and *The Listener*. It is unsurprising, then, that apart from a brief mention in the *Sunday Telegraph* and an oblique reference in *The Guardian*, it was ignored in the national press. *Sweet Songs* would therefore have been known only to loyal listeners of the station that it went out on – Radio Four – and to those who had seen notices in niche publications such as the *Church Times*, which summarised the first programme and wrote later of 'the high standard set by this entertaining and informative series'.

An additional deterrent was the churchy feel of the programmes, with Betjeman speaking as it were from the pulpit, using C. of E. turns of phrase – especially the vicar's first-person plural ('let's start tonight with a hymn written by St. Francis of Assisi') – and breaking off every few minutes for choral examples. Unless they already enjoyed the tone of church services, listeners might well have found the formula of *Sweet Songs* unappetising.

The series was admittedly religious in feel and was meant to celebrate the Church and its history. But unlike the BBC's flagship religious programme *Songs of Praise*, launched on television fourteen years earlier and hugely popular with Christian viewers, *Sweet Songs of Zion* was sufficiently detached for Betjeman to be able to talk about his subject objectively, or as objectively as he wanted, rather than simply preaching on the Church's behalf. To that extent, the programmes made very good listening. Betjeman's commentary ensured that one did not need to be religious to be drawn in by them; he also provided an exceptional opportunity to step back and consider hymns as historical texts rather than presenting them only in the context of religious ceremony.

In spite of its invisibility, *Sweet Songs* was important to Betjeman – and not just as a piece of broadcasting. It was part of his effort to clear his desk and tidy his affairs as he prepared for death. By the mid-1970s, Betjeman was suffering badly from depression and morbidity: in 1974 he wrote of his harvest being over and of losing hold.[1] His greatest fear was that extinction beckoned and he was desperate for assurance that he would continue in some form after

---

[1] 'The Last Laugh', *A Nip in the Air* (London, 1974).

death, even if that meant continuing in Hell. Through *Sweet Songs of Zion* he was able to review the entire sweep of the Christian faith and identify a range of religious role-models – women, evangelists, Calvinists, bishops – who at different times and for different reasons had found it rational to put their faith in Christianity. The British public, embarrassed by manifestations of spirituality and the inner life, may prefer not to think of the ageing Betjeman enthusing about religion in public in this way, as if it pointed to senility. And maybe he harboured the same reservations. And yet, whatever he might or might not have said to the contrary, *Sweet Songs of Zion* shows that there was much that he was burning to say about Christianity when little else still preoccupied him. That forces us to look at him afresh.

BETJEMAN had always had a difficult relationship with religion. Publicly he was a confessing member of the Church of England; privately he was deeply troubled by what he was required to believe and whether church doctrine had any validity. Religion, therefore, was always an effort for him, no matter how much he wished it otherwise. 'Much as I dislike trying to conform to Christian morality,' he wrote in *The Spectator* in 1954, 'the only practical way to face the dreaded lonely journey into Eternity seems to me the Christian one. I therefore try to believe that Christ was God, made Man, and gives Eternal Life and that I may be confirmed in this belief by clinging to the Sacraments and by prayer.' The idea of faith, though attractive to him, was always a struggle and this is reflected in many of his problems.

He traced his theological difficulties back to his 'hateful' nurse, Maud,

> who smelt of soap
> And forced me to eat chewy bits of fish,
> Thrusting me back to babyhood with threats
> Of nappies, dummies and the feeding bottle.[2]

[2] From *Summoned by Bells*, Chap. 1, 'Before MCMXIV'.

Maud was one of many torments that Betjeman suffered as a child and that continued to haunt him in adulthood. He was also bullied and beaten up by fellow schoolboys, demonised for having what was thought to be a German name during the First World War (spelled 'Betjemann' until he dropped the second 'n' later), mocked by a schoolteacher whom he had trusted and looked down on by adults whom he wanted to impress. Each of these abuses came with its own baggage. What made Maud's cruelty distinct was that its baggage was peculiarly Christian:

> She rubbed my face in messes I had made
> And was the first to tell me about Hell,
> Admitting she was going there herself.[3]

'Sadist and puritan' Betjeman called her in his poem 'NW5 & N6' and in a household where his parents gave him no decisive religious direction,[4] he took his cues from her about 'God's dread will' and the punishment of the wicked ('I caught her terror then. I have it still'[5]). These dark associations were compounded by the sadness that church bells roused in him as a small boy at home, making him turn to his teddy bear for comfort. His negativity even spilled over into his first response to the provocative murkiness of Victorian Gothic:

> A silver blight that made my blood run cold
> Hung on a grey house by the cemetery –
> So that for years I only liked red brick.
> The turrets on the chapel for the dead
> And Holly Village[6] with its prickly roofs

---

[3] Ibid.

[4] They were buried not in a church graveyard but in the family plot in Highgate cemetery, a non-denominational burial ground built as a commercial venture in 1839.

[5] From 'NW5 & N6' (*Cornhill Magazine*, Winter 1957–8). Reprinted in *Tennis Whites and Teacakes*.

[6] A group of highly ornamental mock-Gothic almshouses built in 1865 and commissioned by Lady Burdett-Coutts, heir to the Coutts banking fortune.

Against the sky were terrifying shapes.
'Dong!' went the distant cemetery bell
And chilled for good the east side of the hill
And all things east of me.[7]

This contrasts strongly with his anecdote, in a radio talk in 1946,[8] about the poet and vicar William Lisle Bowles who at the age of seven went missing while the family was en route from its old home in Northamptonshire to the father's new living in Somerset. 'He has strolled away! He is lost!' his mother cried but eventually the boy was found 'very peacefully seated, careless of the crowd around, in delight and wonder, listening to the peal from the old tower, on the ancient steps of this churchyard.' There is a strong sense here of the gap between Betjeman's actual childhood and the childhood he would like to have had.

Christianity failed to redeem itself for Betjeman at Marlborough College, where he was shocked by the sanctimony and ingenuousness of 'the old Marlburian bishop', the school's Visitor, who urged the boys to do nothing that would make their mothers blush but failed to speak out against a scandalous regime of bullying that took place under his very nose and with the staff's – and perhaps his own – connivance. The school chapel was the mainspring and the centre of the boys' lives, said the Bishop; Betjeman found that the constant clanging of chapel bells only opened up in him a sense of 'shivering doom'.

Maud and bells are leitmotifs in Betjeman's writings, serving as metaphors for his obvious discomfort with Christian theology and its promotion of man's existential crisis. Betjeman saw Christianity as offering a choice between horror and salvation but he regarded this as a false choice; he believed in the horror but was not convinced that Christianity correctly described it or that salvation was either real in itself or available to him. Belief, then, was one aspect of his difficulty with religion; the other was practice.

[7] From *Summoned by Bells*, Chap 2, 'The Dawn of Guilt'.
[8] Reprinted in *Tennis Whites and Teacakes*.

Betjeman arrived at Magdalen College, Oxford, in 1925 the atheist that Marlborough had made him and threw himself into the social round, acting as court jester and chameleon to win friends among the university's smart set who would make up for his relative loneliness hitherto. Those who were upper crust inspired him to emulate upper crust manners. Those who were practising homosexuals – and homosexuality, according to the historian A. J. P. Taylor, was the norm at Oxford at the time – inspired him to explore homosexuality. Those who were practising Christians awakened him to Christianity. Eventually he gravitated to Anglo-Catholicism which seemed to satisfy all three tendencies at once but also intensified his religious difficulties.

Among the friends who led him to Anglo-Catholicism was Lord Clonmore (William, otherwise 'Billy', 'Dotty' or 'Cracky' Clonmore, later the Earl of Wicklow). Clonmore was a member of the Anglo-Irish aristocracy and found Betjeman's snobbery about lords amusing. He invited Betjeman several times to his home, Shelton Abbey, in Ireland while they were students and sometimes accompanied him on his architecture crawls round Oxford. Clonmore was also an ordinand at St Stephen's House – known in Oxford as 'Staggers', the Anglican theological college started in 1876 by Anglo-Catholics – and got Betjeman to attend an Anglo-Catholic congress in 1927.[9] Through Clonmore Betjeman met various priest-librarians from Pusey House, Oxford's bastion of Anglo-Catholicism, where he received instruction and where he would worship on Sundays.

Anglo-Catholicism – High Church Anglicanism – was an Oxford nineteenth-century creation aimed at reversing the Church of England's drift towards secularism. Betjeman liked it for its traditionalism and because it seemed to be still essentially Victorian in its forms and concepts. He was also attracted to its obscurantism (its commitment to ideas he regarded as false but in

[9] See *Young Betjeman* by Bevis Hillier (John Murray, 1988).

a good cause), to its lush ceremony[10] and to the experience of male intimacy, spiritual and otherwise. In later life, as Roger Lewis observed in *The Independent* in 2004, Betjeman 'liked to ogle choirboys and bell-ringers and employed defrocked clergymen (who had had "a spot of trouble") as private secretaries. His greatest moment of ecstasy ("I was quite spent") was sex in a punt with a vicar's son.'[11] This was not inconsistent with his behaviour as a student. According to John Bowle, a friend of Betjeman's who went with him to Oxford from Marlborough, Betjeman had written long erotic poems about schoolboys while at Magdalen. One of the poems was called 'Bags in Dorm', he told Bevis Hillier, Betjeman's biographer. 'Another, titled "Going back to Bradfield", was a fantasy about John's sitting opposite a boy on a train and noticing from his luggage labels that he was bound for Bradfield School. In the poem "John seduces the boy into going in his car to Reading – then off into the woods where an indecency takes place." Bowle described both poems as "very indecent and very vivid".'[12] During his brief career as a schoolteacher after Oxford, Betjeman also fetishised boys in his charge, posting an eyelash from a boy called Murrant to his friend Patrick Balfour[13] and sending him some of the fourth form's poems, with the hope that 'although they are to me, I sincerely trust that they will cause you an uplift.'[14] While Betjeman's love of the Church – and particularly its outward forms – was deep and scholarly, there was also a strong erotic element in it, making his attendance at choral evensong and the sight of treble voices in surplices doubly compelling.

[10] In *Summoned by Bells*, Chap. 9, 'The Opening World', Betjeman writes about the 'divine baroque' of Pusey House and of the priest's scandalous 'fiddle-back chasuble in mid-Lent pink'.
[11] From 'Cracks in the Façade' (*The Independent*, 17 December 2004), Roger Lewis's review of Bevis Hillier's *Betjeman: The Bonus of Laughter*.
[12] *Young Betjeman* by Bevis Hillier (John Murray, 1988).
[13] Letter to Balfour, Betjeman Archive, University of Victoria (Undated).
[14] Ibid (10 February 1930).

Betjeman's friend Maurice Bowra's casual gloss on Oxford life was that 'buggery was invented to pass the awkward hour between evensong and cocktails.' Betjeman was far less offhand. He felt that however amusing his 'aesthete' friends were, his attraction to homosexuality had hurt his mother and helped destroy his warm relationship with his father. He also felt that his sexual behaviour had made his father into an angry and violent man, turning his parents' marriage into a battleground and driving his father to take mistresses and involve himself in a long-lived extra-marital affair.[15] In this way, the insecurity and guilt that Maud had planted in Betjeman were not existential abstractions: they were part of a perpetual torment about wanting and failing to be a good son. In time, he would take on a further layer of guilt by re-enacting his father's behaviour, driving away his own son (for different reasons), flirting with whomever he could and living as an adulterer. Under the circumstances, could he possibly be saved?

He found an answer to one of his two challenges – the question of how to practise Christianity – through his own *modus operandi* of compensatory expiation. Since he could not erase his past and lacked the will to improve his present, he would serve God in other ways by doing good works in the hope that these would cleanse his sins. After his marriage in 1933, for example, he entered into the life of whichever local parish he happened to be living in: Uffington, Berkshire, which he and his wife Penelope moved to in 1934; Farnborough, from 1945; Wantage, from 1951; or West Smithfield in the City of London, where he lived part-time and without Penelope from 1954. He served as churchwarden, organised youth fellowship groups, attended church bazaars and visited the terminally ill. If the work was more laborious than rewarding, that proved the authenticity of his efforts. Writing to Evelyn Waugh in 1947, he said

---

[15] Said to be bigamous by Alan Pryce-Jones in his autobiography, *The Bonus of Laughter* (Hamish Hamilton, 1987).

In this village which has no Nonconformist chapel, the only bulwark against complete paganism is the church and its chief supporters are Propeller[16] and me. If we were to desert it, there would be no one to whip up people to attend the services, to run the church organisations, to keep the dilatory and woolly-minded incumbent (who lives in another village) to the celebration of Communion services any Sunday. It is just because it is so disheartening and so difficult and so easy to betray, that we must keep this Christian witness going . . . To desert this wounded and neglected church would be to betray Our Lord.[17]

He added that Waugh was wrong to think that Betjeman regarded religion as 'the source of pleasurable emotion and sensation', which is how Anglo-Catholicism had first attracted him. 'I used to, as an undergraduate, but it has been a stern struggle for the last fourteen years. C. of E. village religion is *no* pleasure.'

Parallel to his sense of obligation to the parish was a sense of obligation to the media. He contributed to religious publications, local and national;[18] he also took part in religious broadcasts – and did so in spite of his fight over low pay with other branches of the BBC. When senior management failed to offer him a large enough contract to stop him defecting to commercial television at its birth in 1955, he went on strike. Yet he happily wrote and recited 'verse monologues' for BBC Bristol's Sunday evening series 'The Faith in the West'[19] at just three guineas a time – a fifth of what he was paid elsewhere for easier work; and when asked in August 1952 if he wanted to go ahead with a religious talk in view of the lower fees that the Religious Broadcasting Department paid, he replied 'O Lord yes. Six guineas is jolly good for what is anyhow a duty.'

---

[16] Betjeman's pet name for his wife, Penelope.
[17] *John Betjeman Letters*: Vol. 1, edited by Candida Lycett Green (Methuen, 1994).
[18] Two articles from his parish magazine in Berkshire, *The Country Churchman*, are reprinted in *Tennis Whites and Teacakes*.
[19] In a strand called 'Poems in the Porch'.

In the winter of 1965–6, he took part in an eighteen-part series called *Britain's Cathedrals and their Music* that Radio's Religious Department had devised; in 1967 he contributed to a second, shorter, series: *Church and Collegiate Choirs*. Both programmes were as lacklustre as their names. A decade later, however, *Sweet Songs of Zion* was a triumph. The idea for the programme – a popular history of English hymns – had come from David Winter, a producer who had joined the Religious Broadcasting team in 1971, in consultation with Michael Mayne, then Head of Religious Programmes. Betjeman, who in 1972 had been made poet laureate, would be brought in to write and present the scripts; his remarks would be punctuated by musical illustrations, mostly recorded specially for the programme by the BBC Singers.[20] According to Angela Tilby, who joined the production team as co-producer, 'John Betjeman was very taken with the idea and worked on the scripts with great relish. He was suffering quite badly from Parkinson's disease at the time and came with a bottle of gin as it helped to steady his voice and his gait.'[21]

For the BBC to commission, and for Betjeman to accept, an eleven-part series showed courage on both sides. As Tilby recalls, he was no longer well physically and depended on alcohol to relieve his depression. Equally worrying, he had already shown the BBC, some twenty-five years earlier, that he could be lazy with his writing if he was not fully engaged in it. To lessen the load on him, Winter devised a strict template for the scripts: short blocks of writing alternating with music. Betjeman responded by incorporating the customs of religious broadcasting into his writing – evenness of tone, standard phraseology, balance and inoffensiveness. The style of *Sweet Songs* is therefore not classic Betjeman: it lacks the lyricism of his best broadcasts. On the other hand, it is a

---

[20] Under the direction of Barry Rose, who was organist and director of music for BBC Religious Programmes as well as sub-organist at St Paul's Cathedral where he went on to direct the music at the wedding of the Prince and Princess of Wales in 1981.

[21] Correspondence with Bracha Nemeth.

dynamic and enthralling series with an unexpected informality all his own.

The series was structured around people – individual writers or groups of writers who had made the largest contribution to England's stock of hymns – rather than around church institutions or prayer books. This allowed Betjeman to be more anecdotal and entertaining than might otherwise have been possible. The programmes were also organised thematically. Winter and Tilby worked out a rough outline of each programme and these were then discussed at script meetings with Betjeman. 'I think the unusual element was Betjeman's own Christian faith, for all its eccentricity, which meant that he had a very good knowledge of the subject and of the likely audience,' recalls Winter.[22] 'A lifelong churchgoer of conservative tastes, he had quite strong views about hymn tunes: he was a particular fan, for example, of J. B. Dykes – see Betjeman's satirical poem "The Dear Old Village" and its lines

> No need to hymn the rich uncurling spring
> For DYKES is nowhere near as good as BING.[23]

And then the story he delivered about Sabine Baring-Gould (author, among other gems, of "Onward Christian Soldiers"), as a bachelor curate, lining up a selection of eligible virgins from the village mill and choosing the most fertile-looking to marry was entirely his: even the researcher knew nothing about it.[24] And I recall a beautiful reflection on the early Greek hymn-writers, where Betjeman evoked a moving picture of hymns being chanted as the evening lights were lit – again, entirely his idea.'[25]

The series employed a researcher, Bernard Martin (Winter's

[22] Correspondence with Stephen Games.
[23] Bing Crosby.
[24] This story was added impromptu and therefore does not appear in the scripts from which this book has been compiled. But it also does not appear in Betjeman's earlier radio talk on Baring-Gould in 1945.
[25] Ditto. See *Winter's Tale* by David Winter (Lion, 2001) for an elaboration of this.

father-in-law) who gathered facts, dates and other supporting information which was then sent to Betjeman. In spite of his growing infirmity, Betjeman would write the scripts himself at home, sometimes reworking the material supplied to him and sometimes writing his own material fresh. 'At each recording session we did three programmes and then sat and discussed the next three,' says Winter:

> We'd send J. B. the research material well ahead and he'd come with a script of his 'links'. We'd go through those in the production office and then the PA would re-type them. Sometimes he would ad lib a bit during the recording, usually something a bit whimsical. When his Parkinson's had got really bad, we would type his scripts from his hand-writing (my PA was brilliant at reading the illegible scrawl) but he was wonderfully articulate after a glass or two of bubbly. We recorded some of the programmes at his house in Chelsea.
>
> Mostly the script planning was done at the end of the previous recording session, as I say, but of course we met at length before the first of these to plan the first few scripts. The recording sessions were often fairly hilarious – J. B. in his most mischievous mood at times. The very last of all recedes into an alcoholic haze: the editing took hours and hours!'[26]

Although the 1975 series of *Sweet Songs* consisted of eleven programmes, Betjeman only presented six of them. The other five were presented by Cliff Morgan, the Welsh rugby international who had gone on to become a popular BBC sports commentator. 'Betjeman was very good on the traditional repertoire of hymns and particularly on those in *New English Hymnal* and *Ancient and Modern*,' remembers Tilby, 'but we felt for the programmes which reflected a strongly chapel or Nonconformist tradition we needed a slightly different approach and Cliff Morgan was asked to present those programmes.'[27] Betjeman was due to go to Canada in May

---

[26] Correspondence with Stephen Games.
[27] Op cit.

1975 and was limited in how much time he could devote to the broadcasts. In spite of this he seems to have worked on Morgan's scripts as well as on his own because Morgan was just recovering from a stroke and had to rest. Winter recalls in particular a programme that Morgan presented on mission halls and the American bible bashers, Ira D. Sankey and Dwight L. Moody, the fifth in the first series. 'The whole idea of a programme about Sankey and Moody was Betjeman's,' he says. 'Cliff Morgan was a "stand-in" presenter and didn't know much about the subject. I don't recall him adding very much to the material, if at all.' By contrast 'Betjeman got quite enthusiastic about Sankey and Moody and showed a considerable knowledge of their output.'[28]

Betjeman began his first talk by setting out why hymns mattered: 'Hymns are the poems of the people,' he said, establishing his belief in the bond between English culture and the Church. He went on to explore the vast richness of this bond – the quantity of hymns that make it up, the different origins of their authors, their often conflicting motivations and the surprising diversity of their messages – marvelling at the Church's capacity to absorb creatively, from whatever source. This universality mirrored Betjeman's understanding of what 'Catholicism' really meant. He rejected nothing: even elements of Christianity that no longer appeal, such as the militarism of the Victorian Church and Bishop Heber's celebration of martyrdom, 'The Son of God goes Forth to War', found a place. *Sweet Songs* became an object lesson in how Christianity's numerous strands – often hostile to each other in their origins – now lived together harmoniously on the hymnbook's pages.

It was in this way that Betjeman came to terms with the second of his religious dilemmas: the challenge of how to believe. His own poems had invariably been loaded with uncertainties and anxieties; in *Sweet Songs of Zion*, by contrast, he produced a kaleidoscope of individuals for whom belief was either unproblematic or who had

[28] Ibid.

overcome difficulties in a way that he had not. Instead of challenging them, however, or raising the spectre of his own concerns, he seems instead to have venerated them, as if discovering that while he could not fully believe himself, he could at least worship God through the belief of others. This does not mean that the programmes were impersonal: one feels strongly his identification with William Cowper, who was beset by 'horror of the great darkness waiting to swallow him up' but was able to sublimate his fears in hymns of evangelical certainty. One feels his envy of the Wesleys, who sensed there was something missing from the Church of England into which they were ordained but managed to fill the gap. One feels his affection for the rural deans and inner-city evangelists and great female hymnists in their Victorian crinolines whose hymns reached out to children in a way he felt he had never experienced and which he held himself incapable of ('It is so hard to be kind to children without being frightening (as I am) or unconsciously cruel' he said in a radio talk in 1950.) One feels this but one also feels a letting go as he immerses himself in the faith of the faithful – the closest he can get to a faith of his own.

His fondness for his hymnists was no affectation. 'He was a particular admirer of Fanny Alexander – or "C. F. Alexander" as the older hymn books preferred to call her,' David Winter recalls.

> I can still remember sitting in a studio while he rhapsodised over the sheer verbal facility of verses such as 'There is a green hill far away' and 'All things bright and beautiful': 'Could you imagine better words than *bright and beautiful* or *wise and wonderful* to capture a child's delight in birds and animals?' One week he produced a first edition of a book of Fanny Alexander's verses – not her hymns, which are universally known, but verses on such topics as father coming home from work or the need to be kind to the village idiot. They were utterly charming, echoes of a different era and a culture totally unlike our own. Eventually he inscribed the book and gave it to my daughter, Becky, which she has to this day.'[29]

[29] From *Winter's Tale*, David Winter (Lion, 2001).

Betjeman's seriousness about hymns did not dampen his trademark naughtiness, Winter adds. 'The listener was invited to share his boyish enthusiasms and fascinations. And there was, of course, that quite wicked sense of humour, made all the more mischievous by the artless way in which the barbs were delivered . . . [He] would chuckle quietly [while recording] and then incorporate yet another jolly anecdote into the narrative . . . The more outlandish the ritual or the hymn, the greater its appeal.'[30] These improvisations are now lost, either because they were not transcribed at the time or because the transcripts were not kept. They are therefore sadly absent from the collection that follows. One that remains in Winter's memory is Betjeman's account, referred to above, of Sabine Baring-Gould's unusual way of choosing a wife. Following this broadcast, the BBC received a letter from a descendant of Baring-Gould's, objecting that the story was a slur on the family's reputation. 'When I put it to the poet laureate that his story was being denounced as a malicious invention,' Winter recalls in his autobiography, 'he thought for a moment, sucked his teeth and then muttered something like, "Well, I'm sure I heard the story somewhere. And anyway, it was not malicious. Surely it was rather charming?"'[31]

Sweet Songs of Zion enjoyed an exceptional mailbag and when a second series was planned for 1976, Betjeman presented all eleven programmes. He also presented six more programmes in the half series that he was called back for two years later and in which the emphasis switched slightly from words to music. The last programme aired on September 6, 1978.

Throughout the three series, Betjeman had not kept secret from the production team his anxieties about Christianity and death. Winter was surprised, nonetheless, to get an appreciative letter from him about Winter's book on the Christian case for an afterlife,[32] which he had found more helpful, apparently, than

[30] Ibid.
[31] Ibid.
[32] *Hereafter* by David Winter (Hodder & Stoughton, 1972).

anything he had previously come across. In retrospect, Winter thinks that Betjeman's reading of his book happened to coincide with a period of relative calmness after several years of misery; he does not believe that Betjeman could really have wanted to deny many of the things he most profoundly believed:

> Certainly our last occasion together was marked more by serenity than obsessive fear. It was the recording of the very last edition of *Sweet Songs of Zion*. We did it in his home in Radnor Walk, Chelsea, with the aid of a BBC engineer and my PA, who at that time was a young woman called Maria . . . of decidedly pre-Raphaelite appearance. At any rate, John was entranced by her, even at one point breaking off in the middle of recording to enthuse that she 'looked like an angel, sitting there on the sofa'. At about 4 o'clock he enquired whether we would all agree that the sun was now below the yard-arm . . . At this point Maria was sent downstairs to bring up a couple of bottles of bubbly from the fridge in the kitchen, which we then consumed with much conviviality. He later revealed that these had been flown in from France that morning.
>
> The rest of the recording session was rather difficult, because although the alcohol seemed to help John's Parkinson's, it didn't help either the engineer in his manual dexterity nor Maria and the producer in keeping tabs on the script. Eventually it was all done, though the consequences of our indulgence required several hours in an editing suite to correct. We bade John Betjeman farewell and I did not see him again.

Sweet Songs of Zion was Betjeman's swansong as a broadcaster. It was also the most expansive of all his broadcasting work. Its twenty-eight programmes covered a huge gamut of material from individual heroes of hymnody (Isaac Watts, William Cowper, Augustus Toplady, John and Charles Wesley, Reginald Heber and James Montgomery) to denominational writers (Tractarians, evangelicals, Nonconformists), writers of different ages (pre-medieval, seventeenth century, eighteenth century, Victorian), writers from different nations (Americans, Germans, Scots, Welsh), church functionaries (rectors, bishops, organists and chief musicians) and women. It was not wholly original – Erik Routley,[33] also a Magdalen man, had been writing extensively about hymnody since 1948 – and it was by no means definitive but it was a valiant effort to focus attention on an aspect of England's heritage so embedded as to be overlooked and unvalued.

Sweet Songs of Zion had come to Betjeman out of the blue and at a time when life looked its bleakest. It allowed him to lay Maud's ghost to rest and to sort out his view of the world after a lifetime of disarray. It gives us a similar opportunity to sort out our view of him. We have thought of him mostly in the context of poetry and architecture; *Sweet Songs* forces us to see him also in the context of faith. He had hinted at this thirty years earlier but was not understood at the time. In a radio talk about Swindon in 1948 he had said 'I would sooner be on my knees within the wooden walls of St Saviour's' – one of Swindon's grimmer churches – 'than leaning elegantly forward in a cushioned pew in an Oxford college chapel – that is to say, if I am to realise there is something beyond this world worth thinking about.'[34] *Sweet Songs* shows that Betjeman had a lot beyond this world to think about; we must be indebted to him for giving us a lot to think about too.

[33] 1917–1982. Betjeman refers to him on p. 176.
[34] 'St Mark's, Swindon' (BBC Home Service, 4 August 1948). Reprinted in *Trains and Buttered Toast*.

ISAAC WATTS

From Series 1

BBC Radio Four
Sunday 6 July 1975
Producers: David Winter and Angela Tilby

• • •

Hymns are the poems of the people. From 'Abide with Me' to 'Onward Christian Soldiers', they provide us with memories of happier, more devout days of Sunday School and school assemblies, of weddings and funerals. They've given phrases to the language: 'change and decay', 'bright and beautiful', 'soft refreshing rain', 'all is safely gathered in', 'fir and foe', 'meek and mild', 'God moves in mysterious ways', and dozens of others.

Even today, when it is assumed that we've all given up religion, millions of people enjoy programmes on the radio and television that consist solely of people singing old familiar tunes. And you can still catch milkmen and bus conductors whistling hymn-tunes (especially if they happen to be West Indians).

We're starting this series on hymns and people who wrote them with the man who's credited with being 'the father of all English hymnody' – Isaac Watts. Before him, singing hymns was regarded as a popish aberration, putting 'human words' on a par with Holy Writ. Even the dissenters confined themselves strictly to the Psalter, albeit in a metrical version, and heavy going it was, as young Watts himself is reported to have observed to his father on the way home one Sunday afternoon from the Southampton chapel where they worshipped. 'Then give us something better, young man!' said his father, and was probably shocked to discover the following Sunday that Isaac had brought to chapel with him a brand new hymn, not a paraphrase of a psalm but – horror of horrors! – a hymn of human composition. This is what Isaac Watts, then twenty-two, had written:

> Behold the glory of the Lamb
> Amidst the Father's throne;
> Prepare new honours for his Name
> And songs before unknown.

Very prophetic, because the new honours and the songs before unknown poured from Watts's pen for the next fifty years and it is quite safe to assume that tens of millions of people this very day have been singing one or other of them. They were very different from what had gone before – different in style, in content, in quality and, very strikingly, in cheerfulness.

> COME, LET US JOIN OUR CHEERFUL SONGS
> With angels round the throne.
> Ten thousand thousand are their tongues,
> But all their joys are one.
>
> 'Worthy the Lamb that died,' they cry,
> 'To be exalted thus!'
> 'Worthy the Lamb,' our hearts reply,
> 'For He was slain for us!'
>
> Jesus is worthy to receive
> Honour and power divine;
> And blessings more than we can give
> Be, Lord, forever Thine.
>
> Let all that dwell above the sky
> And air and earth and seas,
> Conspire to lift Thy glories high
> And speak Thine endless praise!

The whole creation join in one
To bless the sacred Name
Of Him Who sits upon the throne
And to adore the Lamb.

There was a sort of confidence and optimism about Watts, whose Calvinism was tempered with just a hint of the universalism that from his day became a feature of much Nonconformity. He had a splendid, universal vision. The next is one of his greatest hymns.

JESUS SHALL REIGN WHERE'ER THE SUN
Does his successive journeys run;
His kingdom stretch from shore to shore
Till moons shall wax and wane no more.

Behold the islands with their kings
And Europe her best tribute brings;
From north to south the princes meet
To pay their homage at His feet.

There Persia, glorious to behold,
There India shines in eastern gold;
And barb'rous nations at His Word
Submit, and bow and own their Lord.

To Him shall endless prayer be made,
And praises throng to crown His head;
His Name like sweet perfume shall rise
With every morning sacrifice.

People and realms of every tongue
Dwell on His love with sweetest song;
And infant voices shall proclaim
Their early blessings on His Name.

Blessings abound wherever He reigns;
The prisoner leaps to lose his chains;
The weary find eternal rest
And all the sons of want are blessed.

Where He displays His healing power,
Death and the curse are known no more:
In Him the tribes of Adam boast
More blessings than their father lost.

Let every creature rise and bring
Peculiar honours to our King;
Angels descend with songs again
And earth repeat the loud 'Amen!'

Great God, whose universal sway
The known and unknown worlds obey,
Now give the kingdom to Thy Son,
Extend His power, exalt His throne.

The sceptre well becomes His hands;
All heav'n submits to His commands;
His justice shall avenge the poor
And pride and rage prevail no more.

With power He vindicates the just
And treads th'oppressor in the dust:
His worship and His fear shall last
Till hours and years and time be past.

As rain on meadows newly mown
So shall He send his influence down:
His grace on fainting souls distills,
Like heav'nly dew on thirsty hills.

The heathen lands, that lie beneath
The shades of overspreading death,
Revive at His first dawning light;
And deserts blossom at the sight.

The saints shall flourish in His days,
Dressed in the robes of joy and praise;
Peace, like a river, from His throne
Shall flow to nations yet unknown.

There's a rather lovely story about that hymn. When Tonga became Christian, the king of the island (George, in fact) arranged a national act of worship on Whit Sunday 1862 in the open air under the banyan trees, and it's said that many of the five thousand Tongans attending this service broke down and wept as they sang this hymn. 'Jesus shall Reign' was one of Watts's 'Christian Psalms': he got around the prohibition of hymns other than those in the Psalter by asserting that all he was doing was re-expressing the Psalms of David in a New Testament idiom. Indeed, the title of his collection published in 1719 is *The Psalms of David, Imitated in the Language of the New Testament*.

When Isaac Watts was born in 1674, just three hundred years ago, his father, who was a deacon of their chapel, was in prison for his religious beliefs. Isaac himself was barred from Oxford and Cambridge and instead went to what was called a 'Dissenting Academy' in Stoke Newington, London. So you see, his Protestant 'dissent' – his own religious beliefs – cost him a great deal. One of his hymns reflects this experience – one shared, of course, at different times in our history by almost all the branches of the Church in Britain. 'I'm not Ashamed to Own My Lord.'

> I'M NOT ASHAMED TO OWN MY LORD;
> Or to defend His cause,
> Maintain the honour of His Word,
> The glory of His cross.
>
> Jesus, my God! I know His Name,
> His Name is all my trust;
> Nor will He put my soul to shame
> Nor let my hope be lost.
>
> Firm as His throne His promise stands
> And He can well secure
> What I've committed to His hands
> Till the decisive hour.

> Then will He own my worthless name
> Before His Father's face
> And in the new Jerusalem
> Appoint my soul a place.

Watts was a pioneer in another field too: poems and songs for children. He compiled a book of *Divine and Moral Songs for the Use of Children* which included such immortal advice as this:

> Let dogs delight to bark and bite
> For 'tis their nature to.

And in the same collection was another poem that enjoyed huge popularity, and I expect you'll recognise the opening lines:

> How doth the little busy bee
> Improve each shining hour?

It's a far cry from that to great national occasions like Remembrance Day at the Cenotaph but Watts manages to bridge the gap. He wrote a hymn that has almost acquired national anthem status: 'O God (or as *he* wrote, Our God) our Help in Ages Past':

> O GOD, OUR HELP IN AGES PAST,
> Our hope for years to come,
> Our shelter from the stormy blast
> And our eternal home.
>
> Under the shadow of Thy throne
> Thy saints have dwelt secure;
> Sufficient is Thine arm alone
> And our defence is sure.
>
> Before the hills in order stood
> Or earth received her frame,
> From everlasting Thou art God
> To endless years the same.

A thousand ages in Thy sight
Are like an evening gone;
Short as the watch that ends the night
Before the rising sun.

Time, like an ever-rolling stream,
Bears all its sons away;
They fly, forgotten, as a dream
Dies at the opening day.

O God, our help in ages past,
Our hope for years to come:
Be Thou our guide while troubles last
And our eternal home.

Interesting, isn't it, that at a festival of remembrance we sing 'They fly forgotten as a dream Dies at the opening day' – but hymn-singing is full of paradoxes like that.

Probably Watts's greatest hymn, and some people think the greatest hymn ever written, is 'When I Survey the Wondrous Cross'. Like many Calvinists, Watts was fascinated by the cross and the whole concept of 'atonement'. But here he enlarges the vision – not only the love of Christ but our love in response, as broad as 'the whole realm of nature'. Incidentally, in the first published version of this hymn in 1707, the opening lines were slightly different:

When I survey the wondrous cross
Where the young Prince of Glory died . . .

I wonder if our slightly more pedantic version ('on which the Prince of Glory died') is *really* an improvement?

WHEN I SURVEY THE WONDROUS CROSS
On which the Prince of Glory died,
My richest gain I count but loss
And pour contempt on all my pride.

Forbid it, Lord, that I should boast
Save in the death of Christ my God!
All the vain things that charm me most
I sacrifice them to His blood.

See from His head, His hands, His feet,
Sorrow and love flow mingled down!
Did e'er such love and sorrow meet
Or thorns compose so rich a crown?

His dying crimson, like a robe,
Spreads o'er His body on the tree;
Then I am dead to all the globe
And all the globe is dead to me.

Were the whole realm of nature mine,
That were a present far too small;
Love so amazing, so divine,
Demands my soul, my life, my all.

Dr Watts became minister of the renowned Independent Chapel in Mark Lane, London, but ill-health forced him to give this up when he was only thirty-eight and the rest of his life – thirty-six years in fact – he was the guest of Sir Thomas and Lady Abney in their big house at Stoke Newington. The site of the house became a huge public cemetery but Watts himself was buried in the Puritan burial ground, Bunhill Fields in East London, and later on a monument was raised to this notable dissenter in that shrine of the Establishment, Westminster Abbey. Like many of his contemporaries, death was a frequent theme in his hymns – death and the fleeting nature of life and the continuity of praise in heaven.

I'LL PRAISE MY MAKER WHILE I'VE BREATH
And when my voice is lost in death
Praise shall employ my nobler powers;
My days of praise shall ne'er be past,
While life and thought and being last
Or immortality endures.

Why should I make a man my trust?
Princes must die and turn to dust;
Vain is the help of flesh and blood:
Their breath departs, their pomp and power,
And thoughts all vanish in an hour,
Nor can they make their promise good.

Happy the man whose hopes rely
On Israel's God: He made the sky,
And earth and seas with all their train;
His truth for ever stands secure,
He saves th'oppressed, He feeds the poor,
And none shall find His promise vain.

The Lord has eyes to give the blind;
The Lord supports the sinking mind;
He sends the labouring conscience peace;
He helps the stranger in distress,
The widow and the fatherless,
And grants the prisoner sweet release.

He loves His saints, He knows them well,
But turns the wicked down to hell;
Thy God, O Zion! ever reigns:
Let every tongue, let every age,
In this exalted work engage;
Praise Him in everlasting strains.

I'll praise Him while He lends me breath
And when my voice is lost in death
Praise shall employ my nobler powers;
My days of praise shall ne'er be past,
While life and thought and being last
Or immortality endures.

I hope heaven matches Watts's expectations of it, which were sublime. Let's end with one of his 'heaven' hymns, the best of them probably: 'There is a Land of Pure Delight'.

THERE IS A LAND OF PURE DELIGHT
Where saints immortal reign;
Infinite day excludes the night
And pleasures banish pain.

There everlasting spring abides
And never withering flowers:
Death, like a narrow sea, divides
This heavenly land from ours.

Sweet fields beyond the swelling flood
Stand dressed in living green:
So to the Jews old Canaan stood
While Jordan rolled between.

But timorous mortals start and shrink
To cross this narrow sea;
And linger, shivering on the brink,
And fear to launch away.

O could we make our doubts remove
Those gloomy thoughts that rise
And see the Canaan that we love
With unbeclouded eyes!

Could we but climb where Moses stood
And view the landscape o'er,
Not Jordan's stream nor death's cold flood
Should fright us from the shore.

WILLIAM COWPER AND AUGUSTUS TOPLADY

From Series 1

BBC Radio Four
Sunday 13 July 1975
Producers: David Winter and Angela Tilby

• • •

William Cowper is one of the enigmas of English literature and hymnody. He was an intelligent, well-educated man who suffered all his life from bouts of depression, which from time to time were manic. Yet he wrote one or two of the most restful, confident hymns in the English language. During his fits of depression he believed himself to be 'damned above Judas'. But he could still write:

> Can a mother's tender care
> Cease towards the child she bare?
> Yes, she may forgetful be,
> Yet will I remember thee.
>
> Mine is an unchanging love,
> Higher than the heights above,
> Deeper than the depths beneath,
> Free and faithful, strong as death.

Those words appear in a hymn called 'Hark, My Soul! It is the Lord!'

HARK MY SOUL! IT IS THE LORD;
'Tis Thy Saviour, hear His word;
Jesus speaks and speaks to thee,
'Say, poor sinner, lov'st thou me?

'I deliver'd thee when bound,
And when bleeding, heal'd thy wound;
Sought thee wandering, set thee right,
Turn'd thy darkness into light.

'Can a woman's tender care
Cease towards the child she bare?
Yes, she may forgetful be,
Yet will I remember thee.

'Mine is an unchanging love,
Higher than the heights above,
Deeper than the depths beneath,
Free and faithful, strong as death.

'Thou shalt see My glory soon,
When the work of grace is done;
Partner of My throne shalt be;
Say, poor sinner, lov'st thou me?'

Lord it is my chief complaint,
That my love is weak and faint;
Yet I love Thee and adore –
Oh! for grace to love Thee more!

I wonder if that hymn would have been as popular as it is if J. B. Dykes hadn't come along with his famous tune a hundred years after the words were written. All the new hymn-books try to tempt us with new tunes – 'better' ones, as they say – but Dykes reigns triumphant.

Cowper was a convert of the Evangelical Revival and went to live in Olney, in Buckinghamshire, in 1765, just to sit at the feet of the Rev. John Newton, the former slave-trader who was then Rector of Olney. Cowper became the Rector's lay helper and the weekly prayer meeting became so enormously popular that it had to be moved to an empty mansion nearby, called the Great House. A feature of the meeting was that every week a new hymn should be introduced (I can't see a modern congregation welcoming that!) and Cowper and Newton took turns at writing it.

Over the years, Cowper contributed sixty-eight hymns to this Olney collection, most of them almost obsessively concerned with individual piety and the state of his own soul, often capturing his torment of mind as he hovered between evangelical assurance and hideous fears that he was not in fact among the elect at all but predestined to damnation. Out of just such a torment came his best-known hymn 'God Moves in a Mysterious Way'.

> GOD MOVES IN A MYSTERIOUS WAY
> His wonders to perform;
> He plants His footsteps in the sea
> And rides upon the storm.
>
> Deep in unfathomable mines
> Of never failing skill
> He treasures up His bright designs
> And works His sovereign will.
>
> Ye fearful saints, fresh courage take;
> The clouds ye so much dread
> Are big with mercy and shall break
> In blessings on your head.
>
> Judge not the Lord by feeble sense,
> But trust Him for His grace;
> Behind a frowning providence
> He hides a smiling face.

His purposes will ripen fast,
Unfolding every hour;
The bud may have a bitter taste
But sweet will be the flower.

Blind unbelief is sure to err
And scan His work in vain;
God is His own interpreter
And He will make it plain.

For thirty-one years Cowper was cared for by Mary Unwin, a clergyman's widow for whom he had a deep though apparently platonic relationship. In 1767 she was seriously ill and he wrote some verses for his aunt, who had sent him a letter of comfort. 'I began to compose them yesterday morning, before day break,' he said in a covering letter, 'but fell asleep at the end of the first two lines.' Those two lines were:

O for a closer walk with God,
A calm and heavenly frame.

He then explained to his aunt how the rest of the stanza came to him. 'When I awaked again, the third and fourth lines were whispered to my heart in a way which I have often experienced':

A light to shine upon the road
That leads me to the Lamb.

It is truly a sublime hymn, especially when you think of the tensions and fears that constantly beset its author.

O FOR A CLOSER WALK WITH GOD,
A calm and heavenly frame,
A light to shine upon the road
That leads me to the Lamb!

Where is the blessedness I knew
When first I saw the Lord?
Where is the soul-refreshing view
Of Jesus and His Word?

Return, O holy Dove, return,
Sweet messenger of rest;
I hate the sins that made Thee mourn
And drove Thee from my breast.

The dearest idol I have known,
Whate'er that idol be,
Help me to tear it from Thy throne
And worship only Thee.

So shall my walk be close with God,
Calm and serene my frame;
So purer light shall mark the road
That leads me to the Lamb.

Cowper was of course a considerable poet but, unusually, he began as a hymn-writer. His first hymns were published in 1779, his first collection of poems three years later. But the poems give us a fascinating insight into the mind of the hymn-writer. In his long discursive poem 'The Task', for instance, there is a passage where he describes his awful fear of eventual damnation, seeing himself as a 'stricken deer'; and his last poem, 'The Castaway', is appalling in its horror of the great darkness waiting to swallow him up. Yet despite this depression, or perhaps because of it, Cowper's hymns often capture better than anyone else's the note of evangelical certainty. He wrote one hymn under the subtitle 'Joy and Peace in Believing':

SOMETIMES A LIGHT SURPRISES
The Christian while he sings;
It is the Lord who rises
With healing in his wings.

When comforts are declining,
He grants the soul again
A season of clear shining,
To cheer it after rain.

In holy contemplation
We sweetly then pursue
The theme of God's salvation
And find it ever new;
Set free from present sorrow,
We cheerfully can say,
Let the unknown tomorrow
Bring with it what it may.

It can bring with it nothing
But He will bear us through:
Who gives the lilies clothing
Will clothe His people, too:
Beneath the spreading heavens
No creature but is fed;
And He who feeds the ravens
Will give His children bread.

Though vine nor fig tree neither
Their wonted fruit should bear;
Though all the fields should wither,
Nor flocks nor herds be there.
Yet, God the same abiding,
His praise shall tune my voice;
For, while in Him confiding,
I cannot but rejoice.

This same tension between a feeling of his own intense unworthiness and his faith in God's forgiveness runs through almost all of Cowper's hymns. The former expressed itself in the most abject self-abasement; the latter at times in somewhat crude evangelical imagery:

Lord, I believe Thou hast prepared
(Unworthy though I be)
For me a blood-bought free reward,
A golden harp for me!

In the same hymn, there's a typical piece of Cowper self-deprecation:

The dying thief rejoiced to see
That fountain in his day;
And there have I, though vile as he,
Washed all my sins away.[1]

The hymn is 'There Is a Fountain Filled with Blood'.

THERE IS A FOUNTAIN FILLED WITH BLOOD
Drawn from Emmanuel's veins;
And sinners plunged beneath that flood
Lose all their guilty stains.
Lose all their guilty stains,
Lose all their guilty stains;
And sinners plunged beneath that flood
Lose all their guilty stains.

The dying thief rejoiced to see
That fountain in his day;
And there have I, though vile as he,
Washed all my sins away.
Washed all my sins away,
Washed all my sins away;
And there have I, though vile as he,
Washed all my sins away.

Dear dying Lamb, Thy precious blood
Shall never lose its power
Till all the ransomed Church of God

[1] Betjeman's original and more speculative wording – 'and there *may* I, though vile as he, *Wash* all my sins away' – reveals a greater anxiety.

Be saved, to sin no more.
Be saved, to sin no more,
Be saved, to sin no more;
Till all the ransomed Church of God
Be saved, to sin no more.

E'er since, by faith, I saw the stream
Thy flowing wounds supply,
Redeeming love has been my theme,
And shall be till I die.
And shall be till I die,
And shall be till I die;
Redeeming love has been my theme,
And shall be till I die.

Then in a nobler, sweeter song,
I'll sing Thy power to save,
When this poor lisping, stamm'ring tongue
Lies silent in the grave.
Lies silent in the grave,
Lies silent in the grave;
When this poor lisping, stamm'ring tongue
Lies silent in the grave.

Lord, I believe Thou hast prepared
(Unworthy though I be)
For me a blood-bought free reward,
A golden harp for me!
A golden harp for me,
A golden harp for me!
For me a blood-bought free reward,
A golden harp for me!

'Tis strung and tuned for endless years
And formed by power divine
To sound in God the Father's ears
No other name but Thine.
No other name but Thine,

No other name but Thine;
To sound in God the Father's ears
No other name but Thine.

As I've said, Cowper's hymns are obsessed with his own spiritual state, so that many of them are hardly suitable for congregational use. But one that is, and one of his very best, is 'Jesus, Where'er Thy People Meet', written for the occasion when that enormous village prayer meeting moved into the Great House at Olney, which makes the line 'Lord we are few' seem unduly modest. Never mind – it's a great hymn of the church, capturing a profound idea and expressing it with very effective simplicity:

JESUS, WHERE'ER THY PEOPLE MEET,
There they behold Thy mercy seat;
Where'er they seek Thee Thou art found
And every place is hallowed ground.

For Thou, within no walls confined,
Dost dwell with those of humble mind;
Such ever bring Thee where they come
And, going, take Thee to their home.

Great Shepherd of Thy chosen few,
Thy former mercies here renew;
Here, to our waiting hearts, proclaim
The sweetness of Thy saving name.

Here may we prove the power of prayer
To strengthen faith and sweeten care;
To teach our faint desires to rise
And bring all heav'n before our eyes.

Lord, we are few but Thou art near;
Nor short Thine arm nor deaf Thine ear;
O rend the heavens, come quickly down
And make a thousand hearts Thine own!

Contemporary with Cowper was the remarkable Augustus Montague Toplady, also a convert of the revival and also a man of dark and mysterious passions. He became a fervent – one might say rabid – Calvinist, bitterly opposed to John Wesley and everybody whom he supposed guilty of promoting or even tolerating that most British of all heresies, Arminianism – the idea that we might have some small contribution to make towards our own salvation.

Anyway, he was a very vigorous controversialist in this cause, writing such books as *Historic Proof of the Doctrinal Calvinism of the Church of England* and *The Church of England Vindicated from the Charge of Arminianism*. He wrote a lot of hymns but only one is an all-time favourite: 'Rock of Ages'. Toplady was, at one time, a West-Country vicar and there is a widely believed story that 'Rock of Ages' was written while sheltering from a storm in a fissure of a precipitous limestone crag at Burrington Combe in the Mendips.[2] But like so many good stories, it isn't true. It certainly didn't circulate until seventy years after his death.

The actual background to the story is considerably less romantic – indeed it is proof that the oddest and least promising sources sometimes yield pure gold. Toplady, in pursuit of his Arminian prey, wrote an article in the *Gospel* magazine in which he set out to compute the national debt of sin. By heaven knows what mathematics he worked out that by the age of ten each of us would be chargeable with no less than 315,036,000 sins. I hate to imagine what the total is at three score and ten.

Anyway, the point of his article was that Christ's redemption will 'infinitely over-balance all the sins of the whole believing world' – and as an appendix to this amazing article he added the four perfect stanzas of 'Rock of Ages'. Here is the whole hymn.

[2] There is also a legend that Toplady wrote the words on a playing card when a boat he was on was forced to take refuge under a rocky overhang near the Cheddar Gorge.

WILLIAM COWPER AND AUGUSTUS TOPLADY

ROCK OF AGES, CLEFT FOR ME,
Let me hide myself in Thee;
Let the water and the blood
From Thy wounded side which flowed,
Be of sin the double cure,
Save from wrath and make me pure.

Not the labour of my hands
Can fulfil Thy Law's demands;
Could my zeal no respite know,
Could my tears forever flow,
All for sin could not atone;
Thou must save and Thou alone.

Nothing in my hand I bring,
Simply to the cross I cling;
Naked, come to Thee for dress;
Helpless look to Thee for grace;
Foul, I to the fountain fly;
Wash me, Saviour, or I die.

While I draw this fleeting breath,
When my eye-strings break in death,
When I soar to worlds unknown,
See Thee on Thy judgement throne.
Rock of Ages, cleft for me,
Let me hide myself in Thee.

THE WESLEYS

From Series 1

BBC Radio Four
Sunday 20 July 1975
Producers: David Winter and Angela Tilby

• • •

Certainly the most prolific and possibly the most gifted hymn-writer in the history of the Christian church was Charles Wesley: the 'sweet singer of Methodism', as he was called. Although he lived and died an Anglican, it is the worldwide Methodist movement that looks to him and his brother John as its founding fathers but many of the 7,270 published hymns of Charles Wesley are the common property of all Christians all over the world.

Of course, thousands of his hymns are rarely, if ever, sung today. But there are few hymn-books that do not contain more hymns by him than by any other author. A recently published hymn-book has thirty-eight of his hymns, with another seven by his brother John, and at least a dozen of his would be in any list of the world's most popular fifty hymns. And the most popular of all? It's difficult to say, but probably this one, much favoured at weddings and burnt into the memory of many a petrified bride and groom as they've stood together at the altar: 'Love Divine, All Loves Excelling'.

> LOVE DIVINE, ALL LOVES EXCELLING,
> Joy of heaven to earth come down;
> Fix in us Thy humble dwelling;
> All Thy faithful mercies crown!

Jesus, Thou art all compassion,
Pure unbounded love Thou art;
Visit us with Thy salvation;
Enter every trembling heart.

Breathe, O breathe Thy loving Spirit,
Into every troubled breast!
Let us all in Thee inherit;
Let us find that second rest.
Take away our bent to sinning;
Alpha and Omega be;
End of faith, as its beginning,
Set our hearts at liberty.

Come, Almighty to deliver,
Let us all Thy life receive;
Suddenly return and never,
Never more Thy temples leave.
Thee we would be always blessing,
Serve Thee as Thy hosts above.
Pray and praise Thee without ceasing,
Glory in Thy perfect love.

Finish, then, Thy new creation;
Pure and spotless let us be.
Let us see Thy great salvation
Perfectly restored in Thee;
Changed from glory into glory,
Till in heav'n we take our place,
Till we cast our crowns before Thee,
Lost in wonder, love, and praise.

John and Charles Wesley were exceptionally devout young men, members of a 'Holy Club' at Oxford, and eventually ordained in the Church of England. But they both felt there was some vital element missing, something to turn laborious duty and piety into assurance and joy. They found it, eventually, through some German

Moravians. Charles, and then, three days later, his brother John, had an experience of conversion that transformed their whole outlook on life and their life's work. It was one of the Moravians, Peter Bohler, who remarked to Charles, 'If I had a thousand tongues I'd use them all to praise my Redeemer' and Charles took the phrase and turned it into a very great hymn. It almost has a thousand verses.

O FOR A THOUSAND TONGUES TO SING
My great Redeemer's praise,
The glories of my God and King,
The triumphs of His Grace!

My gracious Master and my God,
Assist me to proclaim,
To spread through all the earth abroad
The honours of Thy Name.

Jesus! the name that charms our fears,
That bids our sorrows cease;
'Tis music in the sinner's ears,
'Tis life and health and peace.

He breaks the pow'r of cancelled sin,
He sets the prisoner free;
His blood can make the foulest clean,
His blood availed for me.

He speaks and, listening to His voice,
New life the dead receive;
The mournful, broken hearts rejoice,
The humble poor believe.

Hear Him, ye deaf; His praise, ye dumb,
Your loosened tongues employ;
Ye blind, behold your Saviour come,
And leap, ye lame, for joy.

In Christ your Head, you then shall know,
Shall feel your sins forgiven;
Anticipate your heaven below,
And own that love is heaven.

Glory to God, and praise and love
Be ever, ever giv'n,
By saints below and saints above,
The church in earth and heaven.

On this glad day the glorious sun
Of righteousness arose;
On my benighted soul He shone
And filled it with repose.

Sudden expired the legal strife,
'Twas then I ceased to grieve;
My second, real, living life
I then began to live.

Then with my heart I first believed,
Believed with faith divine,
Power with the Holy Ghost received
To call the Saviour mine.

I felt my Lord's atoning blood
Close to my soul applied;
Me, me He loved, the Son of God,
For me, for me He died!

I found and owned His promise true,
Ascertained of my part,
My pardon passed in heav'n I knew
When written on my heart.

Look unto Him, ye nations, own
Your God, ye fallen race;
Look, and be saved through faith alone,
Be justified by grace.

See all your sins on Jesus laid:
The Lamb of God was slain,
His soul was once an offering made
For every soul of man.

Awake from guilty nature's sleep,
And Christ shall give you light,
Cast all your sins into the deep,
And wash the Ethiop white.

Harlots and publicans and thieves
In holy triumph join!
Saved is the sinner that believes
From crimes as great as mine.

Murderers and all ye hellish crew
In holy triumph join!
Believe the Saviour died for you;
For me the Saviour died.

With me, your Chief, ye then shall know,
Shall feel your sins forgiven;
Anticipate your heaven below,
And own that love is heaven.

Phew! John was the evangelist, travelling thousands of miles on horseback to preach to enormous crowds in the open air. Charles was the movement's psalmist. But John contributed hymns too – mostly translations from the German pietists who had influenced him so profoundly. This one was written by Count Zinzendorf, a Moravian whom John had visited at Herrenhut soon after his conversion.

JESUS, THY BLOOD AND RIGHTEOUSNESS
My beauty are, my glorious dress;
'Midst flaming worlds, in these arrayed,
With joy shall I lift up my head.

Bold shall I stand in Thy great day;
For who aught to my charge shall lay?
Fully absolved through these I am
From sin and fear, from guilt and shame.

The holy, meek, unspotted Lamb,
Who from the Father's bosom came,
Who died for me, e'en me to atone,
Now for my Lord and God I own.

Lord, I believe Thy precious blood,
Which, at the mercy seat of God,
Forever doth for sinners plead,
For me, e'en for my soul, was shed.

Lord, I believe were sinners more
Than sands upon the ocean shore,
Thou hast for all a ransom paid,
For all a full atonement made.

When from the dust of death I rise
To claim my mansion in the skies,
Ev'n then this shall be all my plea,
Jesus hath lived, hath died, for me.

This spotless robe the same appears,
When ruined nature sinks in years;
No age can change its glorious hue:
The robe of Christ is ever new.

Jesus, be endless praise to Thee,
Whose boundless mercy hath for me,
For me a full atonement made,
An everlasting ransom paid.

O let the dead now hear Thy voice;
Now bid Thy banished ones rejoice;
Their beauty this, their glorious dress,
Jesus, Thy Blood and Righteousness.

Perhaps John could have been as prolific and successful a hymn-writer as Charles but he was preoccupied with the work of evangelism and the writing was left to his brother. Hymns flowed from Charles's pen and were taken up by the thousands of Methodist groups that were formed as a result of John's preaching. But in no sense were Charles Wesley's hymns narrow or superficial. They were catholic in scope, profound in their exploration of Christian experience and genuinely poetic in their imagery. They truly enlarged the whole concept of hymns in worship.

> CHRIST, WHOSE GLORY FILLS THE SKIES,
> Christ, the true, the only light,
> Sun of righteousness, arise,
> Triumph o'er the shades of night:
> Dayspring from on high, be near;
> Day-star, in my heart appear.
>
> Dark and cheerless is the morn
> Unaccompanied by Thee;
> Joyless is the day's return
> Till Thy mercy's beams I see,
> Till they inward light impart,
> Glad my eyes and warm my heart.
>
> Visit then this soul of mine,
> Pierce the gloom of sin and grief;
> Fill me, radiancy divine,
> Scatter all my unbelief;
> More and more Thyself display,
> Shining to the perfect day.

Hymns for special occasions, and especially for the Church year, were one of Charles's specialities. He wrote 'Hark the Herald Angels Sing' (or rather, he wrote 'Hark How All the Welkin[1]

---

[1] The vault of heaven (archaic).

Rings') and he also wrote the great Ascension-tide hymn 'Hail the Day that Sees Him Rise'.

> HAIL THE DAY THAT SEES HIM RISE, HALLELUJAH!
> To His throne above the skies, Hallelujah!
> Christ, awhile to mortals given, Hallelujah!
> Re-ascends His native heaven, Hallelujah!
>
> There the glorious triumph waits, Hallelujah!
> Lift your heads, eternal gates, Hallelujah!
> Christ hath conquered death and sin, Hallelujah!
> Take the King of Glory in, Hallelujah!
>
> Circled round with angel powers, Hallelujah!
> Their triumphant Lord, and ours, Hallelujah!
> Conqueror over death and sin, Hallelujah!
> Take the King of Glory in, Hallelujah!
>
> Him though highest heav'n receives, Hallelujah!
> Still He loves the earth He leaves, Hallelujah!
> Though returning to His throne, Hallelujah!
> Still He calls mankind His own, Hallelujah!
>
> See! He lifts His hands above, Hallelujah!
> See! He shows the prints of love, Hallelujah!
> Hark! His gracious lips bestow, Hallelujah!
> Blessings on His church below, Hallelujah!
>
> Still for us His death He pleads, Hallelujah!
> Prevalent He intercedes, Hallelujah!
> Near Himself prepares our place, Hallelujah!
> Harbinger of the human race, Hallelujah!
>
> Master (will we ever say), Hallelujah!
> Taken from our head today, Hallelujah!
> See Thy faithful servants, see, Hallelujah!
> Ever gazing up to Thee, Hallelujah!

Grant, though parted from our sight, Hallelujah!
Far above yon azure height, Hallelujah!
Grant our hearts may thither rise, Hallelujah!
Seeking Thee beyond the skies, Hallelujah!

Ever upward let us move, Hallelujah!
Wafted on the wings of love, Hallelujah!
Looking when our Lord shall come, Hallelujah!
Longing, gasping, after home, Hallelujah!

There we shall with Thee remain, Hallelujah!
Partners of Thine endless reign, Hallelujah!
There Thy face unclouded see, Hallelujah!
Find our heaven of heavens in Thee, Hallelujah!

Charles Wesley was one of the first writers to use military metaphors for the Christian battle, a theme devotedly pursued by many Victorian writers. Based on St Paul's words about 'putting on the whole armour of God', he wrote the stirring 'Soldiers of Christ Arise, and Put Your Armour on.'

SOLDIERS OF CHRIST, ARISE, AND PUT YOUR ARMOUR ON,[2]
Strong in the strength which God supplies through His eternal
Son.
Strong in the Lord of hosts, and in His mighty power,
Who in the strength of Jesus trusts is more than conqueror.

Stand then in His great might, with all His strength endued,
But take, to arm you for the fight, the panoply of God;
That, having all things done, and all your conflicts passed,
Ye may o'ercome through Christ alone and stand entire at last.

Stand then against your foes, in close and firm array;
Legions of wily fiends oppose throughout the evil day.
But meet the sons of night, and mock their vain design,
Armed in the arms of heavenly light, of righteousness divine.

[2] A different, shorter version of this hymn appears on p. 126.

Leave no unguarded place, no weakness of the soul,
Take every virtue, every grace, and fortify the whole;
Indissolubly joined, to battle all proceed;
But arm yourselves with all the mind that was in Christ, your
                                                    head.

But, above all, lay hold on faith's victorious shield;
Armed with that adamant and gold, be sure to win the field:
If faith surround your heart, Satan shall be subdued,
Repelled his every fiery dart, and quenched with Jesu's blood.

Jesus hath died for you! What can His love withstand?
Believe, hold fast your shield, and who shall pluck you from His
                                                    hand?
Believe that Jesus reigns; all power to Him is giv'n:
Believe, till freed from sin's remains; believe yourselves to heav'n.

To keep your armour bright, attend with constant care,
Still walking in your Captain's sight, and watching unto prayer.
Ready for all alarms, steadfastly set your face,
And always exercise your arms, and use your every grace.

Pray without ceasing, pray, your Captain gives the Word;
His summons cheerfully obey and call upon the Lord;
To God your every want in instant prayer display,
Pray always; pray and never faint; pray, without ceasing, pray!

In fellowship alone, to God with faith draw near;
Approach His courts, besiege His throne with all the powers of
                                                    prayer:
Go to His temple, go, nor from His altar move;
Let every house His worship know, and every heart His love.

To God your spirits dart, your souls in words declare,
Or groan, to Him who reads the heart, the unutterable prayer:
His mercy now implore, and now show forth His praise,
In shouts, or silent awe, adore His miracles of grace.

Charles Wesley was probably at his best when putting theology to music. No one has surpassed him as a populariser of Christian doctrine – a valuable contribution, of course, to the work of his brother. One of his most popular hymns is so tightly packed with theology that in places it verges on obscurity but always the vivid phrase, the telling image, rescues it: 'And Can It Be that I Should Gain an Interest in the Saviour's Blood?'

> AND CAN IT BE THAT I SHOULD GAIN
> An interest in the Saviour's blood?
> Died He for me? – who caused his pain!
> For me? – who Him to death pursued?
> Amazing love! How can it be
> That Thou, my God, shouldst die for me?
> Amazing love! How can it be
> That Thou, my God, shouldst die for me?
>
> 'Tis mystery all: th'Immortal dies!
> Who can explore His strange design?
> In vain the firstborn seraph tries
> To sound the depths of love divine.
> 'Tis mercy all! Let earth adore;
> Let angel minds inquire no more.
> 'Tis mercy all! Let earth adore;
> Let angel minds inquire no more.
>
> He left his Father's throne above
> (So free, so infinite His grace!),
> Emptied Himself of all but love,
> And bled for Adam's helpless race.
> 'Tis mercy all, immense and free,
> For O my God, it found out me!
> 'Tis mercy all, immense and free,
> For O my God, it found out me!
>
> Long my imprisoned spirit lay,
> Fast bound in sin and nature's night;
> Thine eye diffused a quickening ray;

I woke, the dungeon flamed with light;
My chains fell off, my heart was free,
I rose, went forth, and followed Thee.
My chains fell off, my heart was free,
I rose, went forth, and followed Thee.

No condemnation now I dread;
Jesus, and all in Him, is mine;
Alive in Him, my living Head,
And clothed in righteousness divine,
Bold I approach th'eternal throne,
And claim the crown, through Christ my own.
Bold I approach th'eternal throne,
And claim the crown, through Christ my own.

One hymn of Charles Wesley's is remarkable, even within his opus, for its intensity of feeling. It's often sung nowadays at ordination services and you can see why. It's all about sacrifice, dedication and total commitment. The tune invariably associated with it was written by his grandson, the Victorian composer Samuel Sebastian Wesley. What a family!

O THOU WHO CAMEST FROM ABOVE
The pure celestial fire to impart,
Kindle a flame of sacred love
On the mean altar of my heart.

There let it for Thy glory burn
With inextinguishable blaze[3]
And trembling to its source return,
In humble prayer and fervent praise.

Jesus, confirm my heart's desire
To work and speak and think for Thee;
Still let me guard the holy fire,
And still stir up Thy gift in me.

[3] Or 'Unquenched, undimmed, in darkest days'.

Ready for all Thy perfect will,
My acts of faith and love repeat,
Till death Thine endless mercies seal,
And make my sacrifice complete.

Hymns of pure worship as opposed to hymns of exhortation and advice are probably the most difficult to write. Wesley, however, made them sound very easy, combining biblical phrases and images with his own flashes of spiritual insight. All of these qualities are found in our next hymn, with which we end: 'Ye Servants of God, Your Master Proclaim'.

YE SERVANTS OF GOD, YOUR MASTER PROCLAIM,
And publish abroad His wonderful Name;
The Name all victorious of Jesus extol;
His kingdom is glorious and rules over all.

God ruleth on high, almighty to save;
And still He is nigh – His presence we have;
The great congregation His triumph shall sing,
Ascribing salvation to Jesus our King.

'Salvation to God, who sits on the throne,'
Let all cry aloud, and honour the Son;
The praises of Jesus the angels proclaim,
Fall down on their faces and worship the Lamb.

Then let us adore, and give Him His right:
All glory and power, all wisdom and might,
All honour and blessing, with angels above,
And thanks never ceasing and infinite love.

REGINALD HEBER AND JAMES MONTGOMERY

From Series 1

BBC Radio Four
Sunday 27 July 1975
Producers: David Winter and Angela Tilby

•   •   •

R eginald Heber was an Anglican clergyman, later a bishop, and he's important because he was probably the first High Churchman to have written hymns. In fact, his hymns weren't published until after his death in 1826 because he wasn't at all sure about the reaction they would get. He mentioned in a letter in 1819 that he had for some time been engaged in arranging his hymns but had 'some High Church scruples against using them in public'. He had for some time admired the 'Olney Hymns' of Newton and Cowper and was convinced of their value in worship and in communicating Christian truth and wanted to introduce this evangelical innovation to the rest of the Church.

Heber was a poet of some distinction but he had never tried his hand at writing hymns until his father-in-law Dr Shipley, who was vicar of Wroxham, asked him to write a hymn for a special missionary service in his church. He gave him just one day's notice! Reginald, it is reported, retired to the far end of the room and produced 'From Greenland's Icy Mountains' – just about the most popular missionary hymn ever written, even allowing for its imperialistic undertones and rather patronising references to the 'heathen in his blindness' who 'bows down to wood and stone'. It included, of course, the immortal lines:

> Though every prospect pleases,
> And only man is vile.

Here is the whole hymn.

> FROM GREENLAND'S ICY MOUNTAINS,
> From India's coral strand,
> Where Afric's sunny fountains
> Roll down their golden sand;
> From many an ancient river,
> From many a palmy plain,
> They call us to deliver
> Their land from error's chain.
>
> What though the spicy breezes
> Blow soft o'er Ceylon's isle;
> Though every prospect pleases,
> And only man is vile?
> In vain with lavish kindness
> The gifts of God are strown;
> The heathen in his blindness
> Bows down to wood and stone.
>
> Shall we, whose souls are lighted
> With wisdom from on high,
> Shall we to those benighted
> The lamp of life deny?
> Salvation! O Salvation!
> The joyful sound proclaim,
> Till earth's remotest nation
> Has learned Messiah's Name.
>
> Waft, waft, ye winds, His story,
> And you, ye waters, roll

Till, like a sea of glory,
It spreads from pole to pole:
Till o'er our ransomed nature
The Lamb for sinners slain,
Redeemer, King, Creator,
In bliss returns to reign.

It is obvious from that hymn that Heber had a more literary style of hymn-writing than most of his predecessors. For him, poetic imagery was as important as didactic truth. He liked the well-turned phrase, the carefully chosen adjective and the telling figure of speech. His really were 'hymns of human composition'. Take, as an example of the literary hymn, 'By Cool Siloam's Shady Rill':

By COOL SILOAM'S SHADY RILL
How fair the lily grows!
How sweet the breath, beneath the hill,
Of Sharon's dewy rose!

Lo! such the child whose early feet
The paths of peace have trod,
Whose secret heart, with influence sweet,
Is upward drawn to God.

By cool Siloam's shady rill
The lily must decay;
The rose that blooms beneath the hill
Must shortly fade away.

And soon, too soon, the wintry hour
Of man's maturer age
Will shake the soul with sorrow's power
And stormy passion's rage.

O Thou whose infant feet were found
Within Thy Father's shrine,
Whose years with changeless virtue crowned,
Were all alike divine.

> Dependent on Thy bounteous breath,
> We seek Thy grace alone,
> In childhood, manhood, age and death
> To keep us still Thine own.

That hymn was apportioned by Heber to the first Sunday after Epiphany: all his fifty-seven hymns were allotted to days in the Church calendar or to specific services. In this, too, he was an innovator – the first specifically liturgical hymn-writer of the Church of England. One of his eucharistic hymns is still deservedly popular, 'Bread of the World in Mercy Broken'.

> BREAD OF THE WORLD IN MERCY BROKEN,
> Wine of the soul in mercy shed,
> By whom the words of life were spoken
> And in whose death our sins are dead;
>
> Look on the heart by sorrow broken,
> Look on the tears by sinners shed;
> And be Thy feast to us the token
> That by Thy grace our souls are fed.

Heber was consecrated Bishop of Calcutta in 1823. His diocese covered the whole of the subcontinent and it's hardly surprising that he was desperately overworked. In fact, the work killed him in three years at the age of forty-three and the hymns he had written in England, mostly during his sixteen years as Vicar of Hodnet in Shropshire, became his memorial. One of the most popular of them today is an Epiphany hymn, 'Brightest and Best of the Sons of the Morning':

> BRIGHTEST AND BEST OF THE SONS OF THE MORNING,
> Dawn on our darkness and lend us Thine aid;
> Star of the East, the horizon adorning,
> Guide where our infant Redeemer is laid.

Cold on His cradle the dewdrops are shining;
Low lies His head with the beasts of the stall;
Angels adore Him in slumber reclining,
Maker and Monarch and Saviour of all!

Say, shall we yield Him, in costly devotion,
Odours of Edom and offerings divine?
Gems of the mountain and pearls of the ocean,
Myrrh from the forest or gold from the mine?

Vainly we offer each ample oblation,
Vainly with gifts would His favour secure;
Richer by far is the heart's adoration,
Dearer to God are the prayers of the poor.

Heber wrote several hymns for saint's days hitherto largely unmarked by hymn-writers including one that has been the occasion over the years of a good deal of parody – notably by Dean Inge, who used to misquote the last four lines thus:

They climbed the steep ascent of heaven
Through peril, toil and pain:
O God, to us may grace be given
To follow in the train.

The hymn, dedicated to all the martyrs and saints of the Church, is 'The Son of God Goes Forth to War'.

THE SON OF GOD GOES FORTH TO WAR,
A kingly crown to gain;
His blood-red banner streams afar:
Who follows in His train?
Who best can drink His cup of woe,
Triumphant over pain,
Who patient bears His cross below,
He follows in His train.

That martyr first, whose eagle eye
Could pierce beyond the grave;
Who saw his Master in the sky,
And called on Him to save.
Like Him, with pardon on His tongue,
In midst of mortal pain,
He prayed for them that did the wrong:
Who follows in His train?

A glorious band, the chosen few
On whom the Spirit came;
Twelve valiant saints, their hope they knew,
And mocked the cross and flame.
They met the tyrant's brandished steel,
The lion's gory mane;
They bowed their heads the death to feel:
Who follows in their train?

A noble army, men and boys,
The matron and the maid,
Around the Saviour's throne rejoice
In robes of light arrayed.
They climbed the steep ascent of heaven,
Through peril, toil and pain:
O God, to us may grace be given
To follow in their train.

Like many hymn-writers of the eighteenth and nineteenth centuries, Heber had a highly-cultivated awareness of the imminence of death. Awareness wasn't, for him at least, a morbid preoccupation but a realistic acceptance of what was for his contemporaries an everyday part of human experience. Like other writers, he compares the onset of evening to the approach of death. The two lines:

When the last dread call shall wake us
Do not Thou our God forsake us

are from his evening hymn 'God that Madest Earth and Heaven', which becomes a hymn of preparation for the last things.

> GOD, THAT MADEST EARTH AND HEAVEN,
> Darkness and light;
> Who the day for toil hast given,
> For rest the night;
> May Thine angel guards defend us,
> Slumber sweet Thy mercy send us;
> Holy dreams and hopes attend us,
> All through the night.[1]
>
> And when morn again shall call us,
> To run life's way,
> May we still, whate'er befall us,
> Thy will obey.
> From the power of evil hide us,
> In the narrow pathway guide us,
> Nor Thy smile be e'er denied us
> All through the day.[2]
>
> Guard us waking, guard us sleeping,
> And when we die,
> May we in Thy mighty keeping
> All peaceful lie;
> When the last dread call shall wake us,
> Do not Thou, our God, forsake us,
> But to reign in glory take us
> With Thee on high.

Undoubtedly the good Bishop Heber's finest hymn and the one most often sung today is 'Holy, Holy, Holy'. It is based on a phrase in the book of Revelation but it goes far beyond the letter of scripture in its imagery. Once again the inevitable J. B. Dykes

---

[1] Or 'This livelong night'.
[2] Or 'The livelong day'.

wrote the definitive tune that has fought off all rivals for over a century.

> HOLY, HOLY, HOLY, LORD GOD ALMIGHTY!
> Early in the morning our song shall rise to Thee;
> Holy, holy, holy, merciful and mighty!
> God in three Persons, blessèd Trinity!
>
> Holy, holy, holy! All the saints adore Thee,
> Casting down their golden crowns around the glassy sea;
> Cherubim and seraphim falling down before Thee,
> Who was, and is, and evermore shall be.
>
> Holy, holy, holy! Though the darkness hide Thee,
> Though the eye of sinful man Thy glory may not see;
> Only Thou art holy; there is none beside Thee,
> Perfect in power, in love and purity.
>
> Holy, holy, holy! Lord God Almighty!
> All Thy works shall praise Thy Name, in earth and sky
>   and sea;
> Holy, holy, holy; merciful and mighty!
> God in three Persons, blessèd Trinity!

Heber was a missionary at the start of the great period of church growth when Britain sent out thousands of her finest clergymen and lay workers to the four corners of the earth to spread the gospel. 'From Greenland's Icy Mountains' is typical of one kind of missionary hymn – the descriptive and comparative approach (look how poor, ignorant and deprived the heathen are; see what blessings we civilised Christians enjoy – and be generous). But in the year that Heber became Bishop of Calcutta, a British journalist from Sheffield, James Montgomery, wrote an outstanding missionary hymn of another kind – the triumphant, universal approach that sees evangelisation in terms of a mighty war between darkness and light, culminating in the inevitable victory of Christ.

Montgomery, like Heber, faced some disapproval over the

publication of his hymns but, unlike the Bishop, pressed ahead and the appearance of *Selection of Psalms and Hymns* by himself and Thomas Cotterill in 1819 led in effect to the legalisation of hymn-singing in Church of England services. His great missionary hymn is 'O Spirit of the Living God'. Let it stand as a memorial not only to himself as a pioneer of hymnody but also to the overworked Bishop of Calcutta, the first of our missionary hymn-writers.

O SPIRIT OF THE LIVING GOD,
Thou light and fire divine,
Descend upon Thy church once more,
And make it truly Thine.
Fill it with love and joy and power,
With righteousness and peace;
Till Christ shall dwell in human hearts
And sin and sorrow cease.

Blow, wind of God! With wisdom blow
Until our minds are free
From mists of errors, clouds of doubt,
Which blind our eyes to Thee.
Burn, winged fire! Inspire our lips
With flaming love and zeal,
To preach to all Thy great good news,
God's glorious common weal.

Teach us to utter living words
Of truth which all may hear,
The language all may understand
When love speaks loud and clear;
Till every age and race and clime
Shall blend their creeds in one,
And earth shall form one family
By whom Thy will is done.

So shall we know the power of Christ
Who came this world to save;

So shall we rise with Him to life
Which soars beyond the grave;
And earth shall win true holiness,
Which makes Thy children whole;
Still, perfected by Thee, we reach
Creation's glorious goal!

HYMNS OF THE MISSION

From Series 1

BBC Radio Four
Sunday 3 August 1975
Producers: David Winter and Angela Tilby

• • •

Of all the strands that make up the picture of English hymnody, probably the most often overlooked is the mission hall. You can still see them in the poorer parts of our cities: street corner conventicles with names like Hope Mission, Zion Hall, Bethel and Bethesda. They even had one in *Coronation Street*. They were a vital part of Victorian religion – for many people, the only bit of colour and excitement and hope in a life of otherwise unremitting toil and tedium. Here there was hot soup for the men, buns for the children and marvellous singing, mostly about heaven.

> BLESSED ASSURANCE, JESUS IS MINE!
> O, what a foretaste of glory divine!
> Heir of salvation, purchase of God,
> Born of His Spirit, washed in His Blood.
>> *This is my story, this is my song,*
>> *Praising my Saviour all the day long;*
>> *This is my story, this is my song,*
>> *Praising my Saviour all the day long.*
>
> Perfect submission, perfect delight,
> Visions of rapture now burst on my sight;

Angels descending bring from above
Echoes of mercy, whispers of love.
Chorus

Perfect submission, all is at rest;
I in my Saviour am happy and blest,
Watching and waiting, looking above,
Filled with his goodness, lost in His love.
Chorus

That hymn is by probably the best of all the writers of hymns for
the mission halls, Fanny J. Crosby – and, for good measure, the tune
was written by a woman too: Mrs J. F. Knapp. Fanny Crosby was
an American, born in New York, who lost her sight when she was
just six weeks old. She married another blind person, the musician
Alexander van Alstyne, and, encouraged by him, wrote about two
thousand hymns during her long life (she died in 1915 at the age
of ninety-five).

Looking forward to heaven was one of her great themes;
looking out to the world around, to the millions in the cities living
in squalor and poverty, ignorant of God and even of common
decency, was another.

RESCUE THE PERISHING, CARE FOR THE DYING,
Snatch them in pity from sin and the grave;
Weep o'er the erring one, lift up the fallen,
Tell them of Jesus, the mighty to save.
Rescue the perishing, care for the dying,
Jesus is merciful, Jesus will save.

Though they are slighting Him, still He is waiting,
Waiting the penitent child to receive;
Plead with them earnestly, plead with them gently;
He will forgive if they only believe.
Chorus

Down in the human heart, crushed by the tempter,

Feelings lie buried that grace can restore;
Touched by a loving heart, wakened by kindness,
Chords that were broken will vibrate once more.
　　Chorus

Rescue the perishing, duty demands it;
Strength for thy labour the Lord will provide;
Back to the narrow way patiently win them;
Tell the poor wanderer a Saviour has died.
　　Chorus

'Rescue the Perishing' – and that was the overwhelming ambition of the mission halls. They saw their work in terms of finding the lost sheep that had gone astray and bringing them safely back to the fold. It was another lady hymn-writer who wrote the best-known hymn on that subject – Elizabeth Clephane.

It was a far cry from the slums of East London, Manchester or New York to the green hills of Galilee but the imagery is so powerful that this hymn often reduced whole congregations to tears.

THERE WERE NINETY AND NINE THAT SAFELY LAY
In the shelter of the fold.
But one was out on the hills away,
Far off from the gates of gold.
Away on the mountains wild and bare,
Away from the tender Shepherd's care,
Away from the tender Shepherd's care.

'Lord, Thou hast here Thy ninety and nine;
Are they not enough for Thee?'
But the Shepherd made answer: 'This of Mine
Has wandered away from Me;
And although the road be rough and steep,
I go to the desert to find My sheep,
I go to the desert to find My sheep.'

But none of the ransomed ever knew
How deep were the waters crossed;
Nor how dark was the night the Lord passed through
Ere He found His sheep that was lost.
Out in the desert He heard its cry,
Sick and helpless and ready to die,
Sick and helpless and ready to die.

'Lord, whence are those blood drops all the way
That mark out the mountain's track?'
'They were shed for one who had gone astray
Ere the Shepherd could bring him back.'
'Lord, whence are Thy hands so rent and torn?'
'They are pierced tonight by many a thorn,
They are pierced tonight by many a thorn.'

And all through the mountains, thunder riven
And up from the rocky steep,
There arose a glad cry to the gate of heaven,
'Rejoice! I have found My sheep!'
And the angels echoed around the throne,
'Rejoice, for the Lord brings back His own!
Rejoice, for the Lord brings back His own!'

The tune to that hymn is by Ira D. Sankey, a name to conjure with in the music of the mission. He was, of course, the 'other half' of Dwight L. Moody and together they conducted their evangelistic campaigns all over America, Britain and other countries. It was reckoned that during his life Moody travelled more than a million miles and addressed more than a hundred million people – quite a record in the pre-aeroplane age. And always at the evangelist's side was his 'musical associate', Sankey, ready with an appropriate song, often to music composed for the occasion and accompanying himself on a small reed organ.

There is a sort of vigour about the hymns of the Sankey and Moody kind. Many of them captured the dance rhythms of the popular ballads of the day, on that well-known principle of denying the devil all the best tunes. 'Standing on the Promises' by R. Kelso Carter is a good example. He wrote the words, which are a serious and closely argued expression of the evangelical doctrine of 'assurance', and then set them to a tune that bounces along in what we would now call Country and Western style.

STANDING ON THE PROMISES OF CHRIST MY KING,
Through eternal ages let His praises ring,
Glory in the highest, I will shout and sing,
Standing on the promises of God.
Standing, standing,
Standing on the promises of God my Saviour;
Standing, standing,
I'm standing on the promises of God.

Standing on the promises that cannot fail,
When the howling storms of doubt and fear assail,
By the living word of God I shall prevail,
Standing on the promises of God.
Chorus

Standing on the promises I now can see,
Perfect, present cleansing in the blood for me,
Standing in the liberty where Christ makes free,
Standing on the promises of God.
Chorus

Standing on the promises of Christ the Lord,
Bound to Him eternally by love's strong cord,
Overcoming daily with the Spirit's sword,
Standing on the promises of God.
Chorus

Standing on the promises I cannot fall,
Listening every moment to the Spirit's call,
Resting in my Saviour as my all in all,
Standing on the promises of God.
Chorus

A few of the mission hall hymns have gone into our standard hymn-books. Of course, there's a lot of overlapping too, because many of the hymns of the Wesleys, Newton and Watts from an earlier era were put to new tunes in the great decades of the missions. One hymn very popular in the campaigns and also deservedly popular almost everywhere else is Frances Ridley Havergal's robust call to decision, 'Who is on the Lord's side?'

> WHO IS ON THE LORD'S SIDE? WHO WILL SERVE THE KING?
> Who will be His helpers, other lives to bring?
> Who will leave the world's side? Who will face the foe?
> Who is on the Lord's side? Who for Him will go?
> By Thy call of mercy, by Thy grace divine,
> We are on the Lord's side – Saviour, we are Thine!
>
> Not for weight of glory, nor for crown and palm,
> Enter we the army, raise the warrior psalm;
> But for love that claimeth lives for whom He died:
> He whom Jesus nameth must be on His side.
> By Thy love constraining, by Thy grace divine,
> We are on the Lord's side – Saviour, we are Thine!
>
> Jesus, Thou hast bought us, not with gold or gem,
> But with Thine own life blood, for Thy diadem;
> With Thy blessing filling each who comes to Thee,
> Thou hast made us willing, Thou hast made us free.
> By Thy grand redemption, by Thy grace divine,
> We are on the Lord's side – Saviour, we are Thine!
>
> Fierce may be the conflict, strong may be the foe,
> But the King's own army none can overthrow;
> 'Round His standard ranging, victory is secure,
> For His truth unchanging makes the triumph sure.
> Joyfully enlisting, by Thy grace divine,
> We are on the Lord's side – Saviour, we are Thine!
>
> Chosen to be soldiers, in an alien land,
> Chosen, called and faithful, for our Captain's band

In the service royal, let us not grow cold;
Let us be right loyal, noble, true and bold.
Master, Thou wilt keep us, by Thy grace divine,
Always on the Lord's side – Saviour, always Thine!

Frances Ridley Havergal was the daughter of an English clergyman and represents the strong revivalist element in the Church of England that had its source in the Methodist movement of the previous century. But most of the mission hymns came across the Atlantic in Sankey's luggage – among them many hymns by a Pennsylvanian evangelist, P. P. Bliss. One of them is found in several hymn-books today: 'Man of Sorrows'.

MAN OF SORROWS! WHAT A NAME
For the Son of God, who came
Ruined sinners to reclaim!
Alleluia! What a Saviour!

Bearing shame and scoffing rude,
In my place condemned He stood;
Sealed my pardon with His blood:
Alleluia! What a Saviour!

Guilty, helpless, lost were we;
Spotless Lamb of God was He.
Full atonement – can it be?
Alleluia! What a Saviour!

Lifted up was He to die;
'It is finished!' was His cry;
Now in heaven exalted high:
Alleluia! What a Saviour!

When He comes, our glorious King,
All His ransomed home to bring,
Then anew this song we'll sing:
Alleluia! What a Saviour!

Bliss gave away the royalties from his gospel songs – $30,000 dollars in all, which is some indication of their popularity, not far short of a quarter of a million pounds in today's inflated values. He died at the age of thirty-eight, trying to save his wife in a railway disaster in Ohio.

Probably the best-known hymn from the mission halls is 'Tell me the old, old Story' – at any rate, it has given a valuable prize to the English language, even if it is usually used cynically. The hymn itself is by another woman, Arabella Hankey. It's a masterpiece of simplicity and it had the ideal tune written for it by one of the main contributors to Sankey and Moody's *Sacred Songs and Solos*, W. H. Doane.

> TELL ME THE OLD, OLD STORY OF UNSEEN THINGS ABOVE,
> Of Jesus and His glory, of Jesus and His love.
> Tell me the story simply, as to a little child,
> For I am weak and weary, and helpless and defiled.
>> *Tell me the old, old story, tell me the old, old story,*
>> *Tell me the old, old story, of Jesus and His love.*
>
> Tell me the story slowly, that I may take it in,
> That wonderful redemption, God's remedy for sin.
> Tell me the story often, for I forget so soon;
> The early dew of morning has passed away at noon.
>> *Chorus*
>
> Tell me the story softly, with earnest tones and grave;
> Remember I'm the sinner whom Jesus came to save.
> Tell me the story always, if you would really be,
> In any time of trouble, a comforter to me.
>> *Chorus*
>
> Tell me the same old story when you have cause to fear
> That this world's empty glory is costing me too dear.
> Yes, and when that world's glory is dawning on my soul,
> Tell me the old, old story: 'Christ Jesus makes thee whole.'
>> *Chorus*

Many of the hymns that were most popular in the Victorian mission halls are never heard today, mainly because they were concerned with aspects of life and attitudes peculiar to their day. 'Where is my Wandering Boy, Tonight?' was paralleled by 'Tell Mother I'll be There' and songs about drunkenness; and the evils of alcohol were matched by calls to

> Dare to be a Daniel,
> Dare to stand alone,
> Dare to have a purpose true
> And dare to make it known.

But we end with two mission hymns that are still in use. The first one was very popular during Billy Graham's crusade in Britain:

> TO GOD BE THE GLORY, GREAT THINGS HE HATH DONE,
> So loved He the world that He gave us His Son,
> Who yielded His life our redemption to win,
> And opened the life-gate that all may go in.
> *Praise the Lord, praise the Lord,*
> *Let the earth hear His voice;*
> *Praise the Lord, praise the Lord,*
> *Let the people rejoice;*
> *Oh, come to the Father, through Jesus the Son,*
> *And give Him the glory; great things He hath done.*
>
> Oh, perfect redemption, the purchase of blood,
> To every believer the promise of God;
> The vilest offender who truly believes,
> That moment from Jesus a pardon receives.
> *Chorus*
>
> Great things He hath taught us, great things He hath done,
> And great our rejoicing through Jesus the Son;
> But purer, and higher and greater will be
> Our wonder, our transport when Jesus we see.
> *Chorus*

Our last hymn has the authentic Victorian ring about it. It is unashamedly sentimental and it is addressed to the inevitable wandering sinner but it has the note of infinite forgiveness that runs through so many of these hymns that sprang from the apparently loveless soil of the vast industrial slums of a hundred years ago.

SOFTLY AND TENDERLY JESUS IS CALLING,
Calling for you and for me;
See, on the portals He's waiting and watching,
Watching for you and for me.
> *Come home, come home,*
> *You who are weary, come home;*
> *Earnestly, tenderly, Jesus is calling,*
> *Calling, O sinner, come home!*

Why should we tarry when Jesus is pleading,
Pleading for you and for me?
Why should we linger and heed not His mercies,
Mercies for you and for me?
> *Chorus*

Time is now fleeting, the moments are passing,
Passing from you and from me;
Shadows are gathering, deathbeds are coming,
Coming for you and for me.
> *Chorus*

O for the wonderful love He has promised,
Promised for you and for me!
Though we have sinned, He has mercy and pardon,
Pardon for you and for me.
> *Chorus*

WELSH HYMNS

From Series 1

BBC Radio Four
Sunday 10 August 1975
Producers: David Winter and Angela Tilby

•   •   •

This week we're going to look at the Welsh influence on English hymns. Not surprisingly, that influence is most obvious where music is concerned: very few Welsh hymns have been translated into English. But we start with one that has: 'Guide me O Thou Great Jehovah', written in Welsh by the great William Williams Pantycelin and translated twenty-five years later, in 1771, by P. Williams.

> GUIDE ME, O THOU GREAT JEHOVAH,[1]
> Pilgrim through this barren land.
> I am weak but Thou art mighty;
> Hold me with Thy powerful hand.
> Bread of Heaven, Bread of Heaven,
> Feed me till I want no more;
> Feed me till I want no more.
>
> Open now the crystal fountain,
> Whence the healing stream doth flow;
> Let the fire and cloudy pillar

[1] Or 'Guide me, O Thou Great Redeemer.'

Lead me all my journey through.
Strong Deliverer, strong Deliverer,
Be Thou still my strength and shield;
Be Thou still my strength and shield.

Lord, I trust Thy mighty power,
Wondrous are Thy works of old;
Thou deliver'st Thine from thralldom,
Who for naught themselves had sold:
Thou didst conquer, Thou didst conquer,
Sin and Satan and the grave;
Sin and Satan and the grave.

When I tread the verge of Jordan,
Bid my anxious fears subside;
Death of deaths, and hell's destruction,
Land me safe on Canaan's side.
Songs of praises, songs of praises,
I will ever give to Thee;
I will ever give to Thee.

Musing on my habitation,
Musing on my heav'nly home,
Fills my soul with holy longings:
Come, my Jesus, quickly come.
Vanity is all I see;
Lord, I long to be with Thee!
Lord, I long to be with Thee!

William Williams was the Charles Wesley of Wales, writing hundreds of hymns, many of them still widely used today. But for the most part it is Welsh hymn-tunes that have travelled and English hymn-books would be sadly depleted without them. Take, for instance, the hymn 'Jesu, Lover of My Soul' – words by Charles Wesley but the tune 'Aberystwyth' by Joseph Parry giving them a touch of extra grandeur.

JESU, LOVER OF MY SOUL,
Let me to Thy Bosom fly,
While the nearer waters roll,
While the tempest still is high:
Hide me, O my Saviour, hide,
Till the storm of life be past!
Safe into the haven guide,
Oh, receive my soul at last!

Other refuge have I none,
Hangs my helpless soul on Thee;
Leave, ah! leave me not alone,
Still support and comfort me:
All my trust on Thee is stayed,
All my help from Thee I bring;
Cover my defenceless head
With the shadow of thy wing.

Thou, O Christ, art all I want;
More than all in Thee I find!
Raise the fallen, cheer the faint,
Heal the sick and lead the blind:
Just and holy is Thy Name,
I am all unrighteousness;
False and full of sin I am,
Thou art full of truth and grace.

Plenteous grace with Thee is found,
Grace to cover all my sin,
Let the healing streams abound;
Make and keep me pure within:
Thou of life the fountain art,
Freely let me take of Thee,
Spring Thou up within my heart,
Rise to all eternity.

There is a note of sadness, a sort of ever-present minor key, in much Welsh music. 'Bryn Calfaria' – the hill of Calvary – is just such a tune, perfectly suited to the English words with which it is usually associated outside Wales:

COME YE SINNERS, POOR AND NEEDY,
Weak and wounded, sick and sore;
Jesus ready stands to save you
Full of pity, love and power:
   I will arise and go to Jesus,
   He will embrace me in His arms;
   In the arms of my dear Saviour,
   O there are ten thousand charms.

Come, ye thirsty, come and welcome,
God's free bounty glorify;
True belief and true repentance,
Every grace that brings you nigh.
   Chorus

Come, ye weary, heavy laden,
Lost and ruined by the fall;
If you tarry till you're better,
You will never come at all.
   Chorus

View Him prostrate in the garden;
On the ground your Maker lies.
On the bloody tree behold Him;
Sinner, will this not suffice?
   Chorus

Lo! th'incarnate God ascended,
Pleads the merit of His blood:
Venture on Him, venture wholly,
Let no other trust intrude.
   Chorus

Let not conscience make you linger,
Not of fitness fondly dream;

All the fitness He requireth
Is to feel your need of Him.
    Chorus

To get that note of profound sorrow married to a deep reverence and sense of the power of God – a note that seems to haunt Welsh hymn-tunes – you really have to hear the original words sung to them. You don't have to understand Welsh, I think, to get the heart of this hymn, 'O Jesu Mawr' – 'O Great Jesus' – to the tune 'Llef'.

O! Jesu mawr, rho d'anian bur
I eiddil gwan mewn, anial dir,
I'w nerthu drwy'r holl rwystrau sy
Ar ddyrys i'r Ganaan fry.

Pob gras sydd yn yr Eglwys fawr,
Fry yn y nef, neu ar y llawr,
Caf feddu ull, eu meddu'n un,
Wrth feddu d'annian Di dy Hun.

Mi lyna'n dawel wrth dy draed,
Mi ganaf am rinweddau'r gwaed,
Mi garia'r groes, mi nofia'r don,
Ond cael dy anian dan fy mron.

O Jesus, let Thy spirit bless
This frail one in the wilderness
To guide him through the snares that lie
On Canaan's way to Thee on high.

All grace that through Thy Church doth flow,
In heaven above and here below,
All shall I have, all shall be mine,
If I but have Thy grace divine.

To Thy most holy feet I'll cling,
The virtues of Thy blood I'll sing,

The cross I'll bear, the wave I'll ride,
If Thou but with me now abide.

'What a Friend We Have in Jesus' is a simple enough hymn and used
to be classified in the Children's section of most hymn-books. But
since people started singing it to 'Blaenwern' it has really sounded
like a different hymn altogether: much more imposing, somehow.
Here it is, words by J. M. Scriven, tune by William P. Rowlands.

WHAT A FRIEND WE HAVE IN JESUS,
All our sins and griefs to bear!
What a privilege to carry
Everything to God in prayer!
O what peace we often forfeit,
O what needless pain we bear,
All because we do not carry
Everything to God in prayer.

Have we trials and temptations?
Is there trouble anywhere?
We should never be discouraged;
Take it to the Lord in prayer.
Can we find a friend so faithful
Who will all our sorrows share?
Jesus knows our every weakness;
Take it to the Lord in prayer.

Are we weak and heavy laden,
Cumbered with a load of care?
Precious Saviour, still our refuge,
Take it to the Lord in prayer.
Do your friends despise, forsake you?
Take it to the Lord in prayer!
In His arms He'll take and shield you;
You will find a solace there.

Blessed Saviour, Thou hast promised
Thou wilt all our burdens bear

May we ever, Lord, be bringing
All to Thee in earnest prayer.
Soon in glory bright unclouded
There will be no need for prayer
Rapture, praise and endless worship
Will be our sweet portion there.

Another hymn transformed by a Welsh tune is 'I will Sing the Wondrous Story', written in 1886 by F. H. Rowley. The tune that is now inescapably associated with it is 'Hyfrydol', written by R. H. Prichard a hundred years ago. The chorus has a wonderful note of triumph that suits the words perfectly.

I WILL SING THE WONDROUS STORY
Of the Christ Who died for me.
How He left His home in glory
For the cross of Calvary.
Yes, I'll sing the wondrous story
Of the Christ Who died for me,
Sing it with the saints in glory,
Gathered by the crystal sea.

I was lost but Jesus found me,
Found the sheep that went astray,
Threw His loving arms around me,
Drew me back into His way.[2]
Chorus

I was bruised but Jesus healed me,
Faint was I from many a fall,
Sight was gone and fears possessed me,
But He freed me from them all.
Chorus

Faint was I and fears possessed me,
Bruised was I from many a fall,

[2] Or 'Back into the narrow way'.

Hope was gone and shame distressed me,
But His love has pardoned all.
Chorus

Days of darkness still come o'er me,
Sorrow's path I often tread,
But His presence still is with me;
By His guiding hand I'm led.
Chorus

He will keep me till the river
Rolls its waters at my feet;
Then He'll bear me safely over,
Where the loved ones I shall meet.
Chorus

Traditional Welsh melodies have also been pressed into service as tunes for English hymns – and very effectively, too. That hymn associated with school assemblies, 'Immortal, Invisible, God only wise', is set to a Welsh folk melody, 'St Denio'. The words are by the Victorian hymn-writer W. Chalmers Smith.

IMMORTAL, INVISIBLE, GOD ONLY WISE,
In light inaccessible hid from our eyes,
Most blessèd, most glorious, the Ancient of Days,
Almighty, victorious, Thy great Name we praise.

Unresting, unhasting and silent as light,
Nor wanting, nor wasting, Thou rulest in might;
Thy justice, like mountains, high soaring above
Thy clouds, which are fountains of goodness and love.

To all, life Thou givest, to both great and small;
In all life Thou livest, the true life of all;
We blossom and flourish as leaves on the tree,
And wither and perish – but naught changeth Thee.

Great Father of glory, pure Father of light,
Thine angels adore Thee, all veiling their sight;
All laud we would render; O help us to see
'Tis only the splendour of light hideth Thee.

Another traditional Welsh melody has become associated with H. Scott Holland's hymn 'Judge Eternal, Throned in Splendour'. This is a hymn for the nation – for the weary folk trapped in the 'city's crowded clangour', for the 'body of this nation' to be purged of 'bitter things'. And the tune: 'Rhuddlan'.

JUDGE ETERNAL, THRONED IN SPLENDOUR,
Lord of lords and King of kings,
With Thy living fire of judgement
Purge this land of bitter things;
Solace all its wide dominion
With the healing of Thy wings.

Still the weary folk are pining
For the hour that brings release,
And the city's crowded clangour
Cries aloud for sin to cease;
And the homesteads and the woodlands
Plead in silence for their peace.

Crown, O God, Thine own endeavour;
Cleave our darkness with Thy sword;
Feed all those who do not know Thee
With the richness of Thy Word;
Cleanse the body of this nation
Through the glory of the Lord.

Anna Laetitia Waring only wrote one hymn that has got into our hymn-books but it has become more and more popular over the last decade or so, over a century after it was written. This may well be because Miss Waring's hymn 'In Heavenly Love Abiding' was waiting for David Jenkins's beautiful tune 'Penlan'. They certainly seem to go together perfectly, capturing in our last hymn this week that marriage of Welsh music and English words that has enriched this hymnody of English-speaking people all over the world.

> IN HEAVENLY LOVE ABIDING,
> No change my heart shall fear.
> And safe in such confiding,
> For nothing changes here.
> The storm may roar without me,
> My heart may low be laid,
> But God is round about me,
> And can I be dismayed?
>
> Wherever He may guide me,
> No want shall turn me back.
> My Shepherd is beside me,
> And nothing can I lack.
> His wisdom ever waking,
> His sight is never dim.
> He knows the way He's taking,
> And I will walk with Him.
>
> Green pastures are before me,
> Which yet I have not seen.
> Bright skies will soon be o'er me,
> Where darkest clouds have been.
> My hope I cannot measure,
> My path to life is free.
> My Saviour has my treasure,
> And He will walk with me.

HYMNS OF THE OXFORD MOVEMENT

From Series 1

BBC Radio Four
Sunday 17 August 1975
Producers: David Winter and Angela Tilby

• • •

They were the cause of enormous controversy during the nineteenth century but they wrote some marvellous hymns – 'they' being the Tractarians: the Anglo-Catholics who wanted to make the Church of England more Catholic, less under the State and more spiritual. They included some famous names – John Henry (later Cardinal) Newman, John Mason Neale, F. W. Faber – and they brought a new kind of hymn to England: the hymns of the early church and the medieval church, translated without being marred.

Prince of these translations was undoubtedly John Mason Neale. He ransacked the treasures of the Greek Church and the Latin hymnaries and sequences[1] and in between he even wrote a few hymns of his own. Perhaps the best known of his translations from Latin is 'Jerusalem the Golden', translated – transformed, actually – from Bernard of Cluny's 'De Contemptus Mundi'.

JERUSALEM THE GOLDEN, WITH MILK AND HONEY BLEST,
  Beneath thy contemplation sink heart and voice oppressed.

---

[1] Sequences are religious verses made up of rhythmical prose, unrhymed of (later) rhymed, dating from the ninth century.

SWEET SONGS OF ZION

I know not, O I know not, what joys await us there,
What radiancy of glory, what bliss beyond compare.

They stand, those halls of Zion, all jubilant with song,
And bright with many an angel, and all the martyr throng;
The Prince is ever in them, the daylight is serene.
The pastures of the blessèd are decked in glorious sheen.

There is the throne of David; and there, from care released,
The shout of them that triumph, the song of them that feast.
And they, who with their Leader, have conquered in the fight,
Forever and forever are clad in robes of white.

O sweet and blessèd country, the home of God's elect!
O sweet and blessèd country, that eager hearts expect!
Jesus, in mercy bring us to that dear land of rest,
Who art, with God the Father, and Spirit, ever blessed.

Brief life is here our portion, brief sorrow, short lived care;
The life that knows no ending, the tearless life, is there.
O happy retribution! Short toil, eternal rest;
For mortals and for sinners, a mansion with the blest.

That we should look, poor wanderers, to have our home on high!
That worms should seek for dwellings beyond the starry sky!
And now we fight the battle, but then shall wear the crown
Of full and everlasting, and passionless renown.

And how we watch and struggle, and now we live in hope,
And Zion in her anguish with Babylon must cope;
But He whom now we trust in shall then be seen and known,
And they that know and see Him shall have Him for their own.

For thee, O dear, dear country, mine eyes their vigils keep;
For very love, beholding, thy happy name, they weep:
The mention of thy glory is unction to the breast,
And medicine in sickness, and love and life and rest.

O one, O only mansion! O paradise of joy!
Where tears are ever banished, and smiles have no alloy;
The cross is all thy splendour, the Crucified thy praise,
His laud and benediction thy ransomed people raise.

Jerusalem the glorious! Glory of the elect!
O dear and future vision that eager hearts expect!
Even now by faith I see thee, even here thy walls discern;
To thee my thoughts are kindled, and strive and pant and yearn.

Jerusalem the only, that look'st from heaven below,
In thee is all my glory, in me is all my woe!
And though my body may not, my spirit seeks thee fain,
Till flesh and earth return me to earth and flesh again.

Jerusalem, exulting on that securest shore,
I hope thee, wish thee, sing thee, and love thee evermore!
I ask not for my merit: I seek not to deny
My merit is destruction, a child of wrath am I.

But yet with faith I venture and hope upon the way,
For those perennial guerdons[2] I labour night and day.
The best and dearest Father who made me and who saved,
Bore with me in defilement, and from defilement laved.

When in His strength I struggle, for very joy I leap;
When in my sin I totter, I weep, or try to weep:
And grace, sweet grace celestial, shall all its love display,
And David's royal fountain purge every stain away.

O sweet and blessèd country, shall I ever see thy face?
O sweet and blessèd country, shall I ever win thy grace?
I have the hope within me to comfort and to bless!
Shall I ever win the prize itself? O tell me, tell me, Yes!

[2] Rewards.

Strive, man, to win that glory; toil, man, to gain that light;
Send hope before to grasp it, till hope be lost in sight.
Exult, O dust and ashes, the Lord shall be thy part:
His only, His forever thou shalt be, and thou art.

Of Neale's Greek hymns, none is more popular than 'O Happy Band of Pilgrims', another phrase from a hymn that has entered the language. The original, on which Neale's version is based, was by Joseph the Hymnographer.

O HAPPY BAND OF PILGRIMS,
If onward you will tread,
With Jesus as your Fellow,
To Jesus as your Head.

O happy if you labour,
As Jesus did for men;
O happy if you hunger
As Jesus hungered then.

The cross that Jesus carried
He carried as your due;
The crown that Jesus weareth
He weareth it for you.

The faith by which you see Him,
The hope in which you yearn,
The love that through all troubles
To Him alone will turn.

The trials that beset you,
The sorrows you endure,
The manifold temptations
That death alone can cure.

What are they but His jewels
Of right celestial worth?

What are they but the ladder
Set up to heaven on earth?

O happy band of pilgrims,
Look upward to the skies,
Where such a light affliction
Shall win you such a prize.

To Father, Son and Spirit,
The God whom we adore,
Be loftiest praises given,
Now and for evermore.

Neale, like all his fellow Tractarians, was a firm believer in the educational value of the Church calendar. His Palm Sunday hymn, 'All Glory, Laud and Honour', is justifiably popular, though most modern hymn-books omit one verse of Neale's original. No prizes for guessing why!

> Be Thou, O Lord, the rider,
> And we the little ass,
> That to God's holy city
> Together we may pass.[3]

Another hymn for the Christian year became one of the few really popular Advent hymns. It was translated from a thirteenth-century Latin text and set to a melody from an old French missal.

> O COME, O COME, EMMANUEL,
> And ransom captive Israel,
> That mourns in lonely exile here
> Until the Son of God appear.
>   *Rejoice! Rejoice!*
>   *Emmanuel shall come to thee, O Israel.*

[3] 'All Glory, Laud and Honour' appears in full on p. 118.

O come, Thou wisdom from on high,
Who orderest all things mightily;
To us the path of knowledge show,
And teach us in her ways to go.
    Chorus

O come, Thou rod of Jesse, free
Thine own from Satan's tyranny;
From depths of hell Thy people save,
And give them victory over the grave.
    Chorus

O come, Thou dayspring, come and cheer
Our spirits by Thine advent here;
Disperse the gloomy clouds of night,
And death's dark shadows put to flight.
    Chorus

O come, Thou key of David, come,
And open wide our heavenly home;
Make safe the way that leads on high,
And close the path to misery.
    Chorus

O come, O come, great Lord of might,
Who to Thy tribes on Sinai's height
In ancient times once gave the Law
In cloud and majesty and awe.
    Chorus

O come, Thou root of Jesse's tree,
An ensign of Thy people be;
Before Thee rulers silent fall;
All peoples on Thy mercy call.
    Chorus

O come, desire of nations, bind
In one the hearts of all mankind;

Bid Thou our sad divisions cease,
And be Thyself our King of Peace.
Chorus

Many of the early Tractarians ended up in the Roman Catholic Church and one at least made the journey very rapidly. F. W. Faber was an Anglican rector at Elton in Huntingdonshire for exactly two years before being received into the Roman Catholic Church in 1845. All his hymns were written after that date. Among the best loved of them is one where he describes the beauty, holiness and awesomeness of God.

My God, how wonderful Thou art,
Thy majesty, how bright;
How beautiful Thy mercy seat
In depths of burning light!

How dread are Thy eternal years,
O everlasting Lord,
By prostrate spirits day and night
Incessantly adored!

How wonderful, how beautiful,
The sight of Thee must be;
Thine endless wisdom, boundless power
And glorious purity!

O how I fear Thee, living God,
With deep and tender fear;
And worship Thee with trembling hope,
And penitential tears!

Yet I may love Thee too, O Lord,
Almighty as Thou art;
For Thou hast stooped to ask of me
The love of my poor heart!

No earthly father loves like Thee,
No mother, e'er so mild,
Bears and forbears as Thou hast done,
With me, Thy sinful child.

Only to sit and think of God,
Oh, what a joy it is!
To think the thought, to breathe the Name,
Earth has no higher bliss.

Father of Jesus, love's Reward!
What rapture it will be
Prostrate before Thy throne to lie,
And gaze, and gaze on Thee!

A friend and contemporary of Faber's was Edward Caswell: they
joined the Roman Catholic Church at about the same time. His
carol 'See amid the Winter's Snow' is still very popular, of course,
but most of his hymns were, like Faber's, translations of Latin. He
published a whole book of them under the title *Lyra Catholica* in
1849. Among these hymns was his best-known one, a translation
from the twelfth-century Latin hymn 'Jesu Dulcis Memoria'.

JESUS THE VERY THOUGHT OF THEE
With sweetness fills my breast.
But sweeter far Thy face to see,
And in Thy presence rest.

Nor voice can sing, nor heart can frame,
Nor can the memory find
A sweeter sound than Thy blest name,
O Saviour of mankind!

O hope of every contrite heart,
O joy of all the meek,
To those who fall, how kind Thou art!
How good to those who seek!

But what to those who find? Ah, this
Nor tongue nor pen can show;
The love of Jesus, what it is,
None but His loved ones know.

Jesus, our only joy be Thou,
As Thou our prize will be;
Jesus be Thou our glory now,
And through eternity.

O Jesus, King most wonderful
Thou Conqueror renowned,
Thou sweetness most ineffable
In whom all joys are found!

When once Thou visitest the heart,
Then truth begins to shine,
Then earthly vanities depart,
Then kindles love divine.

O Jesus, light of all below,
Thou fount of living fire,
Surpassing all the joys we know,
And all we can desire.

Jesus, may all confess Thy name,
Thy wondrous love adore,
And, seeking Thee, themselves inflame
To seek Thee more and more.

Thee, Jesus, may our voices bless,
Thee may we love alone,
And ever in our lives express
The image of Thine own.

O Jesus, Thou the beauty art
Of angel worlds above;
Thy name is music to the heart,
Inflaming it with love.

Celestial sweetness unalloyed,
Who eat Thee hunger still;
Who drink of Thee still feel a void
Which only Thou canst fill.

O most sweet Jesus, hear the sighs
Which unto Thee we send;
To Thee our inmost spirit cries;
To Thee our prayers ascend.

Abide with us and let Thy light
Shine, Lord, on every heart;
Dispel the darkness of our night;
And joy to all impart.

Jesus, our love and joy to Thee,
The Virgin's holy Son,
All might and praise and glory be,
While endless ages run.

Of course, an even more famous Anglican had led the way to Rome in the same year as Faber and Caswell: John Henry Newman. Two of his hymns are still very popular. Here's one of them, from his long work 'The Dream of Gerontius':

PRAISE TO THE HOLIEST IN THE HEIGHT,
And in the depth be praise;
In all His words most wonderful,
Most sure in all His ways.

O loving wisdom of our God!
When all was sin and shame,
A second Adam to the fight
And to the rescue came.

O wisest love! that flesh and blood,
Which did in Adam fail,
Should strive afresh against the foe,
Should strive and should prevail.

And that a higher gift than grace
Should flesh and blood refine;
God's presence and His very self,
And essence all divine.

O generous love! that He who smote
In Man for man the foe,
The double agony in Man
For man should undergo.

And in the garden secretly,
And on the cross on high,
Should teach His brethren, and inspire
To suffer and to die.

Praise to the Holiest in the height,
And in the depth be praise;
In all His words most wonderful,
Most sure in all His ways.

I said earlier that the Tractarians caused controversy but wrote beautiful hymns. In the case of one of their hymns at least, our last one tonight, the two things go together – controversy and beauty, that is. S. J. Stone, like any supporters of the Anglo-Catholic movement, was deeply perturbed at the Bishop Colenso affair. This was a famous church scandal in South Africa and centred on Colenso, who held – and worse, publicised – unorthodox views on the miraculous element in the Gospels. He typified, in the minds of the orthodox, the compromise with modern science and with critical views of the Bible that they feared and deplored. The scandal rocked the Church, which for a while seemed likely to split in two over it. During this period, Stone wrote what must be the greatest hymn on the essential unity of the Church ever written. It may have had its roots in a rather unedifying church row but it captures, in memorable words and phrases, the Church not as we see it, perhaps, but as God sees it – 'the great Church victorious'. This hymn, 'The Church's One Foundation', was sung as a processional at the Lambeth Conference of Anglican Bishops and it is reported that the effect was awesome, the congregation quite overcome by this majestic picture of the Holy Catholic Church.

> Elect from every nation
> Yet One o'er all the earth.
> Her charter of salvation
> One Lord, one faith, one birth.

Perhaps they thought of Bishop Colenso – who broke away from the Church of the Province of South Africa to lead a splinter group of Anglicans – when they sang the fourth verse. Here is the hymn in full:

> THE CHURCH'S ONE FOUNDATION
> Is Jesus Christ her Lord,
> She is His new creation
> By water and the word.
> From heaven He came and sought her
> To be His holy bride;
> With His own blood He bought her
> And for her life He died.
>
> Elect from every nation,
> Yet one o'er all the earth;
> Her charter of salvation,
> One Lord, one faith, one birth;
> One holy name she blesses,
> Partakes one holy food,
> And to one hope she presses,
> With every grace endued.
>
> The Church shall never perish!
> Her dear Lord to defend,
> To guide, sustain and cherish,

Is with her to the end:
Though there be those who hate her,
And false sons in her pale,
Against both foe or traitor
She ever shall prevail.

Though with a scornful wonder
Men see her sore oppressed,
By schisms rent asunder,
By heresies distressed:
Yet saints their watch are keeping,
Their cry goes up, 'How long?'
And soon the night of weeping
Shall be the morn of song!

'Mid toil and tribulation,
And tumult of her war,
She waits the consummation
Of peace for evermore;
Till, with the vision glorious,
Her longing eyes are blest,
And the great Church victorious
Shall be the Church at rest.

Yet she on earth hath union
With God the Three in One,
And mystic sweet communion
With those whose rest is won,
With all her sons and daughters
Who, by the Master's hand
Led through the deathly waters,
Repose in Eden land.

O happy ones and holy!
Lord, give us grace that we
Like them, the meek and lowly,
On high may dwell with Thee:
There, past the border mountains,

Where in sweet vales the bride
With Thee by living fountains
Forever shall abide!

MRS C. F. ALEXANDER AND OTHER WOMEN

From Series 1

BBC Radio Four
Sunday 24 August 1975
Producers: David Winter and Angela Tilby

• • •

Unlike women preachers, who are still a bit suspect, women hymn-writers have been accepted and respected for a century and a half. That's only fair, seeing that women probably make up the majority of hymn-singers. Not the first historically but undoubtedly the first in rank is Cecil Frances Alexander. She was the wife of an Irish clergyman who later became Archbishop of Armagh and her hymns appeared during that purple period of British hymn-writing, the second half of Queen Victoria's reign.

As a matter of fact, her first book of hymns was published before she was married, when she was Miss C. F. Humphreys. Her godsons, so the story goes, complained that the catechism, which they were swotting up for confirmation, was difficult and boring. Her response was to write a set of verses illustrating the different clauses of the Creed for their benefit – verses that were published in 1848 under the title *Hymns for Little Children*. (It is not recorded what her godsons' reaction was to that title.)

Her verses to illustrate the opening clause of the Creed – 'I believe in God the Father Almighty, Creator of heaven and earth' – have achieved their own peculiar brand of immortality.

ALL THINGS BRIGHT AND BEAUTIFUL,
All creatures great and small,
All things wise and wonderful,
The Lord God made them all.

Each little flower that opens,
Each little bird that sings,
He made their glowing colours,
He made their tiny wings.
Chorus

The rich man in his castle,
The poor man at his gate,
He made them, high or lowly,
And ordered their estate.
Chorus

The purple-headed mountains,
The river running by,
The sunset and the morning
That brightens up the sky.
Chorus

The cold wind in the winter,
The pleasant summer sun,
The ripe fruits in the garden,
He made them every one.
Chorus

The tall trees in the greenwood,
The meadows where we play,
The rushes by the water,
To gather every day.
Chorus

He gave us eyes to see them,
And lips that we might tell

How great is God Almighty,
Who has made all things well.
   Chorus

The following section of the Creed deals with the mystery of the
incarnation: the birth of Jesus. Mrs Alexander skipped the bit about
the Virgin Birth, probably to her godsons' disappointment, but in a
hymn that has become a best-loved carol – 'Once in Royal David's
City' – she captured the wonder of it all: 'He came down to earth
from heaven, who is God and Lord of all, and his shelter was a
stable, and his cradle was a stall.'

ONCE IN ROYAL DAVID'S CITY
Stood a lowly cattle shed,
Where a mother laid her Baby
In a manger for His bed:
Mary was that mother mild,
Jesus Christ her little Child.

He came down to earth from heaven,
Who is God and Lord of all,
And His shelter was a stable,
And His cradle was a stall;
With the poor and mean and lowly,
Lived on earth our Saviour holy.

And, through all His wondrous childhood,
He would honour and obey,
Love and watch the lowly maiden,
In whose gentle arms He lay:
Christian children all must be
Mild, obedient, good as He.

For He is our childhood's pattern;
Day by day, like us He grew;
He was little, weak and helpless,
Tears and smiles like us He knew;

And He feeleth for our sadness,
And He shareth in our gladness.

And our eyes at last shall see Him,
Through His own redeeming love,
For that Child so dear and gentle
Is our Lord in heav'n above,
And He leads His children on
To the place where He is gone.

Not in that poor lowly stable,
With the oxen standing by,
We shall see Him; but in heaven,
Set at God's right hand on high;
Where like stars His children crowned
All in white shall wait around.

Going on through the Creed, her godsons will have come to an equally profound clause: 'He suffered under Pontius Pilate, was crucified dead and buried.' To illustrate that, Mrs Alexander wrote some verses that, as an example of profound ideas in simple words, have probably never been surpassed:

THERE IS A GREEN HILL FAR AWAY
Without a city wall,
Where the dear Lord was crucified
Who died to save us all.

We may not know, we cannot tell,
What pains He had to bear,
But we believe it was for us
He hung and suffered there.

He died that we might be forgiv'n,
He died to make us good,
That we might go at last to heav'n,
Saved by His precious blood.

There was no other good enough
To pay the price of sin,
He only could unlock the gate
Of heav'n and let us in.

O dearly, dearly has He loved!
And we must love Him too,
And trust in His redeeming blood,
And try His works to do.

Although she is remembered best for her children's hymns, Mrs Alexander also wrote prolifically for adults: nearly four hundred hymns and poems in all. Of her general hymns, probably the best known is 'Jesus Calls Us', based on the Gospel account of the call of Peter and Andrew at the side of the lake. It's a masterpiece of economical writing and in its own way a devotional classic: 'In our joys and in our sorrows, days of toil and hours of ease, still He calls, in cares and pleasures, "Christian, love Me more than these!"'

JESUS CALLS US O'ER THE TUMULT
Of our life's wild, restless sea;
Day by day His sweet voice soundeth,
Saying, 'Christian, follow me!'

As of old th'Apostles heard it
By the Galilean lake,
Turned from home and toil and kindred,
Leaving all for Jesus' sake.

Jesus calls us from the worship
Of the vain world's golden store,
From each idol that would keep us,
Saying, 'Christian, love Me more!'

In our joys and in our sorrows,
Days of toil and hours of ease,

Still He calls, in cares and pleasures,
'Christian, love Me more than these!'

Jesus calls us! By Thy mercies,
Saviour, may we hear Thy call;
Give our hearts to Thine obedience,
Serve and love Thee best of all.

While Mrs Alexander is probably the most distinguished woman hymn-writer, there are many others of the highest quality. The first woman to achieve distinction in this field was a Baptist, Anne Steele, almost a hundred years before Mrs Alexander. Like several other famous women writers of previous centuries, she was dogged all her life by illness and personal tragedy. She was seriously injured in an accident as a child and later, on the morning of the very day on which she was to be married, her fiancé was drowned. But, like many other hymn-writers, she turned her sorrow into poetic inspiration:

FATHER, WHATE'ER OF EARTHLY BLISS
Thy sov'reign hand denies,
Accepted at Thy throne of grace
Let this petition rise:[1]

Give me a calm and thankful heart,
From every murmur free,
The blessings of Thy grace impart,
And let me live to Thee.

Let the sweet hope that Thou art mine
My life and death attend;

[1] In other versions:
Father, whate'er of earthly bliss
Thy sovereign will denies,
Accepted at Thy throne, let this
My humble prayer, arise.

> Thy presence through my journey shine,
> And crown my journey's end.

The same note runs through Anne Steele's best-known hymn. It's one of the four really satisfying hymns about the Bible, perhaps because it sees it in intensely personal terms:

> FATHER OF MERCIES, IN THY WORD[2]
> What endless glory shines!
> Forever be Thy name adored
> For these celestial lines.
>
> Here may the blind and hungry come
> And light and food receive;
> Here shall the lowliest guest have room
> And taste and see and live.
>
> Here springs of consolation rise
> To cheer the fainting mind,
> And thirsting souls receive supplies
> And sweet refreshment find.
>
> Here the Redeemer's welcome voice
> Spreads heavenly peace around,
> And life and everlasting joys
> Attend the blissful sound.
>
> Oh, may these heavenly pages be
> My ever dear delight;
> And still new beauties may I see
> And still increasing light!
>
> Divine Instructor, gracious Lord,
> Be Thou forever near;
> Teach me to love Thy sacred word
> And view my Saviour here.

[2] In Betjeman's script: 'Father of mercy'.

Also earlier than Mrs Alexander was another invalid, Charlotte Elliott. For fifty years, from the age of thirty-two, she was a permanent invalid and much of her writing was either about suffering or addressed to her fellow-sufferers. *Hours of Sorrow Cheered and Comforted* was the title of one collection of poems and another was called simply *The Invalid's Hymn Book.* The hymn for which she is justly famous came directly out of her own experience. After her illness she went to live at Brighton in her brother's vicarage. One afternoon, he and the rest of the family had gone out to a church bazaar leaving Charlotte, the invalid, at home. As she sat in her chair, waiting for them to return, she was momentarily overwhelmed with a sense of her own loneliness and uselessness. From that came a hymn of total faith and trust: 'Just as I am – poor, wretched, blind; sight, riches, healing of the mind, yea, all I need, in thee to find, O Lamb of God, I come.'

> JUST AS I AM, WITHOUT ONE PLEA
> But that Thy blood was shed for me,
> And that Thou bid'st me come to thee,
> O Lamb of God, I come!
>
> Just as I am and waiting not
> To rid my soul of one dark blot,
> To Thee, whose blood can cleanse each spot,
> O Lamb of God, I come!
>
> Just as I am, though toss'd about,
> With many a conflict, many a doubt,
> Fightings and fears within, without,
> O Lamb of God, I come!
>
> Just as I am – poor, wretched, blind;
> Sight, riches, healing of the mind,
> Yea, all I need, in Thee to find,
> O Lamb of God, I come!

Just as I am, Thou wilt receive,
Wilt welcome, pardon, cleanse, relieve;
Because Thy promise I believe,
O Lamb of God, I come!

Just as I am – Thy love unknown
Has broken every barrier down;
Now to be Thine, yea, Thine alone,
O Lamb of God, I come!

Just as I am, of that free love,
The breadth, length, depth, and height to prove,
Here for a season, then above,
O Lamb of God, I come!

Many of the best-known hymns written by women are hymns of personal devotion and experience. Think of 'Take my Life and Let It Be, Consecrated, Lord, to Thee' by Frances Ridley Havergal or Jane Borthwick's 'Be Still My Soul, the Lord Is on Thy Side' or Elizabeth Clephane's 'Beneath the Cross of Jesus, I Fain Would Take My Stand'. There are exceptions, of course, like Mrs Alexander's hymns on the Creed, but perhaps the strongest hymn of a robust, outward-looking kind to come from a woman's pen was by a contemporary of Mrs Alexander's, Caroline Noel, who, like Anne Steele and Charlotte Elliott, had poor health. At the age of forty, and seriously ill, she turned back to writing poetry, which she had given up for twenty years. The result was a book of hymns entitled *Verses for the Sick and Lonely* but it began with 'At the Name of Jesus', a majestic hymn in quite a different vein:

AT THE NAME OF JESUS, EVERY KNEE SHALL BOW,
Every tongue confess Him, King of glory now;
'Tis the Father's pleasure we should call Him Lord,
Who from the beginning was the mighty word.

Mighty and mysterious in the highest height,
God from everlasting, very Light of light.

In the Father's bosom with the Spirit blest,
Love, in love eternal, rest, in perfect rest.

At His voice creation sprang at once to sight,
All the angel faces, all the hosts of light,
Thrones and dominations, stars upon their way,
All the heavenly orders, in their great array.

Humbled for a season, to receive a name
From the lips of sinners unto whom He came,
Faithfully He bore it, spotless to the last,
Brought it back victorious when from death He passed.

Bore it up triumphant with its human light,
Through all ranks of creatures, to the central height,
To the throne of Godhead, to the Father's breast;
Filled it with the glory of that perfect rest.

Name Him, brothers, name Him, with love strong as death
But with awe and wonder and with bated breath!
He is God the Saviour, He is Christ the Lord,
Ever to be worshipped, trusted and adored.

In your hearts enthrone Him; there let Him subdue
All that is not holy, all that is not true.
Crown Him as your Captain in temptation's hour;
Let His will enfold you in its light and power.

Brothers, this Lord Jesus shall return again,
With His Father's glory, with His angel train;
For all wreaths of empire meet upon His brow,
And our hearts confess Him King of Glory now.

Finally, a hymn about the Ascension – a particularly difficult subject – but not this time primarily for children. It's Catherine Winkworth's translation of a seventeenth-century German hymn by Georg Weissel based on the picturesque imagery of Psalm 24: 'Lift up Your Heads, O Ye Gates'.

LIFT UP YOUR HEADS, YE MIGHTY GATES;
Behold, the King of glory waits;
The King of kings is drawing near;
The Saviour of the world is here!

A helper just He comes to thee,
His chariot is humility,
His kingly crown is holiness,
His sceptre, pity in distress.

O blest the land, the city blest,
Where Christ the Ruler is confessed!
O happy hearts and happy homes
To whom this King in triumph comes!

Fling wide the portals of your heart;
Make it a temple, set apart
From earthly use for heaven's employ,
Adorned with prayer and love and joy.

Redeemer, come, with us abide;
Our hearts to Thee we open wide;
Let us Thy inner presence feel;
Thy grace and love in us reveal.

Thy Holy Spirit lead us on
Until our glorious goal is won;
Eternal praise, eternal fame
Be offered, Saviour, to Thy name!

KEBLE AND OTHER TRACTARIANS

From Series 1

BBC Radio Four
Sunday 31 August 1975
Producers: David Winter and Angela Tilby

• • •

John Keble was one of three men who influenced English
hymnody and the Church in Victorian England as profoundly as
the Wesleys had done almost a century earlier. Keble was the oldest
of them. He was the author of just about the most popular book
of verse published in the nineteenth century and the father of the
Oxford Movement, the Anglo-Catholic movement that was to
change the face of the Anglican Church and introduce a whole
new vein of hymnody to it.

The book was called *The Christian Year* and it was published in
1827, the year that saw the posthumous publication of Bishop
Heber's hymns. Over the next forty years, more than a hundred
editions of it appeared. William Wilberforce recalled how he and
his four sons each agreed to bring a new book on holiday for
reading aloud. It turned out that all five brought *The Christian Year*.
The book contained poems for the fasts and feasts of the church
calendar, a sort of devotional companion to the Prayer Book. It also
contained the words of hymns that were to become part of English
hymnody, none more so than the morning hymn 'New Every
Morning':

New every morning is the love
Our wakening and uprising prove;
Through sleep and darkness safely brought,
Restored to life and pow'r and thought.

New mercies, each returning day,
Hover around us while we pray;
New perils past, new sins forgiven,
New thoughts of God, new hopes of heaven.

If, on our daily course, our mind
Be set to hallow all we find,
New treasures still, of countless price,
God will provide for sacrifice.

Old friends, old scenes, will lovelier be,
As more of heav'n in each we see;
Some softening gleam of love and prayer
Shall dawn on every cross and care.

We need not bid, for cloistered cell,
Our neighbour and our words farewell,
Nor strive to find ourselves too high
For sinful man beneath the sky.

The trivial round, the common task,
Will furnish all we ought to ask;
Room to deny ourselves, a road
To bring us daily nearer God.

Seek we no more: content with these,
Let present rapture, comfort, ease –
As heav'n shall bid them, come and go:
The secret this of rest below.

Only, O Lord, in Thy dear love,
Fit us for perfect rest above,
And help us, this and every day,
To live more nearly as we pray.

Matthew Arnold described *The Christian Year* in these terms: 'The wonderful knowledge of Scripture, the purity of heart and the richness of poetry . . . I never saw equalled.' Well, that may be overstating it a bit but, beyond doubt, there were here verses that had a rare devotional quality. Typical of them is Keble's evening hymn, 'Sun of my Soul'.

SUN OF MY SOUL, THOU SAVIOUR DEAR,
It is not night if Thou be near;
O may no earth-born cloud arise
To hide Thee from Thy servant's eyes!

When the soft dews of kindly sleep
My wearied eyelids gently steep,
Be my last thought, how sweet to rest
Forever on my Saviour's breast.

Abide with me from morn till eve,
For without Thee I cannot live;
Abide with me when night is nigh,
For without Thee I dare not die.

If some poor wandering child of Thine
Has spurned today the voice divine,
Now, Lord, the gracious work begin;
Let him no more lie down in sin.

Watch by the sick, enrich the poor,
With blessings from Thy boundless store;
Be every mourner's sleep tonight,
Like infants' slumbers, pure and right.

Come near and bless us when we wake,
Ere through the world our way we take,
Till in the ocean of Thy love
We lose ourselves in heaven above.

With the proceeds of *The Christian Year*, Keble was able completely to rebuild the church at Hursley, in Hampshire, where he was vicar. Dr Pusey regarded the book as 'one of the most powerful sources of revival in the Church of England'. In the early years of Queen Victoria, no respectable household was without its copy.

So much for the book. But Keble's influence went far beyond that. In 1833, he preached his famous 'Assize' Sermon at Oxford, which is often regarded as the starting point of the Oxford Movement. In it he denounced the State's interference in the affairs of the Church of England and reasserted the authority of the historic Faith. Eventually the movement turned its attention to restoring Catholic doctrine, ceremonial and ritual, to the Church, including confession, the religious life and devotion to the Blessèd Virgin Mary. It was for one of the feasts of Mary in *The Christian Year* that Keble wrote the beautiful verses, paraphrasing the Beatitude, 'Blest are the pure in heart'.

> BLEST ARE THE PURE IN HEART,
> For they shall see our God;
> The secret of the Lord is theirs,
> Their soul is Christ's abode.
>
> The Lord, who left the heav'ns
> Our life and peace to bring,
> To dwell in lowliness with men
> Their pattern and their King.
>
> Still to the lowly soul
> He doth Himself impart;
> And for His cradle and His throne
> Chooseth the pure in heart.
>
> Lord, we Thy presence seek;
> May ours this blessing be;
> Give us a pure and lowly heart,
> A temple meet for Thee.

Among the supporters of the Oxford movement were two other men who were destined to make a lasting impression on the English Church. J. M. Neale was a brilliant scholar – eleven times Seatonian prize winner – but, handicapped by poor health, he was never able to take on a parish. Instead, he became warden of a refuge for indigent old men and founded an order of nuns, the Sisterhood of St Margaret. He knew twenty languages and put that skill to good effect in translating hymns and carols – among them, incidentally, 'Good King Wenceslas' – mostly from the Catholic or Orthodox tradition. But one of his best-known hymns is in fact entirely original: 'Art Thou Weary, Art Thou Languid?'

> ART THOU WEARY, ART THOU LANGUID,
> Art thou sore distressed?
> 'Come to Me,' saith One, 'and coming,
> Be at rest.'
>
> Hath He marks to lead me to Him,
> If He be my guide?
> In His feet and hands are wound prints
> And his side.
>
> Is there diadem, as monarch,
> That His brow adorns?
> Yes, a crown in very surety,
> But of thorns.
>
> If I find Him, if I follow,
> What his guerdon here?
> Many a sorrow, many a labour,
> Many a tear.
>
> If I still hold closely to Him,
> What hath He at last?
> Sorrow vanquished, labour ended,
> Jordan passed.

> If I ask Him to receive me,
> Will He say me nay?
> Not till earth and not till heaven
> Pass away.
>
> Finding, following, keeping, struggling,
> Is He sure to bless?
> Saints, apostles, prophets, martyrs,
> Answer, yes!

Probably Neale's best-known translation is his Palm Sunday hymn 'All Glory, Laud and Honour' from the Latin of St Theodulph of Orleans in the ninth[1] century. Incidentally, the usual tune, 'St Theodulph', was in fact written over 200 years before Neale's translation appeared – a reversal of the usual order.

> *ALL GLORY, LAUD AND HONOUR,*
> *To Thee, Redeemer King,*
> *To whom the lips of children*
> *Made sweet hosannas ring.*
>
> Thou art the King of Israel,
> Thou David's royal Son,
> Who in the Lord's name comest,
> The King and Blessèd One.
> *Chorus*
>
> The company of angels
> Are praising Thee on High,
> And mortal men and all things
> Created make reply.
> *Chorus*
>
> The people of the Hebrews
> With palms before Thee went;

[1] 'Eighth', wrongly, in JB's text. Theodulph wrote *Gloria, Laus et Honor* from a prison cell between 820–821.

Our prayer and praise and anthems
Before Thee we present.
    Chorus

To Thee, before Thy Passion,
They sang their hymns of praise;
To Thee, now high exalted,
Our melody we raise.
    Chorus

Thou didst accept their praises;
Accept the prayers we bring,
Who in all good delightest,
Thou good and gracious King.
    Chorus

Be Thou, O Lord, the Rider,
And we the little ass,
That to God's holy city
Together we may pass.
    Chorus

One area in which Neale broke entirely new ground was in bringing hymns of the Greek Orthodox Church into English hymnody. Here was an untapped vein of devotion, some of it well over a thousand years old. Neale managed to keep the distinctively Greek 'feel' of the hymns while putting them into English metre. A good example is 'The Day Is Past and Over', translated from an anonymous sixth-century source; another is the Lenten hymn 'Christian, Dost Thou See Them', translated from the eighth-century Greek of St Andrew of Crete (660-732).

CHRISTIAN, DOST THOU SEE THEM
On the holy ground,
How the powers of darkness
Rage thy steps around?
Christian, up and smite them,

Counting gain but loss,
In the strength that cometh
By the holy cross.

Christian, dost thou feel them,
How they work within,
Striving, tempting, luring,
Goading into sin?
Christian, never tremble;
Never be downcast;
Gird thee for the battle,
Watch and pray and fast.

Christian, dost thou hear them,
How they speak thee fair?
'Always fast and vigil?
Always watch and prayer?'
Christian, answer boldly:
'While I breathe I pray!'
Peace shall follow battle,
Night shall end in day.

'Well I know thy trouble,
O my servant true;
Thou art very weary,
I was weary, too;
But that toil shall make thee
Some day all Mine own,
At the end of sorrow
Shall be near my throne.'

A third important member of the Oxford movement was John
Henry Newman, at any rate until 1845 when he joined the Roman
Catholic Church. He was not a hymn-writer but two pieces of his
verse, neither intended for use as a hymn, have earned him a place
in every hymnbook. 'Praise to the Holiest in the Height' was part
of a long choral work, 'The Dream of Gerontius' – a work he was

so displeased with that he discarded the manuscript; fortunately a friend rescued it.

> PRAISE TO THE HOLIEST IN THE HEIGHT,
> And in the depth be praise;
> In all His words most wonderful,
> Most sure in all His ways.
>
> O loving wisdom of our God!
> When all was sin and shame,
> A second Adam to the fight
> And to the rescue came.
>
> O wisest love! that flesh and blood,
> Which did in Adam fail,
> Should strive afresh against the foe,
> Should strive and should prevail;
>
> And that the highest gift of grace
> Should flesh and blood refine;
> God's presence and His very self,
> And essence all divine.
>
> O generous love! that He who smote
> In Man for man the foe,
> The double agony in Man
> For man should undergo.
>
> And in the garden secretly,
> And on the cross on high,
> Should teach His brethren, and inspire
> To suffer and to die.
>
> Praise to the Holiest in the height,
> And in the depth be praise;
> In all His words most wonderful,
> Most sure in all His ways.

Newman's other great hymn is 'Lead kindly Light'. As with so
many others, it was the product of a period of deep anxiety. At a
crucial moment in his life he succumbed to fever while on holiday
in Sicily and was thought to be dying. He longed to get back to
England but there was no boat for three weeks. When he did catch
an orange boat to Marseilles, it was becalmed for a week. At that
point, in deep distress, he wrote this great hymn of the seeker – or
perhaps, rather, the follower:

> LEAD, KINDLY LIGHT, AMID THE ENCIRCLING GLOOM
> Lead Thou me on!
> The night is dark and I am far from home –
> Lead Thou me on!
> Keep Thou my feet; I do not ask to see
> The distant scene – one step enough for me.
>
> I was not ever thus, nor prayed that Thou
> Shouldst lead me on;
> I loved to choose and see my path; but now
> Lead Thou me on!
> I loved the garish day and, spite of fears,
> Pride ruled my will: remember not past years!
>
> So long Thy power hath blessed me, sure it still
> Will lead me on.
> O'er moor and fen, o'er crag and torrent, till
> The night is gone,
> And with the morn those angel faces smile,
> Which I have loved long since and lost awhile!

VICTORIANS

From Series 1

BBC Radio Four
Sunday 7 September 1975
Producers: David Winter and Angela Tilby

• • •

This week we're going to look at some of the great Victorian hymn-writers. We've already heard from the Tractarians, those men who explored the riches of Catholic and Orthodox devotion, and we've also heard from some of the Victorian ladies. But now we're going to meet some of those remarkable Victorian clergymen from whose country vicarages and rectories and deaneries – and bishops' palaces – flowed a stream of hymns that have filled out our hymn-books ever since.

And we start with a man who was largely responsible for the most famous of those hymn-books, the redoubtable *Hymns Ancient and Modern*. Sir Henry Williams Baker was a baronet and for most of his life the High Church vicar of Monkland, near Leominster, in Herefordshire. To the first volume of *Hymns Ancient and Modern* Baker contributed twenty-five hymns himself – some translations and some original. Of the latter, probably the most popular today is 'The King of Love my Shepherd Is'.

> THE KING OF LOVE MY SHEPHERD IS,
> Whose goodness faileth never,
> I nothing lack if I am His
> And He is mine forever.

Where streams of living water flow
My ransomed soul He leadeth,
And where the verdant pastures grow,
With food celestial feedeth.

Perverse and foolish oft I strayed,
But yet in love He sought me,
And on His shoulder gently laid,
And home, rejoicing, brought me.

In death's dark vale I fear no ill
With Thee, dear Lord, beside me;
Thy rod and staff my comfort still,
Thy cross before to guide me.

Thou spread'st a table in my sight;
Thine unction grace bestoweth;
And O what transport of delight
From Thy pure chalice floweth!

And so through all the length of days
Thy goodness faileth never;
Good Shepherd, may I sing Thy praise
Within Thy house forever.

One of the most eminent Victorian hymn-writers was William Walsham How, regarded by Bernard Manning[1] as possibly the greatest nineteenth-century hymn-writer. He was Bishop of Bedford, where he was known as 'the poor man's bishop', and of Wakefield. Of all his hymns, perhaps the finest is one he wrote for All Saints-tide and for which Vaughan Williams wrote a perfect tune, 'For All the Saints'.

FOR ALL THE SAINTS, WHO FROM THEIR LABOURS REST,
Who Thee by faith before the world confessed,

[1] Bernard Lord Manning (1892–1941), historian of religion and one of Betjeman's many sources for material in these talks.

Thy Name, O Jesus, be forever blest.
Alleluia, Alleluia!

Thou wast their Rock, their Fortress and their Might;
Thou, Lord, their Captain in the well-fought fight;
Thou, in the darkness drear, their one true Light.
Alleluia, Alleluia!

For the apostles' glorious company,
Who bearing forth the cross o'er land and sea,
Shook all the mighty world, we sing to Thee:
Alleluia, Alleluia!

For the Evangelists, by whose blest word,
Like fourfold streams, the garden of the Lord,
Is fair and fruitful, be Thy Name adored.
Alleluia, Alleluia!

For martyrs, who with rapture-kindled eye,
Saw the bright crown descending from the sky,
And seeing, grasped it, Thee we glorify.
Alleluia, Alleluia!

O blest communion, fellowship divine!
We feebly struggle, they in glory shine;
All are one in Thee, for all are Thine.
Alleluia, Alleluia!

O may Thy soldiers, faithful, true and bold,
Fight as the saints who nobly fought of old,
And win with them the victor's crown of gold.
Alleluia, Alleluia!

And when the strife is fierce, the warfare long,
Steals on the ear[2] the distant triumph song,

---

[2] Or 'Far off we hear'.

And hearts are brave, again, and arms are strong.
Alleluia, Alleluia!

The golden evening brightens in the west;
Soon, soon to faithful warriors comes their rest;
Sweet is the calm of paradise the blessed.
Alleluia, Alleluia!

But lo! there breaks a yet more glorious day;
The saints triumphant rise in bright array;
The King of Glory passes on His way.
Alleluia, Alleluia!

From earth's wide bounds, from ocean's farthest coast,
Through gates of pearl streams in the countless host,
And singing to Father, Son and Holy Ghost:
Alleluia, Alleluia!

Victorian hymn–writers, as befitted the age of imperialism and the Raj, were fascinated by military metaphors for the Christian Church. One sees the Victorian Church of England as one endless processional, terrible with banners. Bishop How wrote one such 'military' hymn, 'Soldiers of Christ, Arise'.[3]

SOLDIERS OF CHRIST, ARISE,[4]
And put your armour on,
Strong in the strength which God supplies
Through his eternal Son;

Strong in the Lord of hosts,
And in His mighty power:
Who in the strength of Jesus trusts
Is more than conqueror.

[3] Other hymns considered by Betjeman for inclusion here were George Duffield Junior's 'Stand up, Stand up for Jesus'.
[4] A longer and different version of this hymn appears on p. 51.

Stand then in His great might,
With all his strength endued,
And take, to arm you for the fight,
The panoply of God.

From strength to strength go on,
Wrestle and fight and pray:
Tread all the pow'rs of darkness down,
And win the well-fought day.

That, having all things done,
And all your conflicts past,
Ye may obtain, through Christ alone,
A crown of joy at last.

Jesus, eternal Son,
We praise Thee and adore,
Who art with God the Father one,
And Spirit evermore.

The definitive military hymn, of course, is 'Onward Christian Soldiers', taken up by the Salvation Army in its early days as a kind of battle song. It was written in fact by an Anglican vicar and medieval scholar, Sabine Baring-Gould, for a Whit-Monday Sunday-School procession in the parish in Yorkshire where he was curate:

ONWARD CHRISTIAN SOLDIERS,
Marching as to war,
With the cross of Jesus
Going on before.
Christ, the royal Master,
Leads against the foe;
Forward into battle
See His banners go!
   Onward Christian soldiers
   Marching as to war,

With the cross of Jesus
Going on before.

At the sign of triumph
Satan's host doth flee;
On then, Christian soldiers,
On to victory!
Hell's foundations quiver
At the shout of praise;
Brothers lift your voices,
Loud your anthems raise.
    Chorus

Like a mighty army
Moves the Church of God;
Brothers, we are treading
Where the saints have trod.
We are not divided,
All one body we,
One in hope and doctrine,
One in charity.
    Chorus

What the saints established
That I hold for true.
What the saints believèd,
That I believe too.
Long as earth endureth,
Men the faith will hold,
Kingdoms, nations, empires,
In destruction rolled.
    Chorus

Crowns and thrones may perish,
Kingdoms rise and wane,
But the Church of Jesus
Constant will remain.
Gates of hell can never

'Gainst that Church prevail;
We have Christ's own promise,
And that cannot fail.
    Chorus

Onward then, ye people,
Join our happy throng,
Blend with ours your voices
In the triumph song.
Glory, laud and honour
Unto Christ the King,
This through countless ages
Men and angels sing.
    Chorus

Later Baring-Gould appointed himself, under the fascinating procedures of patronage, Rector of Lew Trenchard, Devon, which had been his family's seat for three hundred years. As well as many original hymns, he translated another very muscular hymn – appropriately, from the German. It's still deservedly popular:

THROUGH THE NIGHT OF DOUBT AND SORROW
Onward goes the pilgrim band,
Singing songs of expectation
Marching to the Promised Land.
Clear before us through the darkness
Gleams and burns the guiding light:
Trusting God we march together
Stepping fearless through the night.

One the light of God's own presence,
O'er His ransomed people shed,
Chasing far the gloom and terror,
Brightening all the path we tread;
One the object of our journey,
One the faith which never tires,
One the earnest looking forward,
One the hope our God inspires.

One the strain the lips of thousands
Lift as from the heart of one;
One the conflict, one the peril,
One the march in God begun;
One the gladness of rejoicing
On the far eternal shore,
Where the One Almighty Father
Reigns in love for evermore.

Onward, therefore, pilgrim brothers,
Onward with the cross our aid;
Bear its shame, and fight its battle,
Till we rest beneath its shade.
Soon shall come the great awaking,
Soon the rending of the tomb;
Then the scattering of all shadows,
And the end of toil and gloom.

Not all the great clerical hymn-writers of the century were
Anglicans: Horatius Bonar was a minister of the Kirk, described by
James Moffatt as 'the prince of Scottish hymn-writers'. He wrote
over six hundred hymns, of which about one hundred are in
common use. One of his most popular hymns is cast in the form
of a dialogue between the voice of Jesus and the disciples' response:

I HEARD THE VOICE OF JESUS SAY,
'Come unto Me and rest;
Lay down, thou weary one, lay down
Thy head upon My breast.'
I came to Jesus as I was,
Weary and worn and sad;
I found in Him a resting place,
And He has made me glad.

I heard the voice of Jesus say,
'Behold, I freely give
The living water; thirsty one,

Stoop down and drink and live.'
I came to Jesus and I drank
Of that life-giving stream;
My thirst was quenched, my soul revived,
And now I live in Him.

I heard the voice of Jesus say,
'I am this dark world's light;
Look unto Me, thy morn shall rise,
And all thy day be bright.'
I looked to Jesus and I found
In Him my Star, my Sun;
And in that light of life I'll walk,
Till travelling days are done.

Bonar's other very popular hymn is 'Fill Thou my Life':

FILL THOU MY LIFE, O LORD MY GOD,
In every part with praise,
That my whole being may proclaim
Thy being and Thy ways.
Not for the lip of praise alone,
Nor e'en the praising heart
I ask, but for a life made up
Of praise in every part!

Praise in the common words I speak,
Life's common looks and tones,
In fellowship in hearth and board
With my belovèd ones;[5]
Not in the temple crowd alone

[5] An alternative version of this hymn substitutes the following for lines nine to twelve:
Praise in the common things of life,
Its going out and in;
Praise in each duty and each deed,
However small and mean.

Where holy voices chime,
But in the silent paths of earth,
The quiet rooms of time.

Fill every part of me with praise;
Let all my being speak
Of Thee and of Thy love, O Lord,
Poor though I be, and weak.
So shalt Thou, Lord, from me, e'en me,
Receive the glory due;
And so shall I begin on earth
The song forever new.

So shall each fear, each fret, each care
Be turned into a song,
And every winding of the way
The echo shall prolong;
So shall no part of day or night
From sacredness be free;
But all my life, in every step
Be fellowship with Thee.

H. F. Lyte was also a Scot but he studied at Eniskillen and Trinity College, Dublin, and after a curacy in Wexford spent the rest of his life in West-Country parishes. It was while he was vicar of Marazion in Cornwall in 1817 that he underwent a profound emotional experience at the deathbed of a friend. It was said to have changed his whole outlook on life and revitalised his preaching. 'Praise, My Soul, the King of Heaven' is one of the favourite hymns of the English-speaking people.

PRAISE, MY SOUL, THE KING OF HEAVEN;
To His feet thy tribute bring;
Ransomed, healed, restored, forgiven,
Evermore His praises sing:
Alleluia, alleluia!
Praise the everlasting King.

Praise him for His grace and favour
To our fathers in distress;
Praise Him still the same for ever,
Slow to chide and swift to bless:
Alleluia, alleluia!
Glorious in His faithfulness.

Father-like, He tends and spares us;
Well our feeble frame He knows;
In His hand He gently bears us,
Rescues us from all our foes.
Alleluia, alleluia!
Widely yet His mercy flows.

Angels, help us to adore Him;
Ye behold Him face to face;
Sun and moon, bow down before Him,
Dwellers all in time and space.
Alleluia, alleluia!
Praise with us the God of grace.

Whenever people talk about hymns, someone is sure to mention 'Abide with Me', traditionally sung at football cup finals until less godly ballads replaced it in recent times. All sorts of stories are told about its writing but what is beyond doubt is that Lyte, who suffered from ill health most of his life, wrote it a short while before his death in 1847 and that it was a hymn of personal experience and faith written by a man who knew the darkness was drawing in on him.

ABIDE WITH ME; FAST FALLS THE EVENTIDE;
The darkness deepens; Lord with me abide.
When other helpers fail and comforts flee,
Help of the helpless, O abide with me.

Swift to its close ebbs out life's little day;
Earth's joys grow dim; its glories pass away;

Change and decay in all around I see;
O Thou who changest not, abide with me.

Not a brief glance I beg, a passing word;
But as Thou dwell'st with Thy disciples, Lord,
Familiar, condescending, patient, free.
Come not to sojourn but abide with me.

Come not in terrors, as the King of kings,
But kind and good, with healing in Thy wings,
Tears for all woes, a heart for every plea –
Come, Friend of sinners, and thus bide with me.

Thou on my head in early youth didst smile;
And, though rebellious and perverse meanwhile,
Thou hast not left me, oft as I left Thee,
On to the close, O Lord, abide with me.

I need Thy presence every passing hour.
What but Thy grace can foil the tempter's power?
Who, like Thyself, my guide and stay can be?
Through cloud and sunshine, Lord, abide with me.

I fear no foe, with Thee at hand to bless;
Ills have no weight and tears no bitterness.
Where is death's sting? Where, grave, thy victory?
I triumph still if Thou abide with me.

Hold Thou Thy cross before my closing eyes;
Shine through the gloom and point me to the skies.
Heaven's morning breaks and earth's vain shadows flee;
In life, in death, O Lord, abide with me.

'Abide with Me' is a great hymn of course, but I wonder whether it is the greatest *evening* hymn. Many would give that accolade to 'The Day Thou Gavest, Lord, Is Ended', said to have been one of Queen Victoria's favourite hymns. It was written by another English clergyman, John Ellerton, co-editor of *Hymns Ancient and*

Modern. Incidentally, he wrote eighty-six hymns and refused to copyright any of them. This one would have earned him a mint in royalties, I should think. It's a lovely hymn with a beautiful logical shape to it, all about the undeniable fact that the sun never sets on the world-wide Church. In those early days of emigration – voluntary and the other sort – to the Antipodes, it must have warmed many a Victorian heart. There can't be a more consoling way to end the programme.

THE DAY THOU GAVEST, LORD, IS ENDED,
The darkness falls at Thy behest;
To Thee our morning hymns ascended,
Thy praise shall sanctify our rest.

We thank Thee that Thy Church, unsleeping,
While earth rolls onward into light,
Through all the world her watch is keeping
And rests not now by day or night.

As o'er each continent and island
The dawn leads on another day,
The voice of prayer is never silent,
Nor dies the strain of praise away.

The sun that bids us rest is waking
Our brethren 'neath the western sky,
And hour by hour fresh lips are making
Thy wondrous doings heard on high.

So be it, Lord; Thy throne shall never,
Like earth's proud empires, pass away:
Thy kingdom stands and grows forever,
Till all Thy creatures own Thy sway.

MORE VICTORIANS

From Series 1

BBC Radio Four
Sunday 14 September 1975
Producers: David Winter and Angela Tilby

•   •   •

The reign of Queen Victoria was undoubtedly the golden age of the English hymn and by far the biggest contributors to our hymn-books are the men and women of imperialism, enterprise and industry. Some of their hymns, especially the mission hall ones, did reflect the poverty and squalor of life in the big cities but most of them preferred to dwell on the beauty of the English country-side, its streams and woods and meadows and the villages that were rapidly dying as the drift to the industrial towns accelerated.

Typical of these Victorian hymns of nature – though more subtle than most – is Adelaide Proctor's 'My God, I Thank Thee, Who Hast Made the Earth So Bright'.

> MY GOD, I THANK THEE, WHO HAST MADE
> The earth so bright,
> So full of splendour and of joy,
> Beauty and light;
> So many glorious things are here,
> Noble and right.
>
> I thank Thee, too, that Thou hast made
> Joy to abound;

So many gentle thoughts and deeds
Circling us round,
That in the darkest spot of earth
Some love is found.

I thank Thee more that all our joy
Is touched with pain,
That shadows fall on brightest hours,
That thorns remain;
So that earth's bliss may be our guide,
And not our chain.

For Thou who knowest, Lord, how soon
Our weak heart clings,
Hast given us joys, tender and true,
Yet all with wings;
So that we see gleaming on high
Diviner things.

I thank Thee, Lord, that Thou hast kept
The best in store;
We have enough, yet not too much
To long for more:
A yearning for a deeper peace
Not known before.

I thank Thee, Lord, that here our souls,
Though amply blessed,
Can never find, although they seek,
A perfect rest;
Nor ever shall, until they lean
On Jesus' breast.

The other great theme of the Victorian hymn-writers was that of
Christian warfare. They understood marching banners, pipes and
drums, and knees bowed in homage to a conquering power. But
they also understood that battles have to be won. In Victorian
England there were no prizes for losers and precious few for

coming second. God gives us strength, true, but it's up to us to 'Fight the Good Fight'.

> FIGHT THE GOOD FIGHT WITH ALL THY MIGHT;
> Christ is thy strength, and Christ thy right;
> Lay hold on life and it shall be
> Thy joy and crown eternally.
>
> Run the straight race through God's good grace,
> Lift up thine eyes, and seek His face;
> Life with its way before us lies,
> Christ is the path and Christ the prize.
>
> Cast care aside, upon thy Guide
> Lean, and His mercy will provide;
> Lean, and the trusting soul shall prove
> Christ is its Life and Christ its Love.
>
> Faint not nor fear, His arms are near,
> He changeth not and thou art dear.
> Only believe and thou shalt see
> That Christ is all in all to thee.

Many Victorian hymn-writers wrote literally hundreds of hymns. Others are remembered just for one hymn, one that secured its place in our hymn-books and in the hearts of worshippers everywhere. J. D. Burns, for instance, is remembered for a hymn that recalls the story of young Samuel in the Temple: 'Hushed was the Evening Hymn'.

> HUSHED WAS THE EVENING HYMN,
> The temple courts were dark;
> The lamp was burning dim
> Before the sacred ark;
> When suddenly a voice divine
> Rang through the silence of the shrine.

The old man, meek and mild,
The priest of Israel, slept;
His watch the temple child,
The little Levite, kept;
And what from Eli's sense was sealed
The Lord to Hannah's son revealed.

O give me Samuel's ear,
The open ear, O Lord,
Alive and quick to hear
Each whisper of Thy word,
Like him to answer at Thy call,
And to obey Thee first of all.

O give me Samuel's heart,
A lowly heart, that waits
Where in Thy house Thou art,
Or watches at Thy gates;
By day and night, a heart that still
Moves at the breathing of Thy will.

O give me Samuel's mind,
A sweet unmurm'ring faith,
Obedient and resigned
To Thee in life and death,
That I may read with childlike eyes
Truths that are hidden from the wise.

Another Bible story set to music is the best-known hymn of Godfrey Thring. It's also a classic example of the mini-sermon: first the story (the storm on the lake and Jesus calming it) and then the application.

So, when our life is clouded o'er
And storm-winds drift us from the shore,
Say, lest we sink to rise no more,
'Peace, be still.'

The hymn is 'Fierce raged the tempest':

> FIERCE RAGED THE TEMPEST O'ER THE DEEP,
> Watch did Thine anxious servants keep
> But Thou wast wrapped in guileless sleep,
> Calm and still.
>
> 'Save, Lord, we perish,' was their cry,
> 'O save us in our agony!'
> Thy word above the storm rose high,
> 'Peace, be still.'
>
> The wild winds hushed; the angry deep
> Sank, like a little child, to sleep;
> The sullen billows ceased to leap,
> At Thy will.
>
> So, when our life is clouded o'er
> And storm-winds drift us from the shore,
> Say, lest we sink to rise no more,
> 'Peace, be still.'

These were also the great years of the missionary movement. Close behind the red-coated British soldiers – and often ahead of them – went the missionaries: explorers, doctors, teachers but above all evangelists, endlessly searching for lost sheep, endlessly obliged to make the gospel known. Frances Ridley Havergal was a great poet of this movement and wrote this fine 'commissioning' hymn:

> LORD, SPEAK TO ME, THAT I MAY SPEAK
> In living echoes of Thy tone;
> As Thou has sought, so let me seek
> Thy erring children, lost and lone.
>
> O lead me, Lord, that I may lead
> The wandering and the wavering feet;
> O feed me, Lord, that I may feed
> Thy hungering ones with manna sweet.

O strengthen me, that while I stand
Firm on the rock and strong in Thee,
I may stretch out a loving hand
To wrestlers with the troubled sea.

O teach me, Lord, that I may teach
The precious things Thou dost impart;
And wing my words, that they may reach
The hidden depths of many a heart.

O give Thine own sweet rest to me,
That I may speak with soothing power
A word in season, as from Thee,
To weary ones in needful hour.

O fill me with Thy fullness, Lord,
Until my very heart overflow
In kindling thought and glowing word,
Thy love to tell, Thy praise to show.

O use me, Lord, use even me,
Just as Thou wilt and when and where,
Until Thy blessèd face I see,
Thy rest, Thy joy, Thy glory share.

Our next hymn has collected more legends than any other –
except perhaps 'Abide with me'. It's 'O Love that Wilt not Let Me
Go', written by the Scots minister George Matheson. He was
almost completely blind from youth but had a brilliant university
career at Edinburgh and wrote several very fine hymns in addition
to this one, for which he is most famous. He wrote it when he was
a minister at the Clyde resort of Inellan, at the age of forty. There
are many romantic versions of the circumstances that led him to
write it but here is his own account:

Something had happened to me which was known only to myself
and which caused me the most severe mental suffering. It was the
quickest bit of work I ever did in my life. I had the impression

rather of having it dictated to me by some inward voice than of working it by myself. I am quite sure that the whole work was completed in five minutes.

Naturally, people have tried to guess what that 'something' was that happened to him but the widely told story that his fiancée had jilted him because of his near-blindness is now discounted. He had been in that condition for twenty years or more. His sister suggested that it may have been the returning memory of a bereavement. Whatever it was, it led to a hymn of quite extraordinary intensity.

> O LOVE THAT WILT NOT LET ME GO,
> I rest my weary soul in Thee;
> I give Thee back the life I owe,
> That in Thine ocean depths its flow
> May richer, fuller be.
>
> O Light that followest all my way,
> I yield my flickering torch to Thee;
> My heart restores its borrowed ray,
> That in Thy sunshine's blaze its day
> May brighter, fairer be.
>
> O Joy that seekest me through pain,
> I cannot close my heart to Thee;
> I trace the rainbow through the rain
> And feel the promise is not vain,
> That morn shall tearless be.
>
> O Cross that liftest up my head,
> I dare not ask to fly from Thee;
> I lay in dust life's glory dead,
> And from the ground there blossoms red
> Life that shall endless be.

I don't know whether you can really call an American a 'Victorian' but we ought to include at least one of the many American hymn-writers of this period. Ray Palmer, the son of a judge, became a congregational minister and an outstanding preacher. He wrote many original hymns including 'My Faith Looks up to Thee' and 'Jesus These Eyes Have Never Seen' but his best known is a translation of a medieval hymn, 'Jesu, Thou Joy of Loving Hearts'.

> JESUS, THOU JOY OF LOVING HEARTS!
> Thou Fount of life, Thou Light of men!
> From the best bliss that earth imparts
> We turn unfilled to Thee again.
>
> Thy truth unchanged hath ever stood;
> Thou savest those that on Thee call;
> To them that seek Thee Thou art good;
> To them that find Thee all in all.
>
> We taste thee, O Thou living bread,
> And long to feast upon Thee still;
> We drink of thee, the fountainhead,
> And thirst our souls from Thee to fill.
>
> Our restless spirits yearn for Thee,
> Where'er our changeful lot is cast;
> Glad, when Thy gracious smile we see;
> Blest, when our faith can hold Thee fast.
>
> O Jesus, ever with us stay;
> Make all our moments calm and bright;
> Chase the dark night of sin away,
> Shed o'er the world Thy holy light.

We end with two of the many fine evening hymns written by Victorian clergymen (for whom the day's end seems to have had a strange fascination). The first is by Harriet Auber – actually a clergyman's daughter – and is a hymn about the coming of the spirit:

> OUR BLEST REDEEMER, ERE HE BREATHED
> His tender last farewell,

A Guide, a Comforter, bequeathed
With us to dwell.

He came in semblance of a dove,
With sheltering wings outspread,
The holy balm of peace and love
On earth to shed.

He came in tongues of living flame
To teach, convince, subdue;
All powerful as the wind He came,
As viewless too.

He came sweet influence to impart,
A gracious, willing guest,
While He can find one humble heart
Wherein to rest.

And 'tis that gentle voice we hear,
Soft as the breath of even,
That checks each fault, that calms each fear,
And speaks of heaven.

And every virtue we possess,
And every conquest won,
And every thought of holiness,
Are His alone.

Spirit of purity and grace,
Our weakness, pitying, see:
O make our hearts Thy dwelling place
And worthier Thee.

And our last hymn, by Canon Henry Twells, is in the same tradition. It's masterly in its application of a biblical scene – Jesus healing the crowds at sunset – to the various ills and weaknesses we all experience: loss of friends, pain, doubt, temptation. And it ends with a memorable prayer:

AT EVEN, ERE THE SUN WAS SET,
The sick, O Lord, around Thee lay;
O, with how many pains they met!
O, with what joy they went away!

Once more 'tis eventide and we,
Oppressed with various ills, draw near;
What if Thyself we cannot see?
We know that Thou art ever near.

O Saviour Christ, our woes dispel;
For some are sick and some are sad;
And some have never loved Thee well,
And some have lost the love they had.

And some are pressed with worldly care
And some are tried with sinful doubt;
And some such grievous passions tear,
That only Thou canst cast them out.

And some have found the world is vain,
Yet from the world they break not free;
And some have friends who give them pain,
Yet have not sought a friend in Thee.

And none, O Lord, have perfect rest,
For none are wholly free from sin;
And they who fain would serve Thee best
Are conscious most of wrong within.

O Saviour Christ, Thou too art man;
Thou hast been troubled, tempted, tried;
Thy kind but searching glance can scan
The very wounds that shame would hide.

Thy touch has still its ancient power;
No word from Thee can fruitless fall;
Hear in this solemn evening hour,
And in Thy mercy heal us all.

SEVENTEENTH-CENTURY HYMN-WRITERS

From Series 2

BBC Radio Four
Sunday 18 July 1976
Producer: David Winter

•   •   •

Goodness knows how many hymns have already been sung today, or by how many million people in what number of languages, but I hope you'll forgive us for adding a few more to that number as we embark on a new series of *Sweet Songs of Zion*. We shall be looking most of all at the words of the hymns and at the writers and finding out how the great treasury of hymns we have today came into being.

And we start in the seventeenth century – not because hymns started then (we shall look much farther back in a later programme) but because hymns in English, of the kind we are used to singing today, first appeared about three hundred years ago.

Here, for instance, is a very well-known hymn written almost exactly three centuries ago. The original German words, by Joachim Neander, a Lutheran layman, were translated into English by the Victorian writer Catherine Winkworth.

> PRAISE TO THE LORD,
> The Almighty, the King of creation!
> O my soul, praise Him,
> For He is thy health and salvation!

Come ye who hear,
Brothers and sisters draw near,[1]
Praise Him in glad adoration.

Praise to the Lord,
Who ov'r'all things so wondrously reigneth,
Shelters thee under His wings,
Yea, so gently sustaineth!
Hast thou not seen
How thy desires e'er have been[2]
Granted in what He ordaineth?

Praise to the Lord,
Who hath fearfully, wondrously, made thee;
Health hath vouchsafed and,
When heedlessly falling, hath stayed thee.
What need or grief
Ever hath failed of relief?
Wings of His mercy did shade thee.

Praise to the Lord,
Who doth prosper thy work and defend thee;
Surely His goodness and mercy
Here daily attend thee.
Ponder anew
What the Almighty can do,
If with His love He befriend thee.

Praise to the Lord,
Who, when tempests their warfare are waging,
Who, when the elements
Madly around thee are raging,
Biddeth them cease,
Turneth their fury to peace,
Whirlwinds and waters assuaging.

[1] In another version 'All ye who hear, now to His temple draw near'.
[2] In other versions 'How all your longings have been'.

Praise to the Lord,
Who, when darkness of sin is abounding,
Who, when the godless do triumph,
All virtue confounding,
Sheddeth His light,
Chaseth the horrors of night,
Saints with His mercy surrounding.

Praise to the Lord,
O let all that is in me adore Him!
All that hath life and breath,
Come now with praises before Him.
Let the 'Amen!'
Sound from His people again,
Gladly for aye we adore Him.

A generation or two before Neander was one of the great periods of English poetry – Donne, Vaughan, Herrick, Waller, Crashaw, Marvell and of course John Milton, whose paraphrase of Psalm 136 is in just about every hymn-book. It's thought that he wrote it when he was about twelve, which must make it one of the longest-surviving pieces of juvenilia in English literature.

LET US, WITH A GLADSOME MIND,
Praise the Lord, for He is kind.
For His mercies aye endure,
Ever faithful, ever sure.

Let us blaze His Name abroad,
For of gods He is the God.
Chorus

He with all commanding might
Filled the new-made world with light.
Chorus

He hath, with a piteous eye,
Looked upon our misery.
    Chorus

He the golden-tressèd sun
Caused all day his course to run.
    Chorus

Th'horned moon to shine by night;
'Mid her spangled sisters bright.
    Chorus

All things living He doth feed,
His full hand supplies their need.
    Chorus

Let us, with a gladsome mind,
Praise the Lord, for He is kind.
    Chorus

George Herbert was another in that great catalogue of poets and his poems, too, have found their way into our hymn-books, although it's most unlikely that he ever intended them to be sung. If he had, I doubt if he would have included these almost unsingable lines in 'Teach Me, My God and King':

A servant with this clause [3]
Makes drudgery divine;
Who sweeps a room, as for Thy laws,
Makes that and th'action fine.

But one could forgive anything for the splendid, pious optimism of the 'servant' who 'with this clause makes drudgery divine'. No gentleman, of course, was ever involved in 'drudgery' – not in those

[3] The 'clause', as represented by Herbert, is the common man's duty to abide by God's word and accept his lowly place in the world.

days, at any rate. The whole poem repays close attention: each verse is a sort of condensed moral thesis.

> TEACH ME, MY GOD AND KING,
> In all things Thee to see,
> And what I do in anything
> To do it as for Thee.
>
> A man that looks on glass,
> On it may stay his eye;
> Or if he pleaseth, through it pass,
> And then the heav'n espy.
>
> All may of Thee partake;
> Nothing can be so mean,
> Which with this tincture, 'for thy sake',
> Will not grow bright and clean.
>
> A servant with this clause
> Makes drudgery divine;
> Who sweeps a room, as for Thy laws,
> Makes that and th'action fine.
>
> This is the famous stone
> That turneth all to gold;
> For that which God doth touch and own
> Cannot for less be told.

Another of Herbert's poems makes a rather better hymn, perhaps. 'King of Glory, King of Peace' is a song of divine love, in the rather extravagant style of the contemporary love poem. John Donne, of course, moved from human to divine love and back again effortlessly. George Herbert, however, set his sights firmly and exclusively on the angels, while sometimes permitting himself a hint of the language of mortals: 'thou didst note my working breast'. At any rate, it's a beautiful piece of writing and it makes a splendid hymn.

KING OF GLORY, KING OF PEACE,
I will love Thee;
And that love may never cease,
I will move Thee.
Thou hast granted my request,
Thou hast heard me;
Thou didst note my working breast,
Thou hast spared me.

Wherefore with my utmost art
I will sing Thee,
And the cream of all my heart
I will bring Thee.
Though my sins against me cried,
Thou didst clear me;
And alone, when they replied,
Thou didst hear me.

Seven whole days, not one in seven,
I will praise Thee;
In my heart, though not in heaven,
I can raise Thee.
Small it is, in this poor sort
To enroll Thee:
E'en eternity's too short
To extol Thee.

George Herbert was for much of his short life – he died at thirty-nine – rector of Bemerton, near Salisbury. Although not a hymn-writer – only paraphrases of the Psalms were permitted in his life-time – he compiled a book of his verse called *The Temple* and many of these pieces have found their way into our modern hymn-books. In Bemerton church there is a stained-glass window showing Nicholas Ferrer, who was a close friend of Herbert's, holding the manuscript of *The Temple*, which had been entrusted to him for publication. Perhaps the best known of all the hymns taken from that book is another great expression of Christian joy:

LET ALL THE WORLD IN EVERY CORNER SING,
My God and King!
The heavens are not too high,
His praise may thither fly;
The earth is not too low,
His praises there may grow.
Let all the world in every corner sing,
My God and King!

Let all the world in every corner sing,
My God and King!
The church with psalms must shout,
No door can keep them out;
But, above all, the heart
Must bear the longest part.
Let all the world in every corner sing,
My God and King!

Samuel Crossman, like many seventeenth-century clergymen, led a chequered ecclesiastical career – the penalty of consistency in an era when only a Vicar of Bray could survive the abrupt changes of direction in the Church of England. He was ejected from his Essex parish in 1662 but went on to become Dean of Bristol, a seat he still occupied on his death twenty years later. In the intervening years he wrote a pamphlet entitled *The Young Man's Meditation*, described as 'Sacred Poems upon Select Subjects and Scriptures'. In this little book there was a poem that has become one of the great hymns of the English-speaking world: 'My Song is Love Unknown'. Has anyone captured the turncoat side of humanity more vividly than in this verse?

Sometimes they strew His way
And His sweet praises sing;
Resounding all the day
Hosannas to their King;
Then 'Crucify!'
Is all their breath,

> And for His death
> They thirst and cry.

The hymn goes like this:

> MY SONG IS LOVE UNKNOWN,
> My Saviour's love to me;
> Love to the loveless shown,
> That they might lovely be.
> O who am I,
> That for my sake
> My Lord should take,
> Frail flesh and die?
>
> He came from His blest throne
> Salvation to bestow;
> But men made strange and none
> The longed-for Christ would know:
> But O! my Friend,
> My Friend indeed,
> Who at my need
> His life did spend.
>
> Sometimes they strew His way,
> And His sweet praises sing;
> Resounding all the day
> Hosannas to their King:
> Then 'Crucify!'
> Is all their breath
> And for His death
> They thirst and cry.
>
> Why, what hath my Lord done?
> What makes this rage and spite?
> He made the lame to run,
> He gave the blind their sight
> Sweet injuries!
> Yet they at these

Themselves displease
And 'gainst Him rise.

They rise and needs will have
My dear Lord made away;
A murderer they saved,
The Prince of Life they slay,
Yet cheerful He
To suffering goes,
That He His foes
From thence might free.

In life, no house, no home
My Lord on earth might have;
In death no friendly tomb
But what a stranger gave.
What may I say?
Heav'n was His home;
But mine the tomb
Wherein He lay.

Here might I stay and sing,
No story so divine;
Never was love, dear King!
Never was grief like Thine.
This is my friend,
In whose sweet praise
I all my days
Could gladly spend.

John Bunyan was another preacher who fell foul of the authorities. In his case, of course, it meant a spell in Bedford Gaol – and that in turn meant *Pilgrim's Progress*. He wrote the first part of it in prison and completed the second part, which is not so well known, some years later. In this sequel, Christian's wife and children make the pilgrimage to the Holy City and it is this part, which includes the verses that can be found today in almost every hymn-book, 'Who Would True Valour See?' Valiant-for-Truth is recounting to

Mr Greatheart how his parents had given him dire warnings of the perils he would face if he set out on his pilgrimage – including the 'hobgoblins and foul fiends' in the Valley of the Shadow of Death. The 'Pilgrim's Song' follows. Unhappily, the hobgoblins have proved too much for some hymn-book compilers, including the editors of *Hymns Ancient and Modern*, but we offer you the original version, hobgoblins, foul fiends and all.

WHO WOULD TRUE VALOUR SEE,
Let him come hither;
One here will constant be,
Come wind, come weather.
There's no discouragement
Shall make him once relent
His first avow'd intent
To be a pilgrim.

Whoso beset him 'round
With dismal stories
Do but themselves confound;
His strength the more is.
No lion can him fright,
He'll with a giant fight,
But he will have a right
To be a pilgrim.

Hobgoblin nor foul fiend
Can daunt his spirit,
He knows he at the end
Shall life inherit.
Then fancies flee away,
He'll fear not what men say,
He'll labour night and day
To be a pilgrim.[4]

[4] Now more commonly: 'He who would valiant be 'gainst all disaster, Let him in constancy follow the Master. There's no discouragement shall make him once relent his first avowed intent to be a pilgrim. Who so beset him round with dismal

Some rather better verse of Bunyan's in the same book is to be found in only a few hymn-books. It's the song of a shepherd boy and it's really a call to the simple life – very modern, I suppose, in its way.

> HE THAT IS DOWN NEEDS FEAR NO FALL,
> He that is low no pride;
> He that is humble ever shall
> Have God to be his guide.
>
> I am content with what I have,
> Little be it or much;
> And, Lord, contentment still I crave,
> Because Thou savest such.
>
> Fullness to such a burden is
> That go on pilgrimage:
> Here little, and hereafter bliss,
> Is best from age to age.

Finally, this week, let's turn to the great Bishop Thomas Ken – another suffering clergyman, incidentally, who was Chaplain to King Charles II and went on to be Bishop of Bath and Wells but was deprived of his See in 1691 as a non-juror.[5] He was obviously a very strong-willed character: he once refused the King's request for the use of the Deanery at Winchester as a residence for Nell Gwynne! His best-known hymns were written for his pupils at

---

stories. Do but themselves confound – his strength the more is. No foes shall stay his might; though he with giants fight, He will make good his right to be a pilgrim. Since, Lord, Thou dost defend us with Thy Spirit, We know we at the end, shall life inherit. Then fancies flee away! I'll fear not what men say, I'll labour night and day to be a pilgrim.'

[5] Non-jurors were a group of Anglican clergy who refused to swear an oath of obedience to King William and Queen Mary for fear of violating their oath to the previous monarch King James II, who had been ousted by Parliament in the Glorious Revolution of 1688. They were unseated as a result.

Winchester College when he was teaching there and they include this lovely evening hymn with which we end tonight's programme, 'Glory to Thee, My God, this Night'.

> GLORY TO THEE, MY GOD, THIS NIGHT,
> For all the blessings of the light:
> Keep me, O keep me, King of kings,
> Beneath Thine own almighty wings.
>
> Forgive me, Lord, for thy dear Son,
> The ill that I this day have done;
> That with the world, myself and Thee,
> I, ere I sleep, at peace may be.
>
> Teach me to live, that I may dread
> The grave as little as my bed;
> Teach me to die, that so I may
> Rise glorious at the awful day.
>
> O may my soul on Thee repose
> And with sweet sleep mine eyelids close;
> Sleep that shall me more vigorous make
> To serve my God when I awake.
>
> When in the night I sleepless lie,
> My soul with heav'nly thoughts supply;
> Let no ill dreams disturb my rest,
> No powers of darkness me molest.
>
> Praise God, from whom all blessings flow;
> Praise Him, all creatures here below;
> Praise Him above, ye heavenly host:
> Praise Father, Son and Holy Ghost.

SOME POETS LAUREATE

From Series 2

BBC Radio Four
Sunday 25 July 1976
Producer: David Winter

• • •

In tonight's programme we shall be looking at some of the hymns written by England's poets laureate. As it happens, their output of verses suitable for inclusion in hymn-books has been rather limited and the last few incumbents, including the present one,[1] have clearly not regarded writing hymns as part of the duties of their office.

However, my predecessors do include one of the founding fathers of British hymnody and a compiler of a complete, if today largely unknown, hymn-book. That founding father was Nahum Tate, who became Poet Laureate in 1692. He collaborated with Nicholas Brady in producing a new metrical version of the Psalter, in the process giving the Church one of its most durable hymns of faith: 'Through all the Changing Scenes of Life'. Ostensibly a paraphrase of Psalm 34, it is to all intents and purposes an original piece of writing. It employs very effectively the device of repetition:

[1] Betjeman himself, who was Poet Laureate from 1972 until his death in 1984.

O magnify the Lord with me,
With me exalt His name.

and

Fear Him ye saints and you will then
Have nothing else to fear.

Here is the hymn in full:

THROUGH ALL THE CHANGING SCENES OF LIFE,
In trouble and in joy,
The praises of my God shall still
My heart and tongue employ.

Of His deliverance I will boast,
Till all that are distressed
From my example courage take
And soothe their griefs to rest.

O magnify the Lord with me,
With me exalt His name;
When in distress to Him I called,
He to my rescue came.

Their drooping hearts were soon refreshed,
Who looked to Him for aid;
Desired success in every face,
A cheerful air displayed.

'Behold,' they say, 'Behold the man
Whom providence relieved;
The man so dangerously beset,
So wondrously retrieved!'

The hosts of God encamp around
The dwellings of the just;
Deliverance He affords to all
Who on His succour trust.

O make but trial of His love;
Experience will decide
How blest are they, and only they,
Who in His truth confide.

Fear Him, ye saints, and you will then
Have nothing else to fear;
Make you His service your delight;
Your wants shall be His care.

While hungry lions lack their prey,
The Lord will food provide
For such as put their trust in Him,
And see their needs supplied.

The other great hymn from the Tate and Brady partnership is a
more literal paraphrase, this time of Psalm 42, but even here the
authors permit themselves the liberty of originality:

As pants the hart for cooling streams
When heated in the chase,
So longs my soul O God for Thee,
And Thy refreshing grace.

One looks in vain in Psalm 42 for the chase – not a pastime
indulged in widely, one imagines, in ancient Israel but familiar
enough to Messrs Tate and Brady and the congregations who
eagerly took up their new version of the Psalms. Here, by contrast,
is how the parallel verses of Psalm 42 actually run:

[1]As the hart panteth after the water brooks,
So panteth my soul after Thee, O God.
[2]My soul thirsteth for God, for the living God:
'When shall I come and appear before God?' ...
[5]Why art thou cast down, O my soul?
And why moanest thou within me?

Hope thou in God; for I shall yet praise Him
For the salvation of His countenance.

And here is the whole of Tate and Brady's adaptation:

As PANTS THE HART FOR COOLING STREAMS
When heated in the chase,
So longs my soul O God for Thee,
And Thy refreshing grace.

For Thee, my God, the living God,
My thirsty soul doth pine:
O when shall I behold Thy face,
Thou Majesty divine?

Why restless, why cast down, my soul?
Hope still, and thou shalt sing
The praise of Him who is thy God,
Thy health's eternal spring.

To Father, Son, and Holy Ghost,
The God whom we adore,
Be glory, as it was, is now,
And shall be evermore.

Poet Laureate just before Nahum Tate was John Dryden, who ended his life a Roman Catholic. His only contribution to hymnody is a translation of 'Veni, Creator Spiritus'[2] – 'Creator Spirit, by Whose Aid', one of several seventeenth-century translations of which the best known today is John Cosin's 'Come, Holy Ghost, Our Souls Inspire'.

Come, Holy Ghost, our souls inspire,
And lighten with celestial fire;
Thou the anointing Spirit art,
Who dost thy seven-fold gifts impart.

[2] Attributed to Rhabanus Maurus, Archbishop of Mainz (776–856).

But here is Dryden's version, as found today in the *Methodist Hymn Book*.

> CREATOR SPIRIT, BY WHOSE AID
> The world's foundations first were laid,
> Come, visit every humble mind;
> Come, pour Thy joys on humankind;
> From sin and sorrow set us free
> And make Thy temples worthy Thee.[3]
>
> O Source of uncreated light,
> The Father's promised paraclete,[4]
> Thrice holy fount, thrice holy fire,
> Our hearts with heavenly love inspire;
> Come and Thy sacred unction bring
> To sanctify us while we sing.
>
> Plenteous of grace, come from on high,
> Rich in Thy sevenfold energy;
> Make us eternal truths receive
> And practise all that we believe;
> Give us Thyself, that we may see
> The Father and the Son by Thee.
>
> Immortal honour, endless fame,
> Attend th'almighty Father's name;
> The Saviour Son be glorified,
> Who for lost man's redemption died;
> And equal adoration be,
> Eternal paraclete, to Thee.

Alfred, Lord Tennyson, one of the most distinguished of the poets laureate, is named as the author of two hymns in many hymn-books, though neither was intended to be such. 'Strong Son of God, Immortal Love' is the first line of 'In Memoriam', the long

---

[3] Or 'And make us temples worthy Thee'.
[4] Helper; comforter: a New Testament word, used of Jesus in *John* and *Acts*.

poem Tennyson wrote to commemorate his friend Arthur Hallam, who died in 1833 as a young man. The hymn originally consisted of four of the first five stanzas of the poem; since then it has grown.

STRONG SON OF GOD, IMMORTAL LOVE,
Whom we, that have not seen Thy face,
By faith, and faith alone, embrace,
Believing where we cannot prove;[5]

Thou wilt not leave us in the dust:
Thou madest man, he knows not why;
He thinks he was not made to die;
And Thou hast made him: Thou art just.

Thou seemest human and divine,
The highest, holiest manhood, Thou.
Our wills are ours, we know not how;
Ours wills are ours, to make them Thine.

Our little systems have their day;
They have their day and cease to be:
They are but broken lights of Thee,
And Thou, O Lord, art more than they.

We have but faith: we cannot know;
For knowledge is of things we see;
And yet we trust it comes from Thee,
A beam in darkness: let it grow.

Let knowledge grow from more to more,
But more of reverence in us dwell;
That mind and soul, according well,
May make one music as before.

[5] The second verse of 'In Memoriam', missing from this hymn, is: 'Thine are these orbs of light and shade; Thou madest Life in man and brute; Thou madest Death; and lo, Thy foot Is on the skull which Thou hast made.'

But vaster. We are fools and slight;
We mock Thee when we do not fear;
But help Thy foolish ones to bear –
Help Thy vain worlds to bear Thy light.

Forgive my grief for one removed,
Thy creature, whom I found so fair.
I trust he lives in Thee, and there
I find him worthier to be loved.

Forgive these wild and wandering cries,
Confusions of a wasted youth;
Forgive them where they fail in truth,
And in thy wisdom make me wise.

The other hymn attributed to Tennyson is a poem he wrote at the age of eighty: 'Crossing the Bar'. It's about facing death.

SUNSET AND EVENING STAR,
And one clear call for me!
And may there be no moaning of the bar,
When I put out to sea,

But such a tide as moving seems asleep,
Too full for sound and foam,
When that which drew from out the boundless deep
Turns again home.

Twilight and evening bell,
And after that the dark!
And may there be no sadness of farewell,
When I embark;

For tho' from out our bourn of time and place
The flood may bear me far,
I hope to see my Pilot face to face
When I have crossed the bar.

Robert Bridges was Poet Laureate from 1913 to 1930 and he, almost alone among poets laureate, had a real interest in writing and translating hymns. Indeed, during his retirement he took charge of the singing in the parish church of Yattendon in Berkshire where he lived and his hymn-book is called *The Yattendon Hymnal*. It was an attempt – foredoomed to failure – to raise the literary standards of popular hymnody. It contains a hundred hymns in the classical style of which Bridges himself wrote, translated or adapted forty-four. Among them is a free translation of an eighteenth-century Latin hymn which in Bridges' version begins:

> HAPPY ARE THEY, THEY THAT LOVE GOD,
> Whose hearts have Christ confest,
> Who by His cross have found their life,
> And 'neath His yoke their rest.
>
> Glad is the praise, sweet are the songs,
> When they together sing;
> And strong the prayers that bow the ear
> Of heaven's eternal King.
>
> Christ to their homes giveth His peace,
> And makes their loves His own:
> But ah, what tares the evil one
> Hath in his garden sown.
>
> Sad were our lot, evil this earth,
> Did not its sorrows prove
> The path whereby the sheep may find
> The fold of Jesus' Love.
>
> Then shall they know, they that love Him,
> How all their pain is good;
> And death itself cannot unbind
> Their happy brotherhood.

Bridges turned to German for another of his hymns, 'All My Hope on God Is Founded' – another free translation, this time of a German hymn by Joachim Neander.

> ALL MY HOPE ON GOD IS FOUNDED;
> He doth still my trust renew,
> Me through change and chance He guideth,
> Only good and only true.
> God unknown,
> He alone
> Calls my heart to be His own.
>
> Pride of man and earthly glory,
> Sword and crown betray His trust;
> What with care and toil he buildeth,
> Tower and temple fall to dust.
> But God's power,
> Hour by hour,
> Is my temple and my tower.
>
> God's great goodness aye endureth,
> Deep his wisdom, passing thought:
> Splendour, light and life attend Him,
> Beauty springeth out of naught.
> Ever more
> From His store
> Newborn worlds rise and adore.
>
> Daily doth the almighty giver
> Bounteous gifts on us bestow;
> His desire our soul delighteth,
> Pleasure leads us where we go.
> Love doth stand
> At His hand;
> Joy doth wait on His command.
>
> Still from man to God eternal
> Sacrifice of praise be done,

High above all praises praising
For the gift of Christ, his Son.
Christ doth call
One and all:
Ye who follow shall not fall.

'All My Hope on God is Founded', from *The Yattendon Hymnal*, which we shall look at more closely next time.

Probably the best-known hymn by Robert Bridges is 'Rejoice, O Land, in God Thy Might'. It's a national hymn, written in the closing years of Queen Victoria's reign, some time before he became Poet Laureate, though I suppose it could be called a real laureate's hymn. One could not possibly end a programme on a more auspicious note of optimism, even if that Victorian millennium has obstinately failed to turn up.

REJOICE, O LAND, IN GOD THY MIGHT,
His will obey, Him serve aright;
For thee the saints uplift their voice:
Fear not, O land, in God rejoice.

Glad shalt thou be, with blessing crowned,
With joy and peace thou shalt abound;
Yea love with thee shall make his home
Until thou see God's kingdom come.

He shall forgive thy sins untold:
Remember thou His love of old;
Walk in His way, His word adore,
And keep His truth for evermore.

THE YATTENDON HYMNAL

From Series 2

BBC Radio Four
Sunday 1 August 1976
Producer: David Winter

• • •

Last week we heard three hymns written by Robert Bridges. They all came from his *Yattendon Hymnal*, a project aimed at producing a 'classical' hymn-book. In pursuit of literary excellence in the field of hymnody, Bridges searched far and wide for suitable material, some of which he translated, some of which he adapted to make it suitable for inclusion in his collection, which was published in 1899.

One hymn that met his standards, though even here he made extensive alterations, was Edward Caswall's 'When Morning Gilds the Skies' – itself a translation of a Franconian hymn of the eighteenth century.

> WHEN MORNING GILDS THE SKIES
> My heart awaking cries:
> May Jesus Christ be praised!
> Alike at work and prayer,
> To Jesus I repair:
> May Jesus Christ be praised!
>
> When you begin the day,
> O never fail to say,

May Jesus Christ be praised!
And at your work rejoice,
To sing with heart and voice,
May Jesus Christ be praised!

Whene'er the sweet church bell
Peals over hill and dell,
May Jesus Christ be praised!
O hark to what it sings,
As joyously it rings,
May Jesus Christ be praised!

My tongue shall never tire
Of chanting with the choir,
May Jesus Christ be praised!
This song of sacred joy,
It never seems to cloy,
May Jesus Christ be praised!

Does sadness fill my mind?
A solace here I find,
May Jesus Christ be praised!
Or fades my earthly bliss?
My comfort still is this,
May Jesus Christ be praised!

To God, the word, on high,
The host of angels cry,
May Jesus Christ be praised!
Let mortals, too, upraise
Their voice in hymns of praise,
May Jesus Christ be praised!

Be this at meals your grace,
In every time and place;
May Jesus Christ be praised!
Be this, when day is past,
Of all your thoughts the last
May Jesus Christ be praised!

When mirth for music longs,
This is my song of songs:
May Jesus Christ be praised!
When evening shadows fall,
This rings my curfew call,
May Jesus Christ be praised!

When sleep her balm denies,
My silent spirit sighs,
May Jesus Christ be praised!
When evil thoughts molest,
With this I shield my breast,
May Jesus Christ be praised!

The night becomes as day
When from the heart we say:
May Jesus Christ be praised!
The powers of darkness fear
When this sweet chant they hear:
May Jesus Christ be praised!

No lovelier antiphon
In all high heav'n is known
Than, Jesus Christ be praised!
There to th'eternal word
Th'eternal psalm is heard:
May Jesus Christ be praised!

Let all the earth around
Ring joyous with the sound:
May Jesus Christ be praised!
In heaven's eternal bliss
The loveliest strain is this:
May Jesus Christ be praised!

Sing, suns and stars of space,
Sing, ye that see His face,
Sing, Jesus Christ be praised!

God's whole creation o'er,
For aye and evermore
Shall Jesus Christ be praised!

In heav'n's eternal bliss
The loveliest strain is this,
May Jesus Christ be praised!
Let earth and sea and sky
From depth to height reply,
May Jesus Christ be praised!

Be this, while life is mine,
My canticle divine:
May Jesus Christ be praised!
Sing this eternal song
Through all the ages long:
May Jesus Christ be praised!

A hymn in the book that is entirely and originally Bridges is 'Love of Love, and Light of Light'.

LOVE OF LOVE, AND LIGHT OF LIGHT
Heavenly Father, all maintaining;
Wisdom hid in highest height,
To Thy creature fondly deigning;
Maker wonderful and just,
Thou hast called my heart to trust.

What are life's unnumbered cares:
Sorrow, torment, passing measure?
O'er my short-lived pains and fears
Surely ruleth The good pleasure.
Boundless is Thy love for me,
Boundless then my trust shall be.

Every burden weigheth light,
Since in Thee my hope abideth:

Sweetly bright my darkest night,
While on Thee my mind confideth.
Give Thy gift, I Thee implore,
Thee to trust for evermore.

Paulus Gerhardt was a Lutheran pastor for whose literary work
Bridges obviously had a great admiration. Four of Gerhardt's five
children died in childhood and his wife died after a long illness in
Berlin and perhaps because of these experiences he was able to
express in his hymns ideas of suffering and separation – nowhere
more movingly than in his Passion hymn 'O Sacred Head, Sore
Wounded'. This version, found in several of our hymn-books, is
Bridges' translation of the original German.

O SACRED HEAD, SORE WOUNDED,
Defiled and put to scorn;
O kingly head surrounded
With mocking crown of thorn:
What sorrow mars Thy grandeur?
Can death Thy bloom deflower?
O countenance whose splendour
The hosts of heaven adore!

Thy beauty, long-desirèd,
Hath vanished from our sight;
Thy power is all expirèd,
And quenched the light of light.
Ah me! for whom Thou diest,
Hide not so far Thy grace:
Show me, O Love most highest,
The brightness of Thy face.

I pray thee, Jesus, own me,
Me, Shepherd good, for Thine;
Who to Thy fold hast won me,
And fed with truth divine.
Me guilty, me refuse not,

Incline Thy face to me,
This comfort that I lose not,
On earth to comfort Thee.

In Thy most bitter Passion
My heart to share doth cry,
With Thee for my salvation
Upon the cross to die.
Ah, keep my heart thus moved
To stand Thy cross beneath,
To mourn Thee, well-beloved,
Yet thank Thee for Thy death.

My days are few, O fail not,
With Thine immortal power,
To hold me that I quail not
In death's most fearful hour;
That I may fight befriended,
And see in my last strife
To me Thine arms extended
Upon the cross of life.

The Passion Chorale 'O Sacred Head, sore wounded' – incidentally, the music there, which also occurs in the St Matthew Passion, originated in the sixteenth century as the tune of a secular ballad. It was associated with Gerhardt's hymn in about 1656 and taken up by Bach sixty years later.

Another translation to be included by Bridges in *The Yattendon Hymnal* was of the twelfth-century Latin hymn 'Amor Patris et Filii' – his own work, again, set to a tune by the great Orlando Gibbons (1583–1625) who was organist at the Chapel Royal, London: 'Love of the Father, Love of God the Son'.

LOVE OF THE FATHER, LOVE OF GOD THE SON,
From whom all came, in whom was all begun;
Who formest heavenly beauty out of strife,
Creation's whole desire and breath of life:

Thou the All-holy, Thou supreme in might,
Thou dost give peace, Thy presence maketh right;
Thou with Thy favour all things dost enfold,
With Thine all-kindness free from harm wilt hold.

Hope of all comfort, splendour of all aid,
That dost not fail nor leave the heart afraid:
To all that cry Thou dost all help accord,
The angels' armour and the saints' reward.

Purest and highest, wisest and most just,
There is no truth save only in Thy trust;
Thou dost the mind from earthly dreams recall,
And bring, through Christ, to Him for whom are all.

Eternal Glory, all men Thee adore,
Who art and shalt be worshipped evermore:
Us whom Thou madest, comfort with Thy might,
And lead us to enjoy Thy heavenly light.

Bridges, as I have said, searched high and low for suitable material
– some of it among the lesser-known works of great English
hymn-writers. He took a hymn of Charles Wesley's, for example –
'Ye that Do Your Master's Will' – and added an extra verse, in a fair
imitation of Wesley's own style:

> He that comforts all that mourn
> Shall to joy your sorrow turn;
> Joy to know your sins forgiven,
> Joy to keep the way of heaven,
> Joy to win His welcome grace,
> Joy to see Him face to face.

He also took a hymn of Isaac Watts's – 'My Lord, my Life, my Love'
– that had last appeared in a rather obscure collection of religious
verses published in 1880, completely rewrote it and once again
added a verse of his own: the last one. Some might have doubts

about this rather cavalier treatment of another man's work but it is Bridges' version that is in the hymn-books and the original of Isaac Watts that has been forgotten.

> MY LORD, MY LIFE, MY LOVE,
> To Thee, to Thee I call;
> I cannot live if Thou remove:
> Thou art my joy, my all.[1]
>
> The smilings of Thy face,
> How amiable they are!
> 'Tis heav'n to rest in Thine embrace,
> And nowhere else but there.
>
> To Thee and Thee alone,
> The angels owe their bliss;
> They sit around Thy gracious throne,
> And dwell where Jesus is.
>
> Nor earth, nor all the sky.
> Can one delight afford;
> No, not a drop of real joy
> Without Thy presence, Lord.
>
> To Thee my spirits fly
> With infinite desire;
> And yet how far from Thee I lie!
> Dear Jesus, raise me higher.

For our last two hymns this week we have two of the evening hymns from *The Yattendon Hymnal*. The first is another translation by Bridges of a German hymn by Paulus Gerhardt, 'The Duteous Day now Closeth'. Erik Routley said of this hymn that he doubted 'if anything more purely beautiful is to be found in all hymnody'.

---

[1] Or 'For Thou art all in all'.

THE DUTEOUS DAY NOW CLOSETH,
Each flower and tree reposeth,
Shade creeps o'er wild and wood:
Let us, as night is falling,
On God our Maker calling
Give thanks to Him, the Giver good.

Now all the heavenly splendour
Breaks forth in starlight tender
From myriad worlds unknown;
And man, this marvel seeing,
Forget his selfish being
For joy of beauty not his own.

His care he drowneth yonder,
Lost in the abyss of wonder;
To heav'n his soul doth steal:
This life he disesteemeth,
The day it is that dreameth,
That doth from truth his vision seal.

Awhile his mortal blindness
May miss God's loving kindness,
And grope in faithless strife:
But when life's day is over
Shall death's fair night discover
The fields of everlasting life.

Our second evening hymn, and the last one in this week's programme, is probably the oldest of all hymns, taking us back to the days when Greek was the language of Christianity. No one knows who wrote it but it dates from about the third century and was sung at the lighting of the lamps, which explains why it is sometimes called the 'Candlelight Hymn'. John Keble had translated it some years earlier –

Hail, gladdening Light, of His pure glory poured
Who is th'immortal Father, heavenly, blest,
Holiest of Holies – Jesus Christ our Lord!

– but this translation is, once again, by Bridges himself:

O GLADSOME LIGHT, O GRACE
Of God the Father's face,
The eternal splendour wearing;
Celestial, holy, blest,
Our Saviour Jesus Christ,
Joyful in Thine appearing.

Now, ere day fadeth quite
We see the evening light,
Our wonted hymn outpouring;
Father of might unknown,
Thee, His incarnate Son,
And Holy Spirit adoring.

To Thee of right belongs
All praise of holy songs,
O Son of God, Lifegiver;
Thee, therefore, O Most High,
The world doth glorify,
And shall exalt forever.

AMERICAN HYMN-WRITERS

From Series 2

BBC Radio Four
Sunday 8 August 1976
Producer: David Winter

•   •   •

Hymns, like good wine, don't seem to travel very well. The tunes do, of course: change the tempo and J. B. Dykes can provide an African anthem or a Korean jubilate. But the words – the actual expression of belief or worship or prayer – don't adapt so easily. Of course there are, as we have seen, many great translations, though most of them are virtually original pieces of writing. But even where peoples share the same language, as it is alleged we do with the Americans, there is not the degree of shared hymnody that one would expect. On the whole, American and British congregations sing a different set of hymns.

Of course Americans do sing quite a few of our favourites and our hymn-books include several American authors; and it is these that we shall be looking at tonight.

And we begin with what must be one of the best of the American imports, 'Lord of All Being, Thronèd Afar'. It was written by Oliver Wendell Holmes, the son of a congregational minister. Holmes became Professor of Anatomy at Harvard and in fact this piece first appeared as a 'Sunday Hymn' on the last page of a kind of diary of the year, called *The Professor at the Breakfast Table*. It was prefaced by these words:

Forget for the moment the difference in the lines of truth we look at through our human prisms, and join in singing (inwardly) this hymn to the Source of the Light we all need to lead us and the warmth which alone can make us all brothers.

It starts:

> LORD OF ALL BEING, THRONÈD AFAR,
> Thy glory flames from sun and star;
> Centre and soul of every sphere,
> Yet to each loving heart how near!
>
> Sun of our life, Thy quickening ray
> Sheds on our path the glow of day;
> Star of our hope, Thy softened light
> Cheers the long watches of the night.
>
> Our midnight is Thy smile withdrawn,
> Our noontide is Thy gracious dawn,
> Our rainbow arch Thy mercy's sign;
> All, save the clouds of sin, are Thine.
>
> Lord of all life, below, above,
> Whose light is truth, whose warmth is love,
> Before Thy ever-blazing throne
> We ask no lustre of our own.
>
> Grant us Thy truth to make us free,
> And kindling hearts that burn for Thee,
> Till all Thy living altars claim
> One holy Light, one heavenly Flame.

A more distinguished poet than Holmes, though probably a less distinguished anatomist, was his contemporary Henry Wadsworth Longfellow. He was also a professor, incidentally, of modern languages at Harvard. He didn't write any hymns but part of one of his poems does appear as a hymn in several English hymn-books. It's his 'Psalm of Life', subtitled 'What the Heart of the

Young Man Said to the Psalmist' and moral uplift doesn't come more uplifting than this.

> TELL ME NOT, IN MOURNFUL NUMBERS,
> Life is but an empty dream! –
> For the soul is dead that slumbers,
> And things are not what they seem.
>
> Life is real! Life is earnest!
> And the grave is not its goal;
> 'Dust thou art, to dust returnest'
> Was not spoken of the soul.
>
> Not enjoyment and not sorrow
> Is our destined end or way;
> But to act, that each tomorrow
> Find us farther than today.
>
> Art is long and time is fleeting
> And our hearts, though stout and brave,
> Still, like muffled drums, are beating
> Funeral marches to the grave.
>
> In the world's broad field of battle,
> In the bivouac of life,
> Be not like dumb, driven cattle!
> Be a hero in the strife!
>
> Trust no future, howe'er pleasant!
> Let the dead past bury its dead!
> Act, – act in the living present!
> Heart within and God o'erhead!
>
> Lives of great men all remind us
> We can make our lives sublime,
> And, departing, leave behind us
> Footprints on the sands of time;

> Footprints, that perhaps another
> Sailing o'er life's solemn main,
> A forlorn and shipwrecked brother,
> Seeing, shall take heart again.
>
> Let us, then, be up and doing,
> With a heart for any fate;
> Still achieving, still pursuing,
> Learn to labour and to wait.

Another American poet, John Greenleaf Whittier, once said that 'a good hymn is the best use to which poetry can be put.' I don't know whether I agree with that but Whittier was at any rate speaking from experience. Although he never wrote a single stanza for a hymn, his poems have provided us with four very popular hymns, with this one – 'Dear Lord and Father of Mankind' – as, perhaps, the best of them all. I like this verse especially:

> Drop thy still dews of quietness,
> Till all our strivings cease;
> Take from our souls the strain and stress,
> And let our ordered lives confess
> The beauty of Thy peace.

The hymn starts off like this, although it is actually part of a much longer poem called 'The Brewing of Soma', about misguided searches for spirituality outside Christianity:

> DEAR LORD AND FATHER OF MANKIND,
> Forgive our foolish ways;
> Reclothe us in our rightful mind,
> In purer lives Thy service find,
> In deeper reverence, praise.
>
> In simple trust like theirs who heard,
> Beside the Syrian sea,
> The gracious calling of the Lord,

Let us, like them, without a word,
Rise up and follow Thee.

O Sabbath rest by Galilee,
O calm of hills above,
Where Jesus knelt to share with Thee
The silence of eternity,
Interpreted by love!

With that deep hush subduing all
Our words and works that drown
The tender whisper of Thy call,
As noiseless let Thy blessing fall
As fell Thy manna down.

Drop Thy still dews of quietness,
Till all our strivings cease;
Take from our souls the strain and stress,
And let our ordered lives confess
The beauty of Thy peace.

Breathe through the heats of our desire
Thy coolness and Thy balm;
Let sense be dumb, let flesh retire;
Speak through the earthquake, wind and fire,
O still, small voice of calm.

Whittier was a Quaker and at one time was secretary of the Anti-Slavery Society. This hymn perhaps reflects both those elements: the Quaker idea of worship as brotherhood and the zeal of the social reformer. Based on some words of St James's, it deserves a closer read than hymns usually get.

O BROTHER MAN, FOLD TO THY HEART THY BROTHER!
Where pity dwells, the peace of God is there;
To worship rightly is to love each other,
Each smile a hymn, each kindly deed a prayer.

For He whom Jesus loved has truly spoken:
The holier worship which He deigns to bless
Restores the lost, and binds the spirit broken,
And feeds the widow and the fatherless.

Follow with reverent steps the great example
Of Him whose holy work was doing good;
So shall the wide earth seem our Father's temple,
Each loving life a psalm of gratitude.

Then shall all shackles fall; the stormy clangour
Of wild war-music o'er the earth shall cease;
Love shall tread out the baleful fire of anger,
And in its ashes plant the tree of peace.

One more hymn written by Whittier is found in most of our hymn-books. It's from a long poem called 'Our Master' that actually yielded several other hymns as well. It has an amazing economy of language – almost, at times, a sort of biblical shorthand:

But warm, sweet, tender, even yet
A present help is He;
And faith has still its Olivet,[1]
And love its Galilee.

The hymn is called 'Immortal Love, Forever Full':

IMMORTAL LOVE, FOREVER FULL,
Forever flowing free,
Forever shared, forever whole,
A never-ebbing sea!

Our outward lips confess the name
All other names above;
Love only knoweth whence it came,
And comprehendeth love.

[1] The Mount of Olives.

Blow, winds of God, awake and blow
The mists of earth away:
Shine out, O Light divine, and show
How wide and far we stray.

We may not climb the heavenly steeps
To bring the Lord Christ down;
In vain we search the lowest deeps,
For Him no depths can drown.

But warm, sweet, tender, even yet
A present help is He;
And faith still has its Olivet,
And love its Galilee.

The healing of His seamless dress
Is by our beds of pain;
We touch Him in life's throng and press
And we are whole again.

Through Him the first fond prayers are said,
Our lips of childhood frame,
The last low whispers of our dead
Are burdened with His Name.

O Lord and Master of us all,
Whate'er our name or sign,
We own Thy sway, we hear Thy call,
We test our lives by Thine.

The letter fails, the systems fall,
And every symbol wanes;
The Spirit over brooding all,
Eternal Love remains.

James Russell Lowell was, like Longfellow, Professor of Modern Languages at Harvard: he was actually Longfellow's successor. But he was also a poet and a politician – not a usual combination of activities. The one hymn from his pen that can be found in our hymn-books today brings the two together very effectively. It's from a poem called 'The Present Crisis' – there's always a crisis, of course, where politicians are concerned but this one was the war with Mexico in 1845, which Lowell regarded as unjust.

> ONCE TO EVERY MAN AND NATION,
> Comes the moment to decide,
> In the strife of truth with falsehood,
> For the good or evil side;
> Some great cause, some great decision,
> Offering each the bloom or blight,
> And the choice goes by forever,
> 'Twixt that darkness and that light.
>
> Then to side with truth is noble,
> When we share her wretched crust,
> Ere her cause bring fame and profit,
> And 'tis prosperous to be just;
> Then it is the brave man chooses
> While the coward stands aside,
> Till the multitude make virtue
> Of the Faith they had denied.
>
> By the light of burning martyrs,
> Christ, Thy bleeding feet we track,
> Toiling up new Calvaries ever
> With the cross that turns not back;
> New occasions teach new duties,
> Ancient values test our youth;
> They must upward still and onward,
> Who would keep abreast of truth.
>
> Though the cause of evil prosper,
> Yet the truth alone is strong;
> Though her portion be the scaffold,
> And upon the throne be wrong;

Yet that scaffold sways the future
And behind the dim unknown,
Standeth God within the shadow,
Keeping watch above his own.

So far we've looked at hymns written by American men of letters. But, statistically at least, the greatest influence on our hymnody from America has been the revivalist movements. This was largely due to Moody and Sankey, whose missions in the late Victorian years introduced scores of new 'Sacred Songs and Solos'. It's said of the 'Glory Song', for instance, written by Charles Gabriel, that within five years of its composition it had sold a hundred million copies throughout the world. It's best known nowadays for its chorus, 'O that will be, glory for me!'

WHEN ALL MY LABOURS AND TRIALS ARE O'ER,
And I am safe on that beautiful shore,
Just to be near the dear Lord I adore,
Will through the ages be glory for me.
  O that will be, glory for me,
  Glory for me, glory for me,
  When by His grace I shall look on His face,
  That will be glory, be glory for me.

When, by the gift of His infinite grace,
I am accorded in heaven a place,
Just to be there and to look on His face,
Will through the ages be glory for me.
  Chorus

Friends will be there I have loved long ago;
Joy like a river around me will flow;
Yet just a smile from my Saviour, I know,
Will through the ages be glory for me.
  Chorus

To finish with tonight, we have another hymn from the Moody and Sankey tradition. It is a marvellous evocation of the American frontier mentality, applied to the doctrine of final perseverance:

> Hold the Fort, for I am coming
> Jesus signals still.
> Send the answer back to heaven:
> By Thy grace, we will!

I can almost see the heavenly cavalry on the horizon! It's called 'Ho, My Comrades!' and here it is in full:

> Ho, my comrades! see the signal
> Waving in the sky!
> Reinforcements now appearing,
> Victory is nigh.
> > *'Hold the fort, for I am coming,'*
> > *Jesus signals still;*
> > *Wave the answer back to Heaven,*
> > *'By Thy grace we will.'*
>
> See the mighty host advancing,
> Satan leading on;
> Mighty ones around us falling,
> Courage almost gone!
> > *Chorus*
>
> See the glorious banner waving!
> Hear the trumpet blow!
> In our Leader's name we triumph
> Over every foe.
> > *Chorus*
>
> Fierce and long the battle rages,
> But our help is near;
> Onward comes our great Commander,
> Cheer, my comrades, cheer!
> > *Chorus*

MORE TRANSLATIONS

From Series 2

BBC Radio Four
Sunday 15 August 1976
Producer: David Winter

• • •

I was saying last week that hymns don't travel well but I was care-ful to omit from that judgement translations and paraphrases. Because the fact is that a very substantial proportion of the hymns we sing today is based on words or ideas first set down centuries ago and often in German, Latin or Greek. And what a sense of continuity that evokes – the unbroken and unbreakable link with the Church's past, all those mysterious bearded saints of Greece and those unknown monks toiling over their manuscripts in medieval monasteries while war, famine and pestilence raged around them.

So let's start tonight with a hymn written by perhaps the most famous monk of them all, St Francis of Assisi. It's his 'Canticle of Brother Sun', paraphrased by William Draper: 'All Creatures of Our God and King'. There are seven verses.

> ALL CREATURES OF OUR GOD AND KING
> Lift up your voice and with us sing,
> Alleluia! Alleluia!
> Thou burning sun with golden beam,
> Thou silver moon with softer gleam!
> *O praise Him, O praise Him,*
> *Alleluia, Alleluia, Alleluia!*

Thou rushing wind that art so strong,
Ye clouds that sail in heaven along,
O praise Him! Alleluia!
Thou rising moon, in praise rejoice,
Ye lights of evening, find a voice!
    Chorus

Thou flowing water, pure and clear,
Make music for thy Lord to hear,
O praise Him! Alleluia!
Thou fire so masterful and bright,
That givest man both warmth and light.
    Chorus

Dear mother earth, who day by day
Unfoldest blessings on our way,
O praise Him! Alleluia!
The flowers and fruits that in thee grow,
Let them His glory also show.
    Chorus

And all ye men of tender heart,
Forgiving others, take your part,
O sing ye! Alleluia!
Ye who long pain and sorrow bear,
Praise God and on Him cast your care!
    Chorus

And thou most kind and gentle Death,
Waiting to hush our latest breath,
O praise Him! Alleluia!
Thou leadest home the child of God
And Christ our Lord the way hath trod.
    Chorus

Let all things their Creator bless
And worship Him in humbleness,
O praise Him! Alleluia!

Praise, praise the Father, praise the Son,
And praise the Spirit, Three in One!
Chorus

Peter Abelard was also a monk in the Middle Ages, a generation or two before St Francis, in fact. He is best remembered today, of course, for his celebrated love affair with Héloise, a beautiful young girl to whom he was first her tutor and then her lover. They had a son but the ensuing scandal drove Héloise to a convent and Abelard himself to a monastery.

Always a controversial figure, Abelard's theological views were under constant attack and were in fact twice condemned by Councils of the Church. His book on the Trinity was publicly burned by the authorities. Still, he managed to die in his bed and later generations have dealt more kindly with his writings. Indeed in 1854 that apostle of orthodoxy, John Mason Neale, translated one of his hymns: a kind of seal of re-instatement for the turbulent priest of the twelfth century. Here it is: 'O What Their Joy and Their Glory Must Be, those Endless Sabbaths the Blessèd Ones See!'

O WHAT THEIR JOY AND THEIR GLORY MUST BE,
Those endless Sabbaths the blessèd ones see;
Crown for the valiant, to weary ones rest:
God shall be all and in all ever blest.

What are the monarch, his court and his throne?
What are the peace and the joy that they own?
O that the blest ones, who in it have share,
All that they feel could as fully declare!

Truly, 'Jerusalem' name we that shore,
City of peace that brings joy evermore;
Wish and fulfilment are not severed there,
Nor do things prayed for come short of the prayer.

There, where no troubles distraction can bring,
We the sweet anthems of Zion shall sing;
While for Thy grace, Lord, their voices of praise
Thy blessèd people eternally raise.

Now, in the meantime, with hearts raised on high,
We for that country must yearn and must sigh,
Seeking Jerusalem, dear native land,
Through our long exile on Babylon's strand.

Low before Him with our praises we fall,
Of whom and in whom and through whom are all;
Of whom, the Father; and in whom, the Son;
And through whom, the Spirit, with them ever One.

Neale searched extensively through early church literature for
verses to translate. For him it was a vital part of restoring or
reasserting the Church's Catholicity. Among the hundreds of Latin
and Greek hymns that he translated or paraphrased is this lovely
evening hymn, attributed to St Anatolius, who died in 458 –
although it may have been written by a later Anatolius, a ninth-
century hymn-writer. Neale claimed that it was a great favourite
in the Greek Isles.

THE DAY IS PAST AND OVER;
All thanks, O Lord, to Thee;
I pray Thee now that sinless
The hours of dark may be.
O Jesus, keep me in Thy sight,
And guard me through the coming night.

The joys of day are over;
I lift my heart to Thee,
And ask Thee that offenceless
The hours of dark may be.
Chorus

The toils of day are over;
I raise the hymn to Thee,
And ask that free from peril
The hours of dark may be.
   Chorus

Be Thou my soul's preserver,
For Thou alone dost know
How many are the perils
Through which I have to go.
   O loving Jesus, hear my call,
   And guard and save me from them all.

Another of Neale's hymns translated from the Greek has a very touching understanding of human frailty and, as it's a Lenten hymn, that in itself is noteworthy. It's a sort of conversation, or rather, a monologue, not from earth to heaven (like most hymns) but the other way round.

Christian, dost thou see them
On the holy ground,
How the troops of Midian
Prowl and prowl around?

After that spine-chilling warning (who are the 'troops of Midian', I wonder?) we move on to more subtle, inward foes: the voice of Lenten frustration, for example. In this version, the troops of Midian seem to have been replaced by powers of darkness.

CHRISTIAN, DOST THOU SEE THEM
On the holy ground,
How the powers of darkness
Rage thy steps around?
Christian, up and smite them,
Counting gain but loss,
In the strength that cometh
By the holy cross.

Christian, dost thou feel them,
How they work within,
Striving, tempting, luring,
Goading into sin?
Christian, never tremble;
Never be downcast;
Gird thee for the battle,
Watch and pray and fast.

Christian, dost thou hear them,
How they speak thee fair?
'Always fast and vigil?
Always watch and prayer?'
Christian, answer boldly:
'While I breathe I pray!'
Peace shall follow battle,
Night shall end in day.

Well I know thy trouble,
O My servant true;
Thou art very weary,
I was weary, too;
But that toil shall make thee
Some day all Mine own,
At the end of sorrow
Shall be near My throne.

In the Reformation period German hymns appeared in great numbers. The Wesleys introduced some to Britain, but Catherine Winkworth, a century ago, was the one whose translations really popularised them in Britain. In all, she published some five hundred translations, many of them in an anthology called *Lyra Germanica*, which was considered to be one of the great devotional works of the nineteenth century. Here's one of the best of them, a lovely triumphant Easter hymn, 'Christ the Lord is risen again'. The original was by M. Weisse, in 1531.

CHRIST THE LORD IS RISEN AGAIN;
Christ hath broken every chain;
Hark! Angelic voices cry,
Singing evermore on high,
Alleluia!

He, who gave for us His life,
Who for us endured the strife,
Is our Paschal Lamb today;
We, too, sing for joy, and say
Alleluia!

He, who bore all pain and loss
Comfortless upon the cross,
Lives in glory now on high,
Pleads for us and hears our cry;
Alleluia!

He, who slumbered in the grave,
Is exalted now to save;
Now through Christendom it rings
That the Lamb is King of kings.
Alleluia!

He whose path no records tell,
Who descended into hell;
Who the strong man armed hath bound,
Now in highest heaven is crowned.
Alleluia!

Now He bids us tell abroad
How the lost may be restored,
How the penitent forgiven,
How we too may enter heav'n.
Alleluia!

Thou, our Paschal Lamb indeed,
Christ, Thy ransomed people feed:
Take our sins and guilt away,

> Let us sing by night and day
> Alleluia!

Another of Catherine Winkworth's translations has become associated with a tune adapted and harmonised for the original version by J. S. Bach. Johann Franck wrote the words: 'Jesus, Priceless Treasure, Source of Purest Pleasure; Truest Friend to Me'.

> Jesus, priceless Treasure,
> Source of purest pleasure;
> Truest Friend to me.
> Ah, how long in anguish
> Shall my spirit languish,
> Yearning, Lord, for Thee?
> Thou art mine, O Lamb divine!
> I will suffer naught to hide Thee,
> Naught I ask beside Thee.
>
> In Thine arms I rest me;
> Foes who would molest me
> Cannot reach me here.
> Though the earth be shaking,
> Every heart be quaking,
> Jesus calms my fear.
> Lightnings flash and thunders crash;
> Yet, though sin and hell assail me,
> Jesus will not fail me.
>
> Satan, I defy thee;
> Death, I now decry thee;
> Fear, I bid thee cease.
> World, thou shalt not harm me
> Nor thy threats alarm me
> While I sing of peace.
> God's great power guards every hour;
> Earth and all its depths adore Him,
> Silent bow before Him.

Evil world, I leave thee;
Thou canst not deceive me,
Thine appeal is vain.
Sin that once did bind me,
Get thee far behind me,
Come not forth again.
Past thine hour, O pride and power;
Sinful life, thy bonds I sever,
Leave thee now forever.

Hence, all thought of sadness!
For the Lord of gladness,
Jesus, enters in.
Those who love the Father,
Though the storms may gather,
Still have peace within;
Yea, whatever we here must bear,
Still in Thee lies purest pleasure,
Jesus, priceless Treasure!

A hymn from the Italian, translated by Richard Frederick Littledale, has become one of the most popular in English. It's by Bianco da Siena, who died in 1434.

COME DOWN, O LOVE DIVINE,
Seek Thou this soul of mine,
And visit it with Thine own ardour glowing;
O Comforter, draw near,
Within my heart appear,
And kindle it, Thy holy flame bestowing.

O let it freely burn,
Till earthly passions turn
To dust and ashes in its heat consuming;
And let Thy glorious light
Shine ever on my sight,
And clothe me round, the while my path illuming.

Let holy charity
Mine outward vesture be,
And lowliness become mine inner clothing;
True lowliness of heart,
Which takes the humbler part,
And o'er its own shortcomings weeps with loathing.

And so the yearning strong,
With which the soul will long,
Shall far outpass the power of human telling;
For none can guess its grace,
Till he become the place
Wherein the Holy Spirit makes His dwelling.

Finally tonight, another beautiful evening hymn, translated by Ellerton[1] and Hort,[2] its original dating back to the early church: St Ambrose, who lived in the fourth century. We can imagine the darkness drawing in around a Greek monastery – the quiet, the calm unclouded close of the day captured by the writer as he watched the fast-fading light.

O STRENGTH AND STAY UPHOLDING ALL CREATION,
Who ever dost Thyself unmoved abide,
Yet day by day the light in due gradation
From hour to hour through all its changes guide.

Grant to life's day a calm, unclouded ending,
An eve untouched by shadows of decay,
The brightness of a holy death-bed blending
With dawning glories of the eternal day.

Hear us, O Father, gracious and forgiving,
Through Jesus Christ Thy co-eternal Word,
Who, with the Holy Ghost, by all things living
Now and to endless ages art adored.

[1] See p. 134.
[2] Fenton John Anthony Hort was a nineteenth-century Cambridge theologist who carried out controversial work on the Greek origins of the New Testament.

MORE HYMNS OF THE EIGHTEENTH CENTURY

From Series 2

BBC Radio Four
Sunday 22 August 1976
Producer: David Winter

• • •

The eighteenth century was the period when hymn-singing really caught on in England, largely thanks to the writers associated with the Wesleyan revival. Although Charles Wesley stands head and shoulders above the rest, in quantity at any rate, there were several others who were writing very fine hymns, many of which are popular today – and it's some of these men we shall be looking at this week.

Among the most outstanding of them was Philip Doddridge, a Nonconformist minister at Northampton. It was only in his later years – he died in 1751 at the age of forty-nine – that he was associated with John Wesley but his hymns were enthusiastically taken up by the Methodists. Here's one of the best known of them.

> O GOD OF BETHEL, BY WHOSE HAND
> Thy people still are fed.
> Who through this earthly pilgrimage
> Hast all our fathers led.
>
> Our vows, our prayers, we now present
> Before Thy throne of grace:

> O God of Israel, be the God
> Of their succeeding race.
>
> Through each perplexing path of life
> Our wandering footsteps guide;
> Give us each day our daily bread,
> And raiment fit provide.
>
> O spread thy covering wings around,
> Till all our wanderings cease,
> And at our Father's loved abode
> Our souls arrive in peace![1]

Doddridge also wrote a splendid Advent hymn, based on our Lord's words at the start of His ministry.

> HARK THE GLAD SOUND! THE SAVIOUR COMES,
> The Saviour promised long;
> Let every heart prepare a throne,
> And every voice a song.
>
> On Him the Spirit, largely poured,
> Exerts His sacred fire;
> Wisdom and might and zeal and love,
> His holy breast inspire.
>
> He comes the prisoners to release,
> In Satan's bondage held;
> The gates of brass before Him burst,
> The iron fetters yield.
>
> He comes, from thickest films of vice
> To clear the mental ray,
> And on the eyes oppressed with night
> To pour celestial day.

---

[1] A fifth verse is by another author, identity unknown.

He comes the broken heart to bind,
The bleeding soul to cure;
And with the treasures of His grace
To enrich the humble poor.

His silver trumpets publish loud
The jubilee of the Lord;
Our debts are all remitted now,
Our heritage restored.

Our glad hosannas, Prince of peace,
Thy welcome shall proclaim;
And heav'n's eternal arches ring
With Thy belovèd Name.

Thomas Olivers, a young Welshman, set out in 1753 to walk from his home in Montgomeryshire to join John Wesley in Cornwall. When he was the best part of the way there, at Tiverton, he bought a colt for five pounds and it's said he eventually rode a hundred thousand miles on its back. As an itinerant Methodist preacher he covered the country and on one of his visits to London he visited a synagogue where he heard a Rabbi Leoni[2] singing a very beautiful melody. Olivers was so impressed by it that he felt he must write a Christian hymn to it: so in this case, at least, the tune came first and 'The God of Abraham Praise' was the result. The tune is still known as 'Leoni' and the Jewish flavour survives the Christian adaptation very well. It's rather long.

THE GOD OF ABRAHAM PRAISE,
Who reigns enthroned above;
Ancient of everlasting days,
And God of Love;
Jehovah, great I AM!
By earth and heav'n confessed;

[2] Not in fact a rabbi but a cantor, Meir ben Judah or Meir Lyon, also known as Myer or Michael Leoni, who sang at the 'Great Synagogue' as well as at Drury Lane.

I bow and bless the sacred Name
Forever blessed.

The God of Abraham praise,
At whose supreme command
From earth I rise and seek the joys
At His right hand;
I all on earth forsake,
Its wisdom, fame and power;
And Him my only Portion make,
My Shield and Tower.

The God of Abraham praise,
Whose all sufficient grace
Shall guide me all my happy days,
In all my ways.
He calls a worm His friend,
He calls Himself my God!
And He shall save me to the end,
Thro' Jesus' blood.

He by Himself has sworn;
I on His oath depend,
I shall, on eagle wings upborne,
To Heav'n ascend.
I shall behold His face;
I shall His power adore,
And sing the wonders of His grace
For evermore.

Tho' nature's strength decay,
And earth and hell withstand,
To Canaan's bounds I urge my way,
At His command.
The watery deep I pass,
With Jesus in my view;
And thro' the howling wilderness
My way pursue.

The goodly land I see,
With peace and plenty bless'd;
A land of sacred liberty,
And endless rest.
There milk and honey flow,
And oil and wine abound,
And trees of life forever grow
With mercy crowned.

There dwells the Lord our King,
The Lord of Righteousness,
Triumphant o'er the world and sin,
The Prince of Peace;
On Sion's sacred height
His kingdom still maintains,
And glorious with His saints in light
For ever reigns.

He keeps His own secure,
He guards them by His side,
Arrays in garments white and pure
His spotless bride:
With streams of sacred bliss,
With groves of living joys –
With all the fruits of Paradise,
He still supplies.

Before the great Three-One
They all exulting stand;
And tell the wonders He hath done,
Through all their land:
The list'ning spheres attend,
And swell the growing fame;
And sing, in songs which never end,
The wondrous Name.

The God Who reigns on high
The great archangels sing,

And 'Holy, holy, holy!' cry,
'Almighty King!
Who was and is the same,
And evermore shall be:
Jehovah – Father – great I AM,
We worship Thee!'

Before the Saviour's face
The ransomed nations bow;
O'erwhelmed at His almighty grace,
Forever new:
He shows His prints of love –
They kindle to a flame!
And sound thro' all the worlds above
The slaughtered Lamb.

The whole triumphant host
Give thanks to God on high;
'Hail, Father, Son and Holy Ghost,'
They ever cry.
Hail, Abraham's God, and mine!
(I join the heav'nly lays,)
All might and majesty are Thine,
And endless praise.

Edward Perronet was a close friend of the Wesleys and one of their preachers for many years. As his name suggests, he was descended from a family of French refugees who settled in England in the seventeenth century. His best-known hymn is 'All Hail the Power of Jesus' Name' which appeared anonymously in the *Gospel Magazine* for November 1779, complete with the tune 'Miles Lane', to which it is still often sung, by William Shrubsole. Later a noted Baptist hymn editor, Dr Rippon, revised the hymn and added a final verse of his own:

O that with yonder sacred throng
We at his feet may fall!
We'll join the everlasting song . . .

Here are the verses that Perronet wrote:

> ALL HAIL THE POWER OF JESUS' NAME!
> Let angels prostrate fall;
> Bring forth the royal diadem,
>> *And crown Him, crown Him, crown Him,*
>> *Crown Him Lord of all.*
>
> Crown him, you martyrs of our God,
> Who from His altar call;
> Extol the stem of Jesse's rod
>> *Chorus*
>
> Ye chosen seed of Israel's race,
> Ye ransomed from the fall,
> Hail Him who saves you by His grace,
>> *Chorus*
>
> Sinners, whose love can ne'er forget
> The wormwood and the gall,
> Go spread your trophies at His feet,
>> *Chorus*

Another of Wesley's lay preachers was John Cennick, who later became a Moravian and spent some time preaching in Germany. His collection of hymns was titled *Sacred Hymns for the Children of God in the Days of Their Pilgrimage*. Among the hymns under that rather daunting title was this, certainly a pilgrim hymn, but also distinctly jolly.

> CHILDREN OF THE HEAVENLY KING,
> As ye journey, sweetly sing;
> Sing your Saviour's worthy praise,
> Glorious in His works and ways.
>
> We are travelling home to God,
> In the way the fathers trod;

They are happy now, and we
Soon their happiness shall see.

O, ye banished seed, be glad!
Christ our advocate is made;
Us to save, our flesh assumes –
Brother to our souls becomes.

Shout, ye little flock, and blest,
You on Jesus' throne shall rest:
There your seat is now prepared –
There your kingdom and reward.

Lift your eyes, ye sons of light,
Zion's city is in sight:
There our endless home shall be,
There our Lord we soon shall see.

Fear not, brethren; joyful stand
On the borders of your land;
Jesus Christ, your Father's Son,
Bids you undismayed go on.

Lord, obedient we would go,
Gladly leaving all below;
Only Thou our Leader be;
And we will still follow Thee.

Cennick also had a share, with Charles Wesley and Martin Madan, in one of the finest of all the Advent hymns, 'Lo He Comes with Clouds Descending'. Madan seems to have found the tune, which was an English melody of the day, and included it in a collection of hymns for Lock Hospital, at Hyde Park Corner, of which he was founder and chaplain, adapting the words and adding this verse.

Yea, Amen, let all adore Thee,
High on Thine eternal throne;
Saviour, take the power and glory;

Claim the kingdom for Thine own:
    Alleluia!
Thou shalt reign, and Thou alone.

Here is Cennick's original hymn:

LO! HE COMETH, COUNTLESS TRUMPETS,
Blow before His bloody sign!
'Midst ten thousand saints and angels,
See their great exalted head.
Alleluia!
Welcome, welcome bleeding lamb!

Now His merit by the harpers,
Thro' the eternal deeps resounds!
Now resplendent shine his nail-prints,
Ev'ry eye shall see His wounds!
They who pierc'd Him,
Shall at His appearing wail.

Every island, sea and mountain,
Heav'n and earth shall flee away!
All who hate Him must ashamèd,
Hear the trump proclaim the day:
Come to judgement!
Stand before the Son of Man!

All who love Him view His glory
Shining in His bruised face:
His dear person on the rainbow,
Now His people's heads shall raise:
Happy mourners!
Now on clouds He comes! He comes!

Now redemption long expected,
See, in solemn pomp appear;
All His people, once despised,
Now shall meet Him in the air:
Alleluiah! Now the promised kingdom's come!

> View Him smiling, now determin'd,
> Ev'ry evil to destroy!
> All the nations now shall sing Him,
> Songs of everlasting joy!
> O come quickly!
> Alleluia! Come Lord, come!

One of the greatest hymn-writers of the Methodist movement was John Newton who in his later years was Rector of St Mary Woolnoth in the City of London. Among his many well-loved hymns is this one, a picture of the Church – idealised, perhaps, but a great deal more attractive than it is usually depicted as in hymns, with only the tiniest hint of triumphalism:

> On the Rock of Ages founded,
> What can shake Thy sure repose?
> With salvation's walls surrounded,
> Thou may'st smile at all Thy foes.

Here it is in full:

> GLORIOUS THINGS OF THEE ARE SPOKEN,
> Zion, city of our God!
> He, whose Word cannot be broken,
> Formed thee for His own abode.
> On the Rock of Ages founded,
> What can shake thy sure repose?
> With salvation's walls surrounded,
> Thou may'st smile at all thy foes.
>
> See! The streams of living waters,
> Springing from eternal love;
> Well supply thy sons and daughters,
> And all fear of want remove:
> Who can faint while such a river
> Ever flows their thirst to assuage?

Grace, which like the Lord, the Giver,
Never fails from age to age.

Round each habitation hovering,
See the cloud and fire appear!
For a glory and a cov'ring
Showing that the Lord is near.
Thus deriving from our banner
Light by night and shade by day;
Safe they feed upon the manna
Which He gives them when they pray.

Blest inhabitants of Zion,
Washed in the Redeemer's blood!
Jesus, whom their souls rely on,
Makes them kings and priests to God.
'Tis His love His people raises,
Over self to reign as kings,
And as priests, His solemn praises
Each for a thank-offering brings.

Saviour, if of Zion's city,
I through grace a member am,
Let the world deride or pity,
I will glory in Thy Name.
Fading is the worldling's pleasure,
All his boasted pomp and show;
Solid joys and lasting treasure
None but Zion's children know.

And finally, back to John Cennick for an evening hymn, perhaps
originally intended for children but not in any true sense childish:
'Ere I Sleep, for Every Favour.'

ERE I SLEEP, FOR EVERY FAVOUR
This day showed

By my God,
I will bless my Saviour.

O my Lord, what shall I render
To Thy Name,
Still the same,
Gracious, good and tender?

Leave me not, but ever love me;
Let Thy peace
Be my bliss,
Till Thou hence remove me.

FOUR RECTORS

From Series 2

BBC Radio Four
Sunday 15 August 1976
Producer: David Winter

• • •

Not surprisingly, most hymns have been written by clergymen; in fact, by Victorian clergymen. We're going to look this week at the work of four famous rectors all from those rural rectories from which so much of the literature of the eighteenth and nineteenth centuries emanated.

We'll start with the most famous of them all, mentioned last week as the author of 'Glorious Things of Thee Are Spoken' – the redoubtable John Newton. Once a slave-trader, he experienced an evangelical conversion (though partly, we must add, as a result of reading Thomas à Kempis's *Imitation of Christ*) and eventually became Rector of Olney, in Buckinghamshire. While he was there, in association with his most distinguished parishioner, William Cowper, the poet, he contributed 280 of their collection of *Olney Hymns*. 'Glorious Things of Thee are Spoken' was one of them. So was this, one of the great hymns of the English language:

> HOW SWEET THE NAME OF JESUS SOUNDS
> In a believer's ear!
> It soothes his sorrows, heals his wounds,
> And drives away his fear.

It makes the wounded spirit whole,
And calms the troubled breast;
'Tis manna to the hungry soul,
And to the weary, rest.

Dear Name, the rock on which I build,
My shield and hiding place,
My never failing treasury, filled
With boundless stores of grace!

By Thee my prayers acceptance gain,
Although with sin defiled;
Satan accuses me in vain,
And I am owned a child.

Jesus! my Shepherd, Husband, Friend,
O Prophet, Priest and King,
My Lord, my Life, my Way, mine End,
Accept the praise I bring.

Weak is the effort of my heart,
And cold my warmest thought;
But when I see Thee as Thou art,
I'll praise Thee as I ought.

Till then I would Thy love proclaim
With every fleeting breath,
And may the music of Thy Name
Refresh my soul in death!

Another of Newton's hymns related very explicitly to the weekly 'prayer meeting' for which most of the Olney hymns were composed. It's an invitation to prayer, couched in effectively simple language:

Thou art coming to a King;
Large petitions with thee bring;
For His grace and power are such
None can ever ask too much.

Incidentally, the opening couplet of the hymn is a nice example of the perils facing hymn-book editors. Newton wrote:

> Come, my soul, thy suit prepare:
> Jesus loves to answer prayer.

One modern editor clearly found that word 'suit' unacceptable – or perhaps ambiguous – for a modern congregation so he changed it to the rather wooden:

> Come, my soul, thy *plea* prepare.

May he be forgiven! Anyway, here it is, as Newton wrote it:

> COME, MY SOUL, THY SUIT PREPARE:
> Jesus loves to answer prayer;
> He himself has bid thee pray,
> Therefore will not say thee nay.
>
> Thou art coming to a King;
> Large petitions with thee bring;
> For His grace and power are such,
> None can ever ask too much.
>
> With my burden I begin:
> Lord, remove this load of sin;
> Let Thy blood, for sinners spilt,
> Set my conscience free from guilt.
>
> Lord, I come to Thee for rest,
> Take possession of my breast;
> There Thy blood-bought right maintain,
> And without a rival reign.
>
> Show me what I have to do,
> Every hour my strength renew:
> Let me live a life of faith,
> Let me die Thy people's death.

> While I am a pilgrim here,
> Let Thy love my spirit cheer;
> As my guide, my guard, my friend,
> Lead me to my journey's end.

We looked at some of William Cowper's hymns in our last series of *Sweet Songs of Zion*, but there is another Cooper among the English hymn-writers: Edward Cooper, Rector of Yoxall, in Staffordshire, near Lichfield. In fact his collected hymns were published under the title *Lichfield*.

His best-known hymn is couched in a form that at one time threatened to become universal: four verses, the first addressed to the Father, the second to the Son, the third to the Holy Spirit and the fourth to the Trinity. Within this framework, he produced the kind of hymn that will always be associated in the mind of my generation with J. B. Dykes and evensong in the parish church:

> FATHER OF HEAVEN, WHOSE LOVE PROFOUND
> A ransom for our souls hath found,
> Before Thy throne we sinners bend;
> To us Thy pardoning love extend.
>
> Almighty Son, incarnate Word,
> Our Prophet, Priest, Redeemer, Lord,
> Before Thy throne we sinners bend;
> To us Thy saving grace extend.
>
> Eternal Spirit, by whose breath
> The soul is raised from sin and death,
> Before Thy throne we sinners bend;
> To us Thy quickening power extend.
>
> Jehovah – Father, Spirit, Son –
> Mysterious Godhead, Three in One,
> Before Thy throne we sinners bend;
> Grace, pardon, life to us extend.

Among many other English hymns in this Trinitarian format,

probably the best and perhaps best-loved is by John Marriott, who was Rector of Church Lawford, Worcestershire. He was a friend of Sir Walter Scott who refers to him in the second canto of 'Marmion' as someone with whom 'he held poetic talk'.

> Nor hill, nor brook, we passed along
> But had its legend or its song.

Well, the 'song' in question at the moment is 'Thou, Whose Almighty Word'. It is in fact a splendidly poetic hymn, quite majestic in its language – especially Verse Three:

> THOU, WHOSE ALMIGHTY WORD
> Chaos and darkness heard,
> And took their flight;
> Hear us, we humbly pray,
> And, where the gospel day
> Sheds not its glorious ray,
> Let there be light!
>
> Thou who didst come to bring
> On Thy redeeming wing
> Healing and sight,
> Heal to the sick in mind,
> Sight to the in-ly blind,
> Now to all humankind,
> Let there be light!
>
> Spirit of truth and love
> Life-giving, holy dove,
> Speed forth Thy flight;
> Move on the water's face,
> Bearing the lamp of grace,
> And in earth's darkest place
> Let there be light!
>
> Holy and blessèd Three,
> Glorious Trinity,

Wisdom, love, might;
Boundless as ocean's tide,
Rolling in fullest pride,
Through the world far and wide,
Let there be light!

That tune, incidentally, which is inevitably associated with Cooper's words, is based on a melody by Felice de Giardini, the famous Italian violinist who lived in Moscow – hence the title of the tune: 'Moscow'.

John Samuel Bewley Monsell was born in Londonderry but became Rector of St Nicholas, Guildford – a quiet country town in those days (the middle of the nineteenth century). He wrote several very famous hymns that span an enormous variety of styles, from the reflective eucharistic hymn 'I Hunger and I Thirst' to the muscular Christianity of 'Fight the Good Fight with All Thy Might'. Let's take that one first – it's a splendid example of good, economical writing, with a most effective use of repetition and assurance.

FIGHT THE GOOD FIGHT WITH ALL THY MIGHT,
Christ is thy strength and Christ thy right;
Lay hold on life, and it shall be
Thy joy and crown eternally.

Run the straight race, through God's good grace,
Lift up thine eyes and seek his face;
Life with its way before us lies,
Christ is the Path and Christ the Prize.

Cast care aside, lean on thy Guide;
His boundless mercy will provide;
Trust, and thy trusting soul shall prove
Christ is its Life and Christ its Love.[1]

[1] A variant of this verse also illustrates the use of poetical repetition: 'Cast care aside, upon they Guide, Lean, and His mercy will provide; Lean, and the trusting soul shall prove Christ is its Life and Christ its Love.'

> Faint not nor fear, His arms are near;
> He changeth not, and thou art dear;
> Only believe, and thou shalt see
> That Christ is all in all to thee.

It is a far cry from that other hymn I mentioned, 'I Hunger and I Thirst':

> I HUNGER AND I THIRST,
> Jesu, my manna be;
> Ye living waters, burst
> Out of the rock for me.

But the same use of literary and poetic devices – but without any artificiality – marks this hymn too. Here's how it goes on:

> Thou bruised and broken Bread,
> My life-long wants supply;
> As living souls are fed,
> O feed me, or I die.
>
> Thou true life-giving Vine,
> Let me Thy sweetness prove;
> Renew my life with Thine,
> Refresh my soul with love.
>
> Rough paths my feet have trod
> Since first their course began;
> Feed me, Thou Bread of God;
> Help me, Thou Son of Man.
>
> For still the desert lies
> My thirsting soul before;
> O Living Waters, rise
> Within me evermore.

Our last hymn tonight is also by Monsell and it's based on what must be one of the most inspired mistranslations in the history of literature. If we believe modern Hebrew scholars, what the Psalmist actually wrote was something like 'Worship the Lord in splendid array' – that is, put on your finest vestments. But the King James translators, groping in the dark a bit, one guesses, settled for 'Worship the Lord in the beauty of holiness'. I bet that's what the Psalmist *wished* he'd written, anyway. Monsell took the line and made this hymn of it:

O WORSHIP THE LORD IN THE BEAUTY OF HOLINESS!
Bow down before Him, His glory proclaim;
With gold of obedience and incense of lowliness,
Kneel and adore Him: the Lord is His Name!

Low at His feet lay thy burden of carefulness,
High on His heart He will bear it for thee,
And comfort thy sorrows and answer thy prayerfulness,
Guiding thy steps as may best for thee be.

Fear not to enter His courts in the slenderness
Of the poor wealth thou wouldst reckon as thine;
For truth in its beauty and love in its tenderness,
These are the offerings to lay on His shrine.

These, though we bring them in trembling and fearfulness,
He will accept for the Name that is dear;
Mornings of joy give for evenings of tearfulness,
Trust for our trembling and hope for our fear.

O worship the Lord in the beauty of holiness!
Bow down before Him, His glory proclaim;
With gold of obedience and incense of lowliness,
Kneel and adore Him: the Lord is His Name!

SCOTTISH HYMN-WRITERS

From Series 2

BBC Radio Four
Sunday 22 August 1976
Producer: David Winter

• • •

We're going to start the programme with a very popular evening hymn but the reason we've chosen it also is that it's by a Scottish author and all the hymns this week are from Scotland – though, strangely enough, although they're all by Scotsmen (and one Scotswoman), several of them were written while their authors were living in London. I don't know whether the air is more poetic down here: I shouldn't have thought so.

This first one, 'Hushed Was the Evening Hymn', was written while its author, the Reverend James Drummond Burns, was minister of Hampstead Presbyterian Church in London. In fact, he's buried in Highgate cemetery. Apparently he was a tall, lanky, rather serious man who always wore clerical black. In this hymn he took the story of the child Samuel in the temple from the Old Testament and created from it these lovely, simple words:

> HUSHED WAS THE EVENING HYMN,
> The temple courts were dark;
> The lamp was burning dim
> Before the sacred ark;
> When suddenly a voice divine
> Rang through the silence of the shrine.

The old man, meek and mild,
The priest of Israel, slept;
His watch the temple child,
The little Levite, kept;
And what from Eli's sense was sealed
The Lord to Hannah's son revealed.

O give me Samuel's ear,
The open ear, O Lord,
Alive and quick to hear
Each whisper of Thy word,
Like him to answer at Thy call,
And to obey Thee first of all.

O give me Samuel's heart,
A lowly heart, that waits
Where in Thy house Thou art,
Or watches at Thy gates;
By day and night, a heart that still
Moves at the breathing of Thy will.

O give me Samuel's mind,
A sweet unmurm'ring faith,
Obedient and resigned
To Thee in life and death,
That I may read with childlike eyes
Truths that are hidden from the wise.

Some people have asked where we got the title of these programmes from. Well, I'm not sure it wasn't from Robert Murray
McCheyne. He was a minister of the Kirk 150 years ago and he
published a book of hymns, most of them not very distinguished,
with the rather verbose title: *Songs of Zion to Cheer and Guide
Pilgrims on Their Way to the New Jerusalem.* Our title may not be
quite so explicit but it is about eighty per cent shorter.[1] One hymn

[1] In the eleventh talk in this series, 'More Translations', Betjeman quotes the hymn
'O What Their Joy and Their Glory Must Be', which contains the line 'We the
sweet anthems of Zion shall sing'.

in that book has found its way into several hymn-books: 'When this Passing World Is Done'.

WHEN THIS PASSING WORLD IS DONE,
When has sunk yon glaring sun,
When we stand with Christ in glory,
Looking o'er life's finished story,
Then, Lord, shall I fully know –
Not till then – how much I owe.

When I hear the wicked call,
On the rocks and hills to fall,
When I see them start and shrink
On the fiery deluge brink,
Chorus

When I stand before the throne,
Dressed in beauty not mine own,
When I see Thee as Thou art,
Love Thee with unsinning heart,
Chorus

When the praise of heav'n I hear,
Loud as thunders to the ear,
Loud as many waters' noise,
Sweet as harp's melodious voice,
Chorus

Ev'n on earth, as through a glass
Darkly, let Thy glory pass,
Make forgiveness feel so sweet,
Make Thy Spirit's help so meet,
Chorus

Chosen not for good in me,
Wakened up from wrath to flee,
Hidden in the Saviour's side,
By the Spirit sanctified,
Teach me, Lord, on earth to show,
By my love, how much I owe.

Oft I walk beneath the cloud,
Dark, as midnight's gloomy shroud;
But, when fear is at the height,
Jesus comes and all is light;
 Blessed Jesus! bid me show
 Doubting saints how much I owe.

When in flowery paths I tread,
Oft by sin I'm captive led;
Oft I fall – but still arise –
The Spirit comes – the tempter flies;
 Blessed Spirit! bid me show
 Weary sinners all I owe.

Oft the nights of sorrow reign —
Weeping, sickness, sighing, pain;
But a night Thine anger burns —
Morning comes and joy returns;
 God of comforts! bid me show
 To Thy poor, how much I owe.

One always thinks of 'Immortal, Invisible' as the typically English hymn much loved by school chaplains and headmasters and probably heartily hated by schoolboys all over the country. Well, in fact it's not English at all. The words are by another Scot, Walter Chalmers Smith, and the tune, 'St Denio', is very emphatically Welsh. However, like Mr Burns, the Rev. Walter Chalmers Smith did sample the metropolitan delights for a time: he was minister of the Scottish Church in Islington. And while he was there he wrote this very theological hymn about the glory of God.

IMMORTAL, INVISIBLE, GOD ONLY WISE,
In light inaccessible hid from our eyes,
Most blessèd, most glorious, the Ancient of Days,
Almighty, victorious, Thy great Name we praise.

Unresting, unhasting and silent as light,
Nor wanting, nor wasting, Thou rulest in might;

Thy justice, like mountains, high soaring above
Thy clouds, which are fountains of goodness and love.

To all, life Thou givest, to both great and small;
In all life Thou livest, the true life of all;
We blossom and flourish as leaves on the tree,
And wither and perish – but naught changeth Thee.

Great Father of glory, pure Father of light,
Thine angels adore Thee, all veiling their sight;
But of all Thy rich graces this grace, Lord, impart
Take the veil from our faces, the vile from our heart.

All laud we would render; O help us to see
'Tis only the splendour of light hideth Thee,
And so let Thy glory, Almighty, impart,
Through Christ in His story Thy Christ to the heart.

'God only wise' – that phrase must have mystified a few generations of choirboys. Happily, wisdom isn't the only attribute of God
– clever people can be very tiresome – but of course the confusion
is caused by the poetic device of inversion; 'the only wise God'
wouldn't have sounded so good.

Now for our Scottish lady. She's Anne Ross Cousin and her
husband was yet another expatriate preacher – minister of the
Scottish church in Chelsea. Her best-known hymn is 'The Sands
of Time Are Sinking'. It's part of a long poem she wrote based on
some words supposed to have been spoken by the Scottish
Covenanter Samuel Rutherford on his death-bed: 'Glory Shineth
in Emmanuel's Land'. It was published in 1857 and with its
authentic Victorian note of resigned mortality, it was instantly
taken up.

> THE SANDS OF TIME ARE SINKING,
> The dawn of heaven breaks;
> The summer morn I've sighed for –
> The fair, sweet morn awakes:
> Dark, dark hath been the midnight,

But dayspring is at hand,
And glory, glory dwelleth
In Emmanuel's land.

O Christ, He is the fountain,
The deep, sweet well of love!
The streams of earth I've tasted
More deep I'll drink above:
There to an ocean fullness
His mercy doth expand,
And glory, glory dwelleth
In Emmanuel's land.

O! well it is forever,
O! well for evermore,
My nest hung in no forest
Of all this death, doomed shore:
Yea, let the vain world vanish,
As from the ship the strand,
While glory – glory dwelleth
In Emmanuel's land.

The hymn continues for another sixteen verses, but we must leave it there. The Victorians obviously had more time than we do.

The rest of our hymns this week are by the best, as well as the first, of all Scottish hymn-writers, Horatius Bonar. He wrote over six hundred hymns, of which nearly a hundred are still in use. Yet in his first parish, Kelso, where he was the assistant minister, hymns were not yet in favour and Bonar was confined to writing verses for the children to sing. He became increasingly dissatisfied with psalmody as the sole vehicle of worship and turned his hand to providing a more popular alternative. Here's a sample: 'Thy Way, Not Mine, O Lord'.

THY WAY, NOT MINE, O LORD,
However dark it be;
Lead me by Thine own hand,
Choose out the path for me.

Smooth let it be or rough,
It will be still the best;
Winding or straight, it leads
Right onward to Thy rest.

I dare not choose my lot;
I would not, if I might;
Choose Thou for me, my God,
So I shall walk aright.

Take Thou my cup, and it
With joy or sorrow fill,
As best to Thee may seem;
Choose Thou my good and ill.

Choose Thou for me my friends,
My sickness or my health;
Choose Thou my cares for me,
My poverty or wealth.

The kingdom that I seek
Is Thine: so let the way
That leads to it be Thine,
Else I must surely stray.

Not mine, not mine the choice
In things or great or small;
Be Thou my guide, my strength
My wisdom, and my all.

James Moffatt called Bonar 'The prince of Scottish hymn-writers'
but he was more than that. He was also a poet. His hymns sing well
but they also read well:

FILL THOU MY LIFE, O LORD MY GOD
In every part with praise,
That my whole being may proclaim
Thy being and Thy ways.

Not for the lip of praise alone,
Nor e'en the praising heart
I ask, but for a life made up
Of praise in every part!

Praise in the common things of life,
Its goings out and in;
Praise in each duty and each deed,
However small and mean.

Fill every part of me with praise;
Let all my being speak
Of Thee and of Thy love, O Lord,
Poor though I be and weak.

So shalt Thou, Lord, from me, e'en me,
Receive the glory due;
And so shall I begin on earth
The song forever new.

So shall each fear, each fret, each care
Be turned into a song,
And every winding of the way
The echo shall prolong;

So shall no part of day or night
From sacredness be free;
But all my life, in every step
Be fellowship with Thee.

Bonar was a minister of the Kirk but after the Disruption of 1843, when 474 ministers left the Church of Scotland, he joined the newly-formed Free Church. In fact, he became Moderator of the Free Church Assembly in 1883. Several of his hymns have the authentic ring of Scottish Calvinism, including this one: 'Go, Labour on: Spend and Be Spent . . .'

GO, LABOUR ON: SPEND AND BE SPENT,
Thy joy to do the Father's will:
It is the way the Master went;
Should not the servant tread it still?

Go, labour on! 'tis not for naught
Thine earthly loss is heavenly gain;
Men heed Thee, love Thee, praise Thee not;
The Master praises: what are men?

Go, labour on! enough, while here,
If He shall praise thee, if He deign
The willing heart to mark and cheer:
No toil for Him shall be in vain.

Go, labour on! Your hands are weak,
Your knees are faint, your soul cast down;
Yet falter not; the prize you seek
Is near – a kingdom and a crown.

Go, labour on while it is day:
The world's dark night is hastening on;
Speed, speed thy work, cast sloth away;
It is not thus that souls are won.

Men die in darkness at your side,
Without a hope to cheer the tomb;
Take up the torch and wave it wide,
The torch that lights time's thickest gloom.

Toil on faint not, keep watch and pray,
Be wise the erring soul to win;
Go forth into the world's highway,
Compel the wanderer to come in.

Toil on, and in thy toil rejoice!
For toil comes rest, for exile home;
Soon shalt thou hear the Bridegroom's voice,
The midnight peal, 'Behold, I come!'

We've saved till last Bonar's best-known hymn, 'I Heard the Voice of Jesus Say'. This soon had the priceless advantage of the perfect tune: 'Vox Dilecti', by J. B. Dykes, with its dramatic, almost melodramatic, change from minor to major key as the writer records his response to the words of Jesus.

> I HEARD THE VOICE OF JESUS SAY,
> 'Come unto Me and rest;
> Lay down, thou weary one,
> Lay down thy head upon My breast.'
> I came to Jesus as I was,
> Weary and worn and sad;
> I found in Him a resting place,
> And He has made me glad.
>
> I heard the voice of Jesus say,
> 'Behold, I freely give
> The living water; thirsty one,
> Stoop down and drink and live.'
> I came to Jesus and I drank
> Of that life-giving stream;
> My thirst was quenched, my soul revived,
> And now I live in Him.
>
> I heard the voice of Jesus say,
> 'I am this dark world's Light;
> Look unto Me, thy morn shall rise,
> And all thy days be bright.'
> I looked to Jesus and I found
> In Him my Star, my Sun;
> And in that light of life I'll walk
> Till travelling days are done.

SOME BISHOPS

From Series 2

BBC Radio Four
Sunday 29 August 1976
Producer: David Winter

• • •

Last week we looked at hymns from Scotland. I hope all our Scottish Presbyterian listeners won't feel too put out by this week's subject: hymns by English bishops.

We had some of them in our last series, of course, but there are plenty more to choose from. Bishops today, most of them, seem to have no time: they're very busy people with committees and synods and confirmations and so on and they don't appear to have much time for such frivolities as books or poetry. But their earlier predecessors seem to have had time and many of our best-known hymns have come from the episcopal palaces of England – and overseas.

Several of them came from the pen of Christopher Wordsworth, Bishop of Lincoln a century ago. Here's one of his best hymns, that rare thing: a good hymn on the Holy Spirit – a Pentecost hymn:

> GRACIOUS SPIRIT, HOLY GHOST,
> Taught by Thee we covet most,
> Of Thy gifts at Pentecost,
> Holy, heavenly, love.

Love is kind and suffers long,
Love is meek and thinks no wrong,
Love than death itself more strong:
Therefore, give us love.

Prophecy will fade away,
Melting in the light of day;
Love will ever with us stay:
Therefore, give us love.

Faith will vanish into sight;
Hope be emptied in delight;
Love in heaven will shine more bright:
Therefore give us love.

Faith and hope and love we see,
Joining hand in hand agree,
But the greatest of the three,
And the best, is love.

From the overshadowing
Of thy gold and silver wing,
Shed on us, who to Thee sing,
Holy, heavenly love.

One of the more extraordinary hymns of Bishop Wordsworth is designated by the compilers of *Hymns Ancient and Modern* for 'Festivals of Martyrs and other Holy Days'. It includes some action-packed lines describing what some of those martyrs have gone through:

Mocked, imprisoned, stoned, tormented, sawn asunder, slain with
sword,
They have conquered death and Satan by the might of Christ the
Lord.

And there is a rather delicious description of those saints of what used to be called the 'gentler sex':

Saintly maiden, godly matron, widows who have watched to
prayer,
Joined in holy concert, singing to the Lord of all, are there.

The hymn is 'Hark the Sound of Holy Voices'.

HARK! THE SOUND OF HOLY VOICES, CHANTING AT THE CRYSTAL
SEA,
Alleluia! Alleluia! Alleluia! Lord, to Thee;
Multitude, which none can number, like the stars in glory stand,
Clothed in white apparel, holding palms of victory in their hand.

Patriarch and holy prophet, who prepared the way of Christ,
King, apostle, saint, confessor, martyr and evangelist;
Saintly maiden, godly matron, widows who have watched to
prayer
Joined in holy concert, singing to the Lord of all, are there.

They have come from tribulation, and have washed their robes in
blood,
Washed them in the blood of Jesus; tried they were and firm they
stood;
Mocked, imprisoned, stoned, tormented, sawn asunder, slain with
sword,
They have conquered death and Satan by the might of Christ the
Lord.

Marching with Thy cross their banner, they have triumphed,
following
Thee, the Captain of salvation, Thee, their Saviour and their King;
Gladly, Lord, with Thee they suffered; gladly, Lord, with Thee they
died;
And by death to life immortal they were born and glorified.

Now they reign in heav'nly glory, now they walk in golden light,
Now they drink, as from a river, holy bliss and infinite:
Love and peace they taste forever, and all truth and knowledge see
In the beatific vision of the blessèd Trinity.

God of God, the One begotten, Light of light, Emmanuel,
In whose body joined together all the saints forever dwell;
Pour upon us of Thy fullness that we may forevermore
God the Father, God the Son and God the Holy Ghost adore.

A third hymn by Bishop Wordsworth is considerably simpler and more direct than that one.

> O LORD OF HEAV'N AND EARTH AND SEA,
> To Thee all praise and glory be;
> How shall we show our love to Thee,
> Who givest all?
>
> The golden sunshine, vernal air,
> Sweet flowers and fruits, Thy love declare;
> Where harvests ripen, Thou art there,
> Who givest all.
>
> For peaceful homes and healthful days,
> For all the blessings earth displays
> We owe Thee thankfulness and praise,
> Who givest all.
>
> Thou didst not spare Thine only Son
> But gav'st Him for a world undone,
> And freely, with that blessèd One,
> Who givest all.
>
> Thou giv'st the Spirit's blessèd dower,
> Spirit of life and love and power,
> And dost His sevenfold graces shower
> Upon us all.
>
> For souls redeemed, for sins forgiv'n,
> For means of grace and hopes of heav'n,
> Father, all praise to Thee be giv'n,
> Who givest all.

We lose what on ourselves we spend,
We have as treasure without end
Whatever, Lord, to Thee we lend,
Who givest all.

Whatever, Lord, we lend to Thee
Repaid a thousand-fold will be;
Then gladly will we give to Thee
Who givest all.

To Thee, from whom we all derive
Our life, our gifts, our power to give:
O may we ever with Thee live,
Who givest all.

Edward Bickersteth was Bishop of Exeter at the turn of the century and, unlike some of his successors, a very Protestant evangelical bishop he was. One of his hymns is in just about every hymn-book. It's what you might call the perfect hymn for evensong – quiet, calm, reassuring and just a little bit sentimental: just listen for the fourth verse.

PEACE, PERFECT PEACE, IN THIS DARK WORLD OF SIN?
The blood of Jesus whispers peace within.

Peace, perfect peace, by thronging duties pressed?
To do the will of Jesus, this is rest.

Peace, perfect peace, with sorrows surging round?
On Jesus' bosom naught but calm is found.

Peace, perfect peace, with loved ones far away?
In Jesus' keeping we are safe, and they.

Peace, perfect peace, our future all unknown?
Jesus we know and He is on the throne.

> Peace, perfect peace, death shadowing us and ours?
> Jesus has vanquished death and all its powers.
>
> It is enough: earth's struggles soon shall cease,
> And Jesus call us to heaven's perfect peace.

The Victorians were great ones for children's hymns. You can imagine the rows of boys in Eton suits and girls in stiff Sunday dresses singing about the heathen and heaven and obedience and duty. Well, one hymn they would certainly have been singing was this lovely hymn by William Walsham How, who was a suffragen bishop in London and then Bishop of Wakefield. It's a child's-eye view of the crucifixion:

> I sometimes think about the cross
> And shut my eyes and try to see
> The cruel nails and crown of thorns
> And Jesus crucified for me.

The hymn is 'It Is a Thing Most Wonderful'.

> IT IS A THING MOST WONDERFUL,
> Almost too wonderful to be,
> That God's own Son should come from heaven
> And die to save a child like me.
>
> And yet I know that it is true:
> He chose a poor and humble lot
> And wept and toiled and mourned and died,
> For love of those who loved Him not.
>
> I cannot tell how He would love
> A child so weak and full of sin;
> His love must be most wonderful,
> If He could die my love to win.

I sometimes think about the cross
And shut my eyes and try to see
The cruel nails and crown of thorns
And Jesus crucified for me.

But even could I see Him die,
I could but see a little part
Of that great love which, like a fire,
Is always burning in His heart.

It is most wonderful to know
His love for me so free and sure;
But 'tis more wonderful to see
My love for Him so faint and poor.

And yet I want to love Thee, Lord;
O light the flame within my heart
And I will love Thee more and more
Until I see Thee as thou art.

Bishop How wrote many of our most popular hymns, of course –
among them 'For All the Saints' and 'Summer Suns Are Glowing'.
Handley Moule was Bishop of Durham earlier this century and
another evangelical. He wrote one or two hymns, including this
one, which is in the *Methodist Hymn Book*:

COME IN, O COME! THE DOOR STANDS OPEN NOW;
I knew thy voice; Lord Jesus, it was Thou.
The sun has set long since; the storms begin:
'Tis time for Thee, my Saviour; O come in!

I seek no more to alter things or mend,
Before the coming of so great a Friend:
All were at best unseemly; and 'twere ill,
Beyond all else, to keep Thee waiting still.

Then, as Thou art, all holiness and bliss,
Come in and see my chamber as it is;
I bid Thee welcome boldly, in the name
Of Thy great glory and my want and shame.

Come, not to find but make this troubled heart
A dwelling worthy of Thee as Thou art;
To chase the gloom, the terror and the sin,
Come, all Thyself, yea come, Lord Jesus, in!

I said that modern bishops don't seem to have time to write hymns or perhaps they don't have the inclination. But a couple of hymns by a bishop of recent times are in several of the newer hymn-books. Frank Houghton was a missionary who became Bishop of East Szechwan, in China until the Communists took over and all European clergy had to leave. He died a couple of years ago. From his missionary experience he wrote what is probably the only post-Victorian missionary hymn widely used today: 'Facing a Task Unfinished'.

FACING A TASK UNFINISHED
That drives us to our knees;
A need that, undiminished,
Rebukes our slothful ease.
We, who rejoice to know Thee,
Renew before Thy throne
The solemn pledge we owe Thee
To go and make Thee known.

Where other lords beside Thee
Hold their unhindered sway,
Where forces that defied Thee
Defy Thee still today,
With none to heed their crying
For life and love and light,
Unnumbered souls are dying
And pass into the night.

We bear the torch that flaming
Fell from the hands of those
Who gave their lives proclaiming
That Jesus died and rose.
Ours is the same commission,
The same glad message ours,
Fired by the same ambition,
To Thee we yield our powers.

O Father who sustained them,
O Spirit who inspired,
Saviour, whose love constrained them
To toil with zeal untired,
From cowardice defend us,
From lethargy awake!
Forth on Thy mission send us
To labour for Thy sake.

Bishop Houghton wrote several books of verse and from them has
come this Christmas hymn – almost a carol, really – with a theme
based on some words of St Paul's: 'Though he was rich, yet for our
sakes he became poor'.

THOU WHO WAST RICH BEYOND ALL SPLENDOUR,
All for love's sake becamest poor;
Thrones for a manger didst surrender,
Sapphire-paved courts for stable floor.
Thou who wast rich beyond all splendour,
All for love's sake becomes poor.

Thou who art God beyond all praising,
All for love's sake becamest man;
Stooping so low but sinners raising
Heavenwards by Thine eternal plan.
Thou who art God beyond all praising,
All for love's sake becamest man.

Thou who art love beyond all telling,
Saviour and King, we worship Thee.
Emmanuel, within us dwelling,
Make us what Thou wouldst have us be.
Thou who art love beyond all telling,
Saviour and King, we worship Thee.

FROM THE CATHEDRAL

From Series 2

BBC Radio Four
Sunday 5 September 1976
Producers: David Winter and Hubert Hoskins

• • •

There's something very Church of England about deans: a stroll around the cathedral close and a glass of sherry at the deanery. And the position has always been greatly desired. Think of the bloodless feuding in Walpole's novel *The Cathedral*, or this immortal prayer of an eighteenth-century incumbent:

> O make me, sphere-descended Queen,
> A bishop – or at least a dean.

Actually, English deans have been a very academic lot, on the whole, and rather literary. We're going to look at the hymns of a few of them in this programme, all very clever men. The first of them, in point of time, is Henry Hart Milman who was Dean of St Paul's, London, just over a hundred years ago. His best-known hymn is a Palm Sunday one:

> RIDE ON, RIDE ON IN MAJESTY!
> Hark! all the tribes Hosanna cry;
> O Saviour meek, pursue Thy road
> With palms and scatter'd garments strew'd.

Ride on, ride on, in majesty!
In lowly pomp ride on to die!
O Christ! Thy triumph now begin
Over captive death and conquered sin.

Ride on, ride on, in majesty!
The wingèd squadrons of the sky
Look down with sad and wondering eyes
To see the approaching sacrifice.

Ride on, ride on, in majesty!
Thy last and fiercest strife is nigh;
The Father, on His sapphire throne,
Expects His own anointed Son.

Ride on, ride on, in majesty!
In lowly pomp ride on to die;
Bow Thy meek head to mortal pain,
Then take, O God, Thy power, and reign.

Dean Milman was a very academic man. He translated Sanskrit poems, was Professor of Poetry at Oxford for ten years, edited Gibbon's *Decline and Fall* and wrote Gibbon's biography and a *History of Latin Christianity*. So you may wonder how he found time to write hymns, let alone do whatever duties a dean has to do. Still, there wouldn't have been problems with tourists in those days.

Milman was a broad churchman and very keen on German biblical criticism so it's a bit of a surprise to find him writing what is really a very simple, devout hymn like our next one:

O HELP US LORD, EACH HOUR OF NEED
Thy heavenly succour give;
Help us in thought and word and deed,
Each hour on earth we live.

O help us, when our spirits cry
With contrite anguish sore;
And when our hearts are cold and dry,
O help us, Lord, the more!

O help us, through the prayer of faith,
More firmly to believe;
For still the more the servant hath,
The more shall he receive.

O help us, Jesus, from on high:
We know no help but Thee;
O help us so to live and die
As Thine in heaven to be.

Henry Alford was another very clever man – in fact, he wrote Latin odes and a history of the Jews before he was ten. That must have got him in the right mood for his main life's work, an enormous edition of the New Testament that appeared in instalments between 1849 and 1861. Eventually he became Dean of Canterbury – the best of all places to be dean, I should have thought – and he managed to find time to write some very popular hymns. One of them is a marvellous example of Victorian triumphalism. Even *Ancient and Modern*, which advises the most exotic contrasts of volume in most hymns, marks the greater part of this hymn simply as '*forte*'. And what else could it be?

TEN THOUSAND TIMES TEN THOUSAND
In sparkling raiment bright,
The armies of the ransomed saints
Throng up the steps of light:
'Tis finished, all is finished,
Their fight with death and sin;
Fling open wide the golden gates,
And let the victors in.

What rush of alleluias
Fills all the earth and sky!
What ringing of a thousand harps
Bespeaks the triumph nigh!
O day, for which creation
And all its tribes were made;
O joy, for all its former woes
A thousandfold repaid!

O then what raptured greetings
On Canaan's happy shore;
What knitting severed friendships up
Where partings are no more!
Then eyes with joy shall sparkle,
That brimmed with tears of late;
Orphans no longer fatherless,
Nor widows desolate.

Bring near thy great salvation,
Thou Lamb for sinners slain;
Fill up the roll of Thine elect,
Then take Thy power and reign;
Appear, Desire of nations:
Thine exiles long for home;
Show in the heaven Thy promised sign;
Thou Prince and Saviour, come.

Dean Alford also wrote one of the most popular of our harvest hymns: harvest festivals were a Victorian innovation and one can imagine how enthusiastically hymns like this would have been taken up.

COME, YE THANKFUL PEOPLE, COME –
Raise the song of harvest-home;
All is safely gathered in,
Ere the winter storms begin.
God our Maker doth provide
For our wants to be supplied;

Come to God's own temple, come:
Raise the song of harvest-home.

All the world is God's own field,
Fruit unto His praise to yield;
Wheat and tares together sown,
Unto joy or sorrow grown.
First the blade and then the ear,
Then the full corn shall appear;
Lord of harvest, grant that we,
Wholesome grain and pure may be.

For the Lord our God shall come,
And shall take His harvest-home;
From His field shall in that day
All offences purge away,
Giving angels charge at last
In the fire the tares to cast;
But the fruitful ears to store
In His garner evermore.

Even so, Lord, quickly come,
Bring Thy final harvest home;
Gather Thou Thy people in,
Free from sorrow, free from sin,
There, forever purified,
In Thy garner to abide;
Come, with all Thine angels come,
Raise the glorious harvest-home.

Even more remarkable both as a scholar and as a supporter of lost causes was Arthur Penrhyn Stanley, Dean of Westminster. A fervent supporter of German radical theology, he spent his life trying to push back the borders of Anglican comprehensiveness. Even Unitarians were welcomed by him as well as Tractarians and Low Churchmen, though several leading Tractarians refused to preach for him at the Abbey. He was devoted to the State connection and passionately opposed the disestablishment of the Church of Ireland. Queen Victoria liked him (not surprisingly) and would have made him a bishop but for protests by Palmerston and Gladstone. He wrote several hymns but this one, 'The Lord Is Come!', is the only one at all widely used today.

THE LORD IS COME! ON SYRIAN SOIL,
The child of poverty and toil;
The Man of Sorrows, born to know
Each varying shade of human woe:
His joy, His glory, to fulfil,
In earth and heaven, His Father's will;
On lonely mount, by festive board,
On bitter cross, despised, adored.

The Lord is come! In Him we trace
The fullness of God's truth and grace;
Throughout those words and acts divine
Gleams of th'eternal splendour shine;
And from His inmost Spirit flow,
As from a height of sunlit snow,
The rivers of perennial life,
To heal and sweeten nature's strife.

The Lord is come! In every heart
Where truth and mercy claim apart,
In every land where right is might,
And deeds of darkness shun the light,
In every church where faith and love
Lift earthward thoughts to things above,
In every holy, happy home,
We bless Thee, Lord, that Thou hast come.

Dean Stanley was one of the translators of the *Revised Version of the Bible* and so was another scholarly dean, Edward Hayes Plumtre, Dean of Wells. He was perhaps a better poet than the others. There's an economy about his writing that seems to have eluded most Victorian deans. This hymn, for instance, about healing and hospitals, paints a vivid picture of our Lord's ministry:

> THINE ARM, O LORD, IN DAYS OF OLD
> Was strong to heal and save;
> It triumphed o'er disease and death,
> O'er darkness and the grave.
> To Thee they went, the blind, the dumb,
> The palsied and the lame,
> The leper with his tainted life,
> The sick with fevered frame.
>
> And lo! Thy touch brought life and health,
> Gave speech and strength and sight;
> And youth renewed and frenzy calmed
> Owned Thee, the Lord of Light;
> And now, O Lord, be near to bless,
> Almighty as of yore;
> In crowded street, by restless couch,
> As by Gennesareth's shore.[1]
>
> Be Thou our Great Deliverer still,
> Thou Lord of life and death;
> Restore and quicken, soothe and bless,
> With Thine almighty breath:
> To hands that work and eyes that see
> Give wisdom's heavenly lore,
> That whole and sick, and weak and strong,
> May praise Thee evermore.

It's slightly odd that the Victorian age, which saw the Church in England more sharply divided than ever before or since with no-Popery riots and vicars jailed for breaking Church law – it's slightly

---

[1] Lake Kinneret in modern Israel, known in the New Testament both as the Sea of Galilee and the Sea of Gennesareth.

odd that such an age should have produced so many hymns about how wonderfully united the Church really is. Or perhaps it's not surprising at all. Anyway, one of the best of them is by Dean Plumtre, 'Thy Hand, O Lord, Has Guided Thy Flock from Age to Age', with that confident chorus: 'One Church, one Faith, one Lord'. A good note to end on.

THY HAND, O GOD, HAS GUIDED
Thy flock from age to age;
The wondrous tale is written,
Full clear on every page.
Our fathers owned Thy goodness
And we their deeds record;
And both of this bear witness,
'One Church, one Faith, one Lord'.

Thy heralds brought glad tidings
To greatest, as to least;
They bade men rise and hasten
To share the great King's feast;
And this was all their teaching,
In every deed and word,
To all alike proclaiming,
'One Church, one Faith, one Lord'.

When shadows thick were falling
And all seemed sunk in night,
Thou, Lord, didst send Thy servants,
Thy chosen sons of light.
On them and on Thy people
Thy plenteous grace was poured
And this was still their message:
'One Church, one Faith, one Lord'.

Through many a day of darkness,
Through many a scene of strife,
The faithful few fought bravely,

To guard the nation's life;
Their gospel of redemption,
Sin pardoned, man restored,
Was all in this enfolded,
'One Church, one Faith, one Lord'.

And we, shall we be faithless?
Shall hearts fail, hands hang down?
Shall we evade the conflict
And cast away our crown?
Not so: in God's deep counsels
Some better thing is stored:
We will maintain, unflinching,
'One Church, one Faith, one Lord'.

Thy mercy will not fail us
Nor leave Thy work undone;
With Thy right hand to help us
The victory shall be won;
And then, by men and angels,
Thy Name shall be adored,
And this shall be their anthem,
'One Church, one Faith, one Lord'.

Just for contrast, we've added one hymn this week that is not by a
dean but an archdeacon (there's a very English title!) – and a living
one at that. Timothy Dudley-Smith is Archdeacon of Norwich and
he's written one of the very few new hymns really to establish
themselves in recent years. It's based on the words of the Magni-
ficat in the *New English Bible*: 'Tell Out, My Soul, the Greatness of
the Lord'.

TELL OUT, MY SOUL, THE GREATNESS OF THE LORD!
Unnumbered blessings give my spirit voice;
Tender to me the promise of His Word;
In God my Saviour shall my heart rejoice.

Tell out, my soul, the greatness of His Name!
Make known His might, the deeds His arm has done;
His mercy sure, from age to age to same;
His holy Name – the Lord, the Mighty One.

Tell out, my soul, the greatness of His might!
Powers and dominions lay their glory by.
Proud hearts and stubborn wills are put to flight,
The hungry fed, the humble lifted high.

Tell out, my soul, the glories of His Word!
Firm is His promise and His mercy sure.
Tell out, my soul, the greatness of the Lord
To children's children and for evermore!

SOME NONCONFORMISTS

From Series 2

BBC Radio Four
Sunday 12 September 1976
Producers: David Winter and Hubert Hoskins

• • •

In this last programme of this series about hymns and their writers, we look at the work of some Nonconformists, as they used to be called. Incidentally, one of the nicest things about hymns is that we all sing one another's: Protestants sing hymns by Papists and Roman Catholics sing hymns by Methodists and everybody the whole world over sings hymns by Anglicans.

Dr Thomas Binney was a famous congregational preacher of the last century: he ended up as Minister of the famous King's Weigh House Chapel in London. It's said that he wrote this hymn while sitting in his study watching the sunset and the stars taking over as the lights of the night sky:

> ETERNAL LIGHT, ETERNAL LIGHT!
> How pure the soul must be,
> When, placed within Thy searching light,
> It shrinks not but with calm delight
> Can live and look on Thee!
>
> O how shall I, whose native sphere
> Is dark, whose mind is dim,
> Before th'Ineffable appear,

And on my naked spirit bear
The uncreated beam?

There is a way for man to rise
To that sublime abode:
An offering and a sacrifice,
A Holy Spirit's energies,
An Advocate with God:

These, these prepare us for the sight
Of holiness above:
The sons of ignorance and night
May dwell in the eternal light,
Through the eternal love!

Dr John Fawcett was a Yorkshireman and a Baptist. In fact for over fifty years he was pastor to a poor little Baptist church at Wainsgate, near Hebdon Bridge. Halfway through that period, he accepted an invitation to succeed the famous Dr Gill as Minister of Carters Lane Chapel, London, but after preaching his farewell sermon, and with his carriage loaded, he changed his mind and decided to stay with his Yorkshire flock. He wrote 166 hymns and of the handful of them still sung, the best known is undoubtedly 'Lord Dismiss Us with Thy Blessing' – a very public school sort of hymn to be written by the pastor of a struggling country chapel in Yorkshire.

LORD, DISMISS US WITH THY BLESSING;
Fill our hearts with joy and peace.
Let us each Thy love possessing
Triumph in redeeming grace.
O refresh us, O refresh us!
Travelling through this wilderness.

Thanks we give and adoration
For Thy gospel's joyful sound;
May the fruits of Thy salvation
In our hearts and lives abound.

Ever faithful, ever faithful,
To the truth may we be found.

So that when Thy love shall call us,
Saviour, from the world away,
Let no fear of death appal us,
Glad Thy summons to obey.
May we ever, may we ever,
Reign with Thee in endless day.

Thomas Kelly was the son of an Irish judge and in fact trained for the Bar himself, but he gave it up to return to Ireland to be ordained in the Church of Ireland. However, he was a bit too evangelical (or 'methodistical', as they might have said) for the then Archbishop of Dublin, who 'inhibited' him − stopped him preaching. With a name like Kelly he obviously wasn't going to accept *that*, so he left the established Church and built four independent chapels in Ireland, where great crowds flocked to hear him.

He also wrote hymns − 765 in all − and among them are some of the real jewels of English hymnody. This hymn, for instance, on the cross − 'We Sing the Praise of Him Who Died' − is about as good a piece of hymn-writing as you could get:

WE SING THE PRAISE OF HIM WHO DIED,
Of Him who died upon the cross;
The sinner's hope let men deride:
For this we count the world but loss.

Inscribed upon the cross we see
In shining letters, 'God is Love';
He bears our sins upon the tree;
He brings us mercy from above.

The cross: it takes our guilt away,
It holds the fainting spirit up;
It cheers with hope the gloomy day
And sweetens every bitter cup.

> It makes the coward spirit brave
> And nerves the feeble arm for fight;
> It takes its terror from the grave
> And fills the bed of death with light.
>
> The balm of life, the cure of woe,
> The measure and the pledge of love,
> The sinner's refuge here below,
> The angel's theme in Heaven above.

There's not much of the hot-headed rebel in that hymn, is there? Nor is there in our next one, which has become the classic hymn for Ascension-tide. It's a hymn full of the contrast between life and death, shame and glory:

> THE HEAD THAT ONCE WAS CROWNED WITH THORNS
> Is crowned with glory now!
> A royal diadem adorns
> The mighty Victor's brow!
>
> The highest place that heav'n affords
> Belongs to Him by right;
> The King of kings and Lord of lords
> And heaven's eternal Light.
>
> The joy of all who dwell above,
> The joy of all below,
> To whom He manifests His love
> And grants His Name to know.
>
> To them the cross with all its shame,
> With all its grace, is given;
> Their name an everlasting name,
> Their joy the joy of heaven.
>
> They suffer with their Lord below,
> They reign with Him above;
> Their profit and their joy to know
> The mystery of His love.

The cross He bore is life and health,
Though shame and death to Him,
His people's hope, His people's wealth,
Their everlasting theme.

Strangely enough, there are only two or three really good
Ascension-tide hymns and Thomas Kelly wrote another of them:

LOOK, YE SAINTS! THE SIGHT IS GLORIOUS,
See the Man of Sorrows now;
From the fight returned victorious,
Every knee to Him shall bow.
Crown Him, crown Him, crown Him, crown Him,
Crowns become the Victor's brow,
Crowns become the Victor's brow.

Crown the Saviour! Angels, crown Him;
Rich the trophies Jesus brings.
In the seat of power enthrone Him,
While the vault of heaven rings.
Crown Him, crown Him, crown Him, crown Him,
Crown the Saviour King of kings,
Crown the Saviour King of kings.

Sinners in derision scorned Him,
Mocking thus the Saviour's claim;
Saints and angels crowd around Him,
Own His title, praise His name.
Crown Him, crown Him, crown Him, crown Him,
Spread abroad the Victor's fame,
Spread abroad the Victor's fame.

Hark, those bursts of acclamation!
Hark, those loud triumphant chords!
Jesus takes the highest station;
O what joy the sight affords!
Crown Him, crown Him, crown Him, crown Him,
King of kings and Lord of lords!
King of kings and Lord of lords!

253

Our next writer was also an Irish Nonconformist. William Young Fullerton was a Baptist, a disciple of the famous Charles Hadden Spurgeon and eventually President of the Baptist Union at the time of the First World War. His only well-known hymn was written to fit that lovely Irish traditional melody, the 'Londonderry Air', and it's a kind of meditation on the idea of the incarnation:

I CANNOT TELL WHY HE, WHOM ANGELS WORSHIP,
Should set His love upon the sons of men;
Or why, as Shepherd, He should seek the wanderers
To bring them back, they know not how or when.
But this I know, that He was born of Mary,
When Bethl'hem's manger was His only home,
And that He lived at Nazareth and laboured
And so the Saviour, Saviour of the world is come.

I cannot tell how silently He suffered
As with His peace He graced this place of tears;
Or how His heart upon the cross was broken
The crown of pain to three and thirty years.
But this I know, He heals the broken-hearted
And stays our sin and calms our lurking fear
And lifts the burden from the heavy laden,
For yet the Saviour, Saviour of the world is here.

I cannot tell how He will win the nations,
How He will claim His earthly heritage,
How satisfy the needs and aspirations
Of east and west, of sinner and of sage.
But this I know, all flesh shall see His glory
And He shall reap the harvest He has sown
And some glad day His sun shall shine in splendour
When He the Saviour, Saviour of the world is known.

I cannot tell how all the lands shall worship
When at His bidding every storm is stilled;
Or who can say how great the jubilation

When all the hearts of men with love are filled.
But this I know, the skies will thrill with rapture
And myriad, myriad human voices sing
And earth to heaven, and heaven to earth will answer
'At last the Saviour, Saviour of the world is King!'

For our last Nonconformist writer, we go back before the Victorian era to a man who lived and worked in the century before that, a contemporary of the evangelical preacher George Whitefield and the Wesleys. Robert Robinson was Minister of the Calvinistic Methodist Chapel at Mildenhall in Suffolk and his most famous hymn is 'Come Thou Fount of Every Blessing'. Strangely, perhaps, from the pen of a Calvinist, it's all about the possibility and danger of wandering away from the grace of God.

In fact, at one point in his life, Robinson did just that. He became, in his own words, 'somewhat frivolous' in his behaviour and one day, travelling in a coach and presumably being somewhat frivolous, he was reproved by a lady traveller who quoted a verse of his own hymn to him; whereupon poor Robinson burst into tears and admitted that he was 'the poor unhappy man who composed it'. Being hoist with your own words must be one of the perils of the hymn-writer, especially when the words are as forthright as these:

COME, THOU FOUNT OF EVERY BLESSING,
Tune my heart to sing Thy grace;
Streams of mercy, never ceasing,
Call for songs of loudest praise.
Teach me some melodious sonnet,
Sung by flaming tongues above.
Praise the mount! I'm fixed upon it,
Mount of Thy redeeming love.

Sorrowing I shall be in spirit
Till released from flesh and sin,
Yet from what I do inherit,

Here Thy praises I'll begin;
Here I raise my Ebenezer;[1]
Here by Thy great help I've come;
And I hope, by Thy good pleasure,
Safely to arrive at home.

Jesus sought me when a stranger,
Wandering from the fold of God;
He, to rescue me from danger,
Interposed His precious blood;
How His kindness yet pursues me
Mortal tongue can never tell;
Clothed in flesh, till death shall loose me
I cannot proclaim it well.

O to grace how great a debtor
Daily I'm constrained to be!
Let that grace now, like a fetter,
Bind my wandering heart to Thee.
Prone to wander, Lord, I feel it,
Prone to leave the God I love;
Here's my heart, O take and seal it,
Seal it for Thy courts above.

O that day when freed from sinning,
I shall see Thy lovely face;
Clothèd then in blood-washed linen
How I'll sing Thy sovereign grace.
Come, my Lord, no longer tarry,
Take my ransomed soul away;
Send Thine angels now to carry
Me to realms of endless day.

[1] A reference to the memorial 'stone of help' (Eben-Ezer) that Samuel placed between the towns of Mizpah and Shen, to mark God's help in a successful rout of the Philistines (1 Samuel 7:12).

SONGS OF OLD

From Series 3

BBC Radio Four
Sunday 2 August 1978
Producer: David Winter

•   •   •

There are two things you need for a jolly good hymn. The first is a set of words that expresses the mood or sentiment of the worshipper. The second – and perhaps even more important – is a good tune. And by a good tune I don't mean some frightfully highbrow composition that only an operatic tenor could sing comfortably but a simple, popular melody. And goodness knows why, because something is popular, the experts have to assume it is also bad.

The fact is, hymn-tunes are the nearest we've got to English folk music. When a football crowd wants to find a tune for its unmentionable slogans, as often as not they choose a hymn-tune. And there can't be many people who don't know at least one irreverent parody of something from our heritage of hymnody, even if it's only those shepherds washing their socks by night or something mildly scandalous about Good King Wenceslas.

At any rate, in this series of programmes we're going to be looking at hymn-tunes as well as words. And we're starting with some of the oldest ones, taken from two of the earliest English hymn-books, *Day's Psalter* and *Hymns and Songs of the Church* by

George Wither. Let's start with one from *Day's Psalter*, 'All People that on Earth Do Dwell'.

ALL PEOPLE THAT ON EARTH DO DWELL,
Sing to the Lord with cheerful voice.
Him serve with mirth,[1] His praise forth tell;
Come ye before Him and rejoice.

The Lord, ye know, is God indeed;
Without our aid He did us make;
We are His folk, He doth us feed,
And for His sheep He doth us take.

O enter then His gates with praise;
Approach with joy His courts unto;
Praise, laud and bless His Name always,
For it is seemly so to do.

For why? the Lord our God is good;
His mercy is for ever sure;
His truth at all times firmly stood
And shall from age to age endure.

To Father, Son and Holy Ghost,
The God whom heaven and earth adore,
From men and from the angel host
Be praise and glory evermore.

The most common tune for that hymn is known as the 'Old Hundredth' because it was set to a metrical version of Psalm 100 in *Day's Psalter*. Mind you, Day wasn't the compiler but the publisher; the compilers were Sternhold and Hopkins, who were Puritans and collected these metrical psalms because they didn't approve of hymns of 'human composition' in church. They got most of the tunes from the Continent – many of them from

---

[1] Now more often 'Him serve with fear'.

Geneva, where Calvin disapproved of the Lutheran type of hymn with tunes based on the old German chorales. He liked straightforward tunes based on the principle of one note, one syllable. Well, whatever you think of predestination, you may reckon he was right there. That tune, like many in *Day's Psalter*, is by the Frenchman, Louis Bourgeois.

Now let's have J. N. Chadwick's hymn, 'Eternal Ruler of the Ceaseless Round', which can be sung to a tune from George Wither's collection – Song Number One.

ETERNAL RULER OF THE CEASELESS ROUND
Of circling planets singing on their way,
Guide of the nations from the night profound
Into the glory of the perfect day,
Rule in our hearts, that we may ever be
Guided and strengthened and upheld by Thee.

We are of Thee, the children of Thy love,
The brothers of Thy well belovèd Son;
Descend, O Holy Spirit, like a dove
Into our hearts, that we may be as one:
As one with Thee, to whom we ever tend;
As one with Him our Brother and our Friend.

We would be one in hatred of all wrong,
One in our love of all things sweet and fair,
One with the joy that breaketh into song,
One with the grief that trembleth into prayer,
One in the power that makes Thy children free
To follow truth and thus to follow Thee.

O clothe us with Thy heavenly armour, Lord,
Thy trusty shield, Thy sword of love divine.
Our inspiration be Thy constant Word;
We ask no victories that are not Thine.
Give or withhold, let pain or pleasure be,
Enough to know that we are serving Thee.

Song One in Wither's *Hymns and Songs of the Church* was composed
by Orlando Gibbons and in fact Wither's collection is chiefly
remembered now for Gibbons's tunes. Wither was not an outstanding poet but he must have been a brave one – not always the
hallmark of the trade. He was an officer in the Civil War and was
captured by the Royalists, which gave rise to an unkind joke that
the King must not hang Wither 'for so long as Wither lived no one
would account himself the worst poet in England'.

Well, he survived and when James II came to the throne he
gave Wither permission to include some original hymns alongside
the inevitable metrical psalms. This led to bitter opposition and the
book might have been completely forgotten but for Gibbons's
marvellous new tunes. Probably the best-known of them, Song
Thirty-Four, can be set to Charles Wesley's words 'Forth in Thy
Name O Lord I Go'.

FORTH IN THY NAME, O LORD, I GO,
My daily labour to pursue;
Thee, only Thee, resolved to know
In all I think or speak or do.

The task Thy wisdom hath assigned,
O let me cheerfully fulfil;
In all my works Thy presence find,
And prove Thy good and perfect will.

Preserve me from my calling's snare,
And hide my simple heart above,
Above the thorns of choking care,
The gilded baits of worldly love.

Thee may I set at my right hand,
Whose eyes mine inmost substance see
And labour on at Thy command,
And offer all my works to Thee.

Give me to bear Thy easy yoke
And every moment watch and pray
And still to things eternal look
And hasten to Thy glorious day.

There's a lovely last verse:

For Thee delightfully employ
Whate'er Thy bounteous grace hath giv'n;
And run my course with even joy
And closely walk with Thee to heav'n.

If one mark of good verse is surprise, then Wesley scores twice here. 'Delightfully' is splendid in that last verse, isn't it? And I love the idea of 'even joy' – nothing extreme, you understand, or enthusiastic: just 'even' joy.

There's one tune, at least, in *Day's Psalter* that's a bit of a surprise too. It's the 'Old 112th' and it dares to break Calvin's rule because it's definitely of German origin and is generally assumed to have been composed by his arch-rival, Luther. In the old *Psalter* it was, of course, assigned to Psalm 112 but here it is set to John Wesley's translation of Gerhard Tersteegen's hymn 'Lo, God is here: let us adore'.

LO, GOD IS HERE: LET US ADORE,
And own how dreadful is this place!
Let all within us feel His power
And humbly bow before His face.
Who know His power, His grace who prove,
Serve Him with awe, with reverence love.

Lo, God is here! Him day and night
United choirs of angels sing;
To Him, enthroned above all height,
Heav'n's host their noblest praises bring.
Disdain not, Lord, our meaner song,
Who praise Thee with a stammering tongue.

Almighty Lord, may this our praise
Thy courts with grateful fragrance fill;
Still may we stand before Thy face,
Still hear and do Thy sovereign will;
To Thee may all our thoughts arise,
Ceaseless, accepted sacrifice.

Bishop Heber wrote some famous hymns, including 'From Greenland's Icy Mountains' but one that was very popular until recent times was 'The Son of God goes Forth to War'. It's a sort of celebration of martyrdom that possibly had more appeal to our forefathers than it does to us.

THE SON OF GOD GOES FORTH TO WAR,
A kingly crown to gain;
His blood-red banner streams afar:
Who follows in His train?
Who best can drink His cup of woe,
Triumphant over pain,
Who patient bears His cross below,
He follows in His train.

That martyr first, whose eagle eye
Could pierce beyond the grave;
Who saw his Master in the sky,
And called on Him to save.
Like Him, with pardon on His tongue,
In midst of mortal pain,
He prayed for them that did the wrong:
Who follows in His train?

A glorious band, the chosen few
On whom the Spirit came;
Twelve valiant saints, their hope they knew,
And mocked the cross and flame.
They met the tyrant's brandished steel,
The lion's gory mane;

They bowed their heads the death to feel:
Who follows in their train?

A noble army, men and boys,
The matron and the maid,
Around the Saviour's throne rejoice
In robes of light arrayed . . .

It concludes with a ringing challenge:

. . . They climbed the steep ascent of heaven
Through peril, toil and pain:
O God, to us may grace be given
To follow in their train.

Dean Inge was naughty enough to parody the last lines for the modern Christian:

O God, to us may grace be given
To follow in the train.

Anyway, Heber's hymn is set, in *Ancient and Modern*, to the 'Old 81st' from Sternhold and Hopkins.

Bishop Heber's militant Christianity, with its 'blood-red banners' and, in the third verse, 'lion's gory mane', might well be set against an equally popular hymn by another Victorian bishop, E. H. Bickersteth, 'Peace, Perfect Peace'. It can be sung to another of Orlando Gibbons's splendid songs in Wither's collection, Song Forty-Six.

PEACE, PERFECT PEACE, IN THIS DARK WORLD OF SIN?
The blood of Jesus whispers peace within.

Peace, perfect peace, by thronging duties pressed?
To do the will of Jesus, this is rest.

Peace, perfect peace, with sorrows surging round?
On Jesus' bosom naught but calm is found.

Peace, perfect peace, with loved ones far away?
In Jesus' keeping we are safe, and they.

Peace, perfect peace, our future all unknown?
Jesus we know, and He is on the throne.

Peace, perfect peace, death shadowing us and ours?
Jesus has vanquished death and all its powers.

It is enough: earth's struggles soon shall cease,
And Jesus call us to heaven's perfect peace.

We're going to end our selection of hymn-tunes from these two very old collections with the 'Old 104th', from *Day's Psalter*. Unlike many of the others it is still often sung to the words for which it was originally composed, William Kethe's 1561 paraphrase of Psalm 104, 'O Worship the King, All Glorious above'.

O WORSHIP THE KING, ALL GLORIOUS ABOVE,
O gratefully sing His power and His love;
Our Shield and Defender, the Ancient of Days,
Pavilioned in splendour and girded with praise.

O tell of His might, O sing of His grace,
Whose robe is the light, whose canopy space;
His chariots of wrath the deep thunderclouds form
And dark is His path on the wings of the storm.

The earth with its store of wonders untold,
Almighty, Thy power hath founded of old;
Established it fast by a changeless decree
And round it hath cast, like a mantle, the sea.

Thy bountiful care, what tongue can recite?
It breathes in the air, it shines in the light;
It streams from the hills, it descends to the plain
And sweetly distils in the dew and the rain.

Frail children of dust and feeble as frail,
In Thee do we trust, nor find Thee to fail;
Thy mercies how tender, how firm to the end,
Our Maker, Defender, Redeemer and Friend.

O measureless might! Ineffable love!
While angels delight to worship Thee above,
The humbler creation, though feeble their lays,
With true adoration shall all sing Thy praise.

FROM THE CHIEF MUSICIANS

From Series 3

BBC Radio Four
Sunday 9 August 1978
Producer: David Winter

• • •

All sorts of people have written hymn-tunes, many of them parsons, of course, presumably filling in a quiet hour or two at the rectory piano. But some of our very best hymn-tunes have been composed by the professionals, men who were by any standards among the great musicians of their time – for example, the tune 'Laudate Dominum' by Sir Charles Parry. It was set to Sir H. W. Baker's splendid words 'O Praise Ye the Lord! Praise Him in the Height'.

> O PRAISE YE THE LORD!
> Praise Him in the height;
> Rejoice in His word,
> Ye angels of light;
> Ye heavens, adore Him
> By whom ye were made
> And worship before Him,
> In brightness arrayed.
>
> O praise ye the Lord!
> Praise Him upon earth,
> In tuneful accord,

Ye sons of new birth;
Praise Him who hath brought you
His grace from above,
Praise Him who hath taught you
To sing of his love.

O praise ye the Lord!
All things that give sound;
Each jubilant chord
Re-echo around;
Loud organs, His glory
Forth tell in deep tone,
And sweet harp, the story
Of what He hath done.

O praise ye the Lord!
Thanksgiving and song
To Him be outpoured
All ages along!
For love in creation,
For heaven restored,
For grace of salvation,
O praise ye the Lord!

That tune began life as the fifth movement of an anthem composed for the Salisbury Diocesan Choral Association's Festival of 1894 but it has all the marks of a really popular hymn-tune, doesn't it?

Parry was a professor of composition at the Royal College of Music in London and one of his students there was Gustav Holst. Despite his Scandinavian name, Holst was born at Cheltenham and his musical output includes one outstanding piece of popular church music – his tune to Christina Rossetti's Christmas carol 'In the Bleak Midwinter'. It's fascinating to see how the poet could take a story from Palestine and decorate it with the imagery of the traditional English Christmas but without making it seem ludicrous:

IN THE BLEAK MIDWINTER
Frosty wind made moan,
Earth stood hard as iron,
Water like a stone;
Snow had fallen, snow on snow,
Snow on snow,
In the bleak midwinter,
Long ago.

Well, I don't think that's Bethlehem. It looks more like those
Victorian pictures of winter scenes with the Thames frozen over.
Yet the carol captures the idea of the incarnation more vividly
perhaps than any other:

Our God, Heav'n cannot hold Him,
Nor earth sustain;
Heaven and earth shall flee away
When He comes to reign.
In the bleak midwinter
A stable place sufficed
The Lord God Almighty,
Jesus Christ.

And it goes on:

Enough for Him, whom cherubim,
Worship night and day,
A breastful of milk,
And a mangerful of hay;
Enough for Him, whom angels
Fall before,
The ox and ass and camel
Which adore.

Angels and archangels
May have gathered there,
Cherubim and seraphim

Thronged the air;
But His mother only,
In her maiden bliss,
Worshipped the Beloved
With a kiss.

What can I give Him,
Poor as I am?
If I were a shepherd,
I would bring a lamb;
If I were a wise man,
I would do my part;
Yet what I can I give Him:
Give my heart.

Martin Shaw was yet another student at the Royal College of Music and afterwards helped Vaughan Williams in the compilation of the *English Hymnal*. He wrote several popular hymn-tunes but one of the best, 'Little Cornard', was composed for use in St Mary's, Primrose Hill, where Shaw was organist for a time (the vicar was Percy Dearmer, who had also worked on the *English Hymnal* and with Shaw and Vaughan Williams later compiled *Songs of Praise*). Little Cornard, incidentally, is a village near Sudbury, Suffolk, where Shaw spent his honeymoon. The tune is usually set to Charles E. Oakley's Advent hymn 'Hills of the North, Rejoice'.

HILLS OF THE NORTH, REJOICE:
River and mountain spring,
Hark to the Advent voice;
Valley and lowland, sing.
Though absent long, your Lord is nigh;
He judgement brings and victory.

Isles of the southern seas,
Deep in your coral caves
Pent be each warring breeze,

Lulled be your restless waves:
He comes to reign with boundless sway,
And makes your wastes His great highway.

Lands of the East, awake:
Soon shall your sons be free;
The sleep of ages break
And rise to liberty.
On your far hills, long cold and gray,
Has dawned the everlasting day.

Shores of the utmost West,
Ye that have waited long,
Unvisited, unblest,
Break forth to swelling song;
High raise the note, that Jesus died,
Yet lives and reigns, the Crucified.

Shout, while ye journey home;
Songs be in every mouth.
Lo, from the North we come,
From East and West and South.
City of God, the bond are free,
We come to live and reign in Thee!

The Rev. Sir Frederick Gore-Ousley was one of the great figures of Victorian church music. He founded a choral school, St Michael's, Tenbury, in Worcestershire, where the youthful John Stainer was the first organist and later became Professor of Music at Oxford. Gore-Ousley was the composer of half-a-dozen very good hymn-tunes including one called 'Contemplation', set to Joseph Addison's poem 'When All Thy Mercies, O My God'.

WHEN ALL THY MERCIES, O MY GOD,
My rising soul surveys,
Transported with the view, I'm lost
In wonder, love and praise.

Thy Providence my life sustained
And all my wants redressed,
While in the silent womb I lay
And hung upon the breast.

To all my weak complaints and cries
Thy mercy lent an ear,
Ere yet my feeble thoughts had learned
To form themselves in prayer.

Unnumbered comforts to my soul
Thy tender care bestowed,
Before my infant heart conceived
From whom those comforts flowed.

I think this next verse deserves singling out:

When in the slippery paths of youth
With heedless steps I ran,
Thine arm unseen conveyed me safe
And led me up to man.

– But hang on – there are another eight verses still to go:

Through hidden dangers, toils and deaths
It gently cleared my way;
And through the pleasing snares of vice,
More to be feared than they.

O how shall words with equal warmth
The gratitude declare,
That glows within my ravished heart?
But Thou canst read it there.

Thy bounteous hand with worldly bliss
Hath made my cup run o'er;
And, in a kind and faithful Friend,
Hath doubled all my store.

Ten thousand thousand precious gifts
My daily thanks employ;
Nor is the last a cheerful heart
That tastes those gifts with joy.

When worn with sickness, oft hast Thou
With health renewed my face;
And, when in sins and sorrows sunk,
Revived my soul with grace.

Through every period of my life
Thy goodness I'll pursue;
And after death, in distant worlds,
The glorious theme renew.

When nature fails and day and night
Divide Thy works no more,
My ever grateful heart, O Lord,
Thy mercy shall adore.

Through all eternity to Thee
A joyful song I'll raise;
For, oh, eternity's too short
To utter all Thy praise!

Gore-Ouseley's protégé John Stainer succeeded him as Professor of Music at Oxford and was, by general consent, a rather better musician. His best-known work is, of course, 'The Crucifixion' – still performed by thousands of church and chapel choirs every Easter – but I want to look instead at a Whitsun hymn, 'Gracious Spirit, Holy Ghost', written by Bishop Wordsworth. It's got a very clever rhyme pattern, though I'm not sure what I think of rhyming 'Ghost' and 'Pentecost'. Stainer's hymn for it is called 'Charity' and it was written for the 1868 'Appendix' to *Hymns Ancient and Modern*.

GRACIOUS SPIRIT, HOLY GHOST,
Taught by Thee, we covet most,
Of Thy gifts at Pentecost,
Holy, heavenly love.

Faith, that mountains could remove,
Tongues of earth or heaven above,
Knowledge – all things – empty prove,
Without heavenly love.

Though I as a martyr bleed,
Give my goods the poor to feed,
All is vain – if love I need;
Therefore, give us love.

Love is kind and suffers long,
Love is meek and thinks no wrong,
Love than death itself more strong;
Therefore, give us love.

Prophecy will fade away,
Melting in the light of day,
Love will ever with us stay;
Therefore, give us love.

Faith will vanish into sight,
Hope be emptied in delight,
Love in heaven will shine more bright;
Therefore, give us love.

Faith and hope and love we see
Joining hand in hand agree;
But the greatest of the three,
And the best, is love.

From the overshadowing
Of Thy gold and silver wing

> Shed on us, who to Thee sing,
> Holy, heavenly love.

Choosing hymns for a wedding is always a bit difficult, mainly because hardly anybody has thought to write a suitable one. There are only three hymns under 'Holy Matrimony' in *Ancient and Modern* and two of them I've never heard sung. So 'The Lord's my Shepherd' and 'Lead Us, Heavenly Father, Lead Us' hold sway, along with the one really popular 'specialist' wedding hymn, 'O Perfect Love'. It was written by Mrs Dorothy F. Gurney for her own sister's wedding in 1883 when it was sung to J. B. Dyke's tune 'Strength and Stay'. But Sir Joseph Barnby (who was organist of St Anne's, Soho) put a new tune to it for the wedding of Princess Louise and the Duke of Fife in 1889 and his tune has achieved the rare distinction of ousting Dykes's one from popular use.

> O PERFECT LOVE, ALL HUMAN THOUGHT TRANSCENDING,
> Lowly we kneel in prayer before Thy throne,
> That theirs may be the love that knows no ending,
> Whom Thou for evermore dost join in one.
>
> O perfect Life, be Thou their full assurance,
> Of tender charity and steadfast faith,
> Of patient hope and quiet, brave endurance,
> With childlike trust that fears nor pain nor death.
>
> Grant them the joy that brightens earthly sorrow;
> Grant them the peace that calms all earthly strife,
> And to life's day the glorious unknown morrow
> That dawns upon eternal love and life.

Another distinguished musician who made a considerable contribution to church music was Sir Henry Walford Davies. He was for a time organist of St George's Chapel, Windsor, and later Master of the King's Musick. Many people know that he wrote the RAF's March Past; some will know that he wrote no less than two good tunes for 'O Little Town of Bethlehem'; but I wonder how many know that he composed the familiar tune to 'God Be in My Head'. The words, of course, are very old – they come from a Sarum Primer – but the tune we all know is Walford Davies's and we end this week's programme with it.

> GOD BE IN MY HEAD,
> And in my understanding;
>
> God be in mine eyes,
> And in my looking;
>
> God be in my mouth,
> And in my speaking;
>
> God be in my heart,
> And in my thinking;
>
> God be at my end
> And at my departing.

An exquisite, perfect prayer.

FROM THE ORGAN LOFT

From Series 3

BBC Radio Four
Sunday 16 August 1978
Producer: David Winter

• • •

Church organists are a splendid breed of people, often eccentric, sometimes doctrinaire, seldom anonymous. It's hard to hide your light under a bushel when all that huge potential of sound is at your fingers – and feet. Organists have done more than their fair share of composing church music and we shall be featuring some of their hymn-tunes in this programme, starting with one that is not only for church worship but about it: 'Angel voices, ever singing', words by Francis Pott, tune by Dr E. G. Monk.

> ANGEL VOICES, EVER SINGING,
> Round Thy throne of light,
> Angel harps, forever ringing,
> Rest not day or night;
> Thousands only live to bless Thee
> And confess Thee
> Lord of might.
>
> Thou who art beyond the farthest
> Mortal eye can scan,
> Can it be that Thou regardest

Songs of sinful man?
Can we know that Thou art near us
And wilt hear us?
Yea, we can.

Yea, we know that Thou rejoicest
O'er each work of Thine;
Thou didst ears and hands and voices
For Thy praise design;
Craftsman's art and music's measure
For Thy pleasure
All combine.

In Thy house, great God, we offer
Of Thine own to Thee;
And for Thine acceptance proffer,
All unworthily,
Hearts and minds and hands and voices
In our choicest
Psalmody.

Honour, glory, might and merit,
Thine shall ever be,
Father, Son and Holy Spirit,
Blessèd Trinity!
Of the best that Thou hast given
Earth and heaven
Render Thee.

Dr Monk, who wrote that tune, was for twenty-five years organist at York Minster. The words were written for the dedication of an organ at Winwick, Lancashire, in 1861 and Dr Monk's tune was composed for them.

Henry Thomas Smart did not have a formal musical education. In fact, he was articled to a solicitor but his love of organs, including their mechanism, lured him away from the legal profession. He was organist at three famous London churches: St Philip's, Regent Street (hence his tune 'Regent Square'),

St Luke's, Clerkenwell and St Pancras. A number of his hymn-tunes are still very popular, among them 'Heathlands', set to H. F. Lyte's words, 'God of Mercy, God of Grace'. I like the second verse especially.

> GOD OF MERCY, GOD OF GRACE,
> Show the brightness of Thy face.
> Shine upon us, Saviour, shine,
> Fill Thy Church with light divine,
> And Thy saving health extend
> Unto earth's remotest end.
>
> Let the people praise Thee, Lord;
> Be by all that live adored.
> Let the nations shout and sing
> Glory to their Saviour-King;
> At Thy feet their tribute pay
> And Thy holy will obey.
>
> Let the people praise Thee, Lord;
> Earth shall then her fruits afford.
> God to man His blessing give,
> Man to God devoted live;
> All below, and all above,
> One in joy and light and love.

There was never an era in Church history when the Church was more divided, nor one when its unity was more eloquently affirmed, than the nineteenth century. The more heresies distressed it, the more schisms rent it asunder, the more they wrote hymns that claimed 'We are not divided, all one body we'. One such hymn, and a very good one too, is Plumptre's 'Thy Hand, O God, Has Guided' with its triumphal (not to say triumphalist) refrain 'One Church, one Faith, one Lord'.[1] The most popular tune to it

---

[1] The first and last verses of the hymn that follows differ slightly from those in the version printed on pages 246–7.

nowadays is undoubtedly 'Thornsbury', composed by Dr Basil Harwood, who was organist at St Barnabas, Pimlico, Ely Cathedral and Christ Church, Oxford.

THY HAND, O GOD, HAS GUIDED
Thy flock, from age to age;
Their wondrous tale is written,
Full clear on every page.
Thy people owned Thy goodness,
And we their deeds record;
And both of this bear witness;
'One Church, one Faith, one Lord.'

Thy heralds brought glad tidings
To greatest, as to least;
They bade men rise and hasten
To share the great King's feast;
And this was all their teaching,
In every deed and word,
To all alike proclaiming
'One Church, one Faith, one Lord.'

When shadows thick were falling,
And all seemed sunk in night,
Thou, Lord, didst send Thy servants,
Thy chosen sons of light.
On them and on Thy people
Thy plenteous grace was poured
And this was still their message,
'One Church, one Faith, one Lord.'

Through many a day of darkness,
Through many a scene of strife,
The faithful few fought bravely,
To guard the nation's life;
Their gospel of redemption,
Sin pardoned, man restored,

Was all in this enfolded,
'One Church, one Faith, one Lord.'

And we, shall we be faithless?
Shall hearts fail, hands hang down?
Shall we evade the conflict
And cast away our crown?
Not so: in God's deep counsels
Some better thing is stored:
We will maintain, unflinching,
'One Church, one Faith, one Lord.'

Thy mercy will not fail us
Nor leave thy work undone;
With Thy right hand to help us
Thy victory shall be won;
And then, by all creation,
Thy Name shall be adored,
And this shall be their anthem:
'One Church, one Faith, one Lord.'

Henry Gauntlett was probably the most prolific composer of hymn-tunes who ever lived. This achievement, or weakness, could be attributed to his father, who was vicar of Olney, in Buckinghamshire, early in the nineteenth century. He was unwise enough to offer young Henry, who was about five at the time, a farthing for every tune he could copy out. Shortly after, Henry presented himself at his father's study door with a chart containing a thousand tunes. They agreed on a guinea as settling the debt. (It should have been £1. 8s. 10d. but probably little Henry was better at music than maths.) But clearly the boy got a taste for hymn-tunes because it is said he wrote in all ten thousand.

At nine years old, he became Olney's first organist and later was organist at St Olave's, Southwark, for twenty years. But the tune we're going to hear now, 'St Albinus', was written while he was organist of the Union Chapel, Islington, and it was sung to these words at the funeral of General Gordon in St Paul's Cathedral.

JESUS LIVES! THY TERRORS NOW
Can no more, O death, appal us;[2]
Jesus lives! By this we know
Thou, O grave, canst not enthral us.
Alleluia!

Jesus lives! Henceforth is death
But the gate of life immortal;
This shall calm our trembling breath
When we pass its gloomy portal.
Alleluia!

Jesus lives! For us He died;
Then, alone to Jesus living,
Pure in heart may we abide,
Glory to our Saviour giving.
Alleluia!

Jesus lives! Our hearts know well
Nought from us His love shall sever;
Life, nor death nor powers of hell
Tear us from His keeping ever.
Alleluia!

Jesus lives! To Him the throne
Over all the world is given:
May we go where He has gone,
Rest and reign with Him in heaven.
Alleluia!

Sir George Elvey was organist at St George's Chapel, Windsor and seems to have specialised in rather splendid, majestic hymn-tunes. One of his, called 'St George's Windsor', is usually sung to the harvest hymn 'Come Ye Thankful People, Come', but his best-

[2] Today more commonly 'Can, O death, no more appal us', or even 'Can no longer, death, appal us'.

known tune is undoubtedly 'Diademata', set to Matthew Bridges' splendid words 'Crown Him with Many Crowns':

CROWN HIM WITH MANY CROWNS,
The Lamb upon His throne;
Hark! How the heavenly anthem drowns
All music but its own:
Awake, my soul, and sing
Of Him who died for thee,
And hail Him as thy matchless King
Through all eternity.

Crown Him the Virgin's Son,
The God incarnate born,
Whose arm those crimson trophies won
Which now His brow adorn;
Fruit of the mystic rose,
As of that rose the stem;
The root whence mercy ever flows,
The Babe of Bethlehem.

Crown Him the Son of God,
Before the worlds began,
And ye who tread where He hath trod,
Crown Him the Son of Man;
Who every grief hath known
That wrings the human breast,
And takes and bears them for His own,
That all in Him may rest.

Crown Him the Lord of life,
Who triumphed over the grave,
And rose victorious in the strife
For those He came to save.
His glories now we sing,
Who died and rose on high,
Who died eternal life to bring
And lives that death may die.

Crown Him the Lord of peace,
Whose power a sceptre sways
From pole to pole, that wars may cease,
And all be prayer and praise.
His reign shall know no end,
And round His piercèd feet
Fair flowers of paradise extend
Their fragrance ever sweet.

Crown Him the Lord of love,
Behold His hands and side:
Those wounds, yet visible above,
In beauty glorified.
No angel in the sky
Can fully bear that sight,
But downward bends His burning eye
At mysteries so bright.

Crown Him the Lord of heaven,
Enthroned in worlds above,
Crown Him the King to whom is given
The wondrous Name of Love.
Crown Him with many crowns,
As thrones before Him fall;
Crown Him, ye kings, with many crowns,
For He is King of all.

Crown Him the Lord of lords,
Who over all doth reign,
Who once on earth, the incarnate Word,
For ransomed sinners slain,
Now lives in realms of light,
Where saints with angels sing
Their songs before Him day and night,
Their God, Redeemer, King.

Crown Him the Lord of years,
The Potentate of time,

Creator of the rolling spheres,
Ineffably sublime.
All hail, Redeemer, hail!
For Thou hast died for me;
Thy praise and glory shall not fail
Throughout eternity.

Sir John Goss was another very eminent church organist at St Andrew's, Lambeth and St Luke's, Chelsea before being appointed to St Paul's Cathedral. He was also, like so many of these composers, a professor – at the Royal Academy of Music. In 1872 he wrote an anthem celebrating the recovery of the Prince of Wales from an illness, which may seem an odd cause of religious celebration; perhaps it was only coincidence that in the same year Queen Victoria knighted him. At any rate by far his best-known hymn-tune was written three years before that, providing Lyte's words 'Praise My Soul the King of Heaven' with the tune they had been waiting for for thirty-five years.

PRAISE, MY SOUL, THE KING OF HEAVEN;
To His feet thy tribute bring.
Ransomed, healed, restored, forgiven,
Who like me His praise should sing?
Praise Him, praise Him,
Praise Him, praise Him,[3]
Praise the everlasting King.

Praise Him for His grace and favour
To our fathers in distress;
Praise Him still the same as ever,
Slow to chide and swift to bless:
Praise Him, praise Him,
Praise Him, praise Him
Glorious in His faithfulness.

[3] Changed in some modern hymnals to 'Alleluia! Alleluia!'

Father-like, He tends and spares us,
Well our feeble frame He knows;
In His hands He gently bears us,
Rescues us from all our foes:
Praise Him, praise Him,
Praise Him, praise Him
Widely as His mercy flows.

Angels, help us to adore Him;
Ye behold Him face to face;
Sun and moon, bow down before Him,
Dwellers all in time and space:
Praise Him, praise Him,
Praise Him, praise Him
Praise with us the God of grace.

We end this week with one of those evening hymns for which the Victorians are justly famous. Perhaps it has something to do with the popularity of Evensong but no one seems to be able to write these evocative candle-lit sort of hymns any more. Or perhaps it's that we don't any longer associate nightfall with thoughts of mortality and the grave. Ellerton[4] wrote the words and Dr Edward Hopkins the tune, which he called 'Ellers' (which sounds like an awful public school abbreviation of the author's name). Hopkins was organist at St Mary's, Islington – then, as now, very 'low' – and for fifty-four years at the famous Temple Church, London. The hymn is 'Saviour, Again to Thy Dear Name We Raise' and I think its true flavour is captured in the third verse, where the themes of darkness and light are neatly counterpoised:

SAVIOUR, AGAIN TO THY DEAR NAME WE RAISE
With one accord our parting hymn of praise.
Once more we bless Thee ere our worship cease,
Then, lowly bending, wait Thy word of peace.

[4] See p. 134-135.

Grant us Thy peace upon our homeward way;
With Thee began, with Thee shall end, the day;
Guard Thou the lips from sin, the hearts from shame,
That in this house have called upon Thy Name.

Grant us Thy peace, Lord, through the coming night;
Turn Thou for us its darkness into light.
From harm and danger keep Thy children free,
For dark and light are both alike to Thee.

Grant us Thy peace throughout our earthly life,
Our balm in sorrow and our stay in strife;
Then, when Thy voice shall bid our conflict cease,
Call us, O Lord, to Thine eternal peace.

FROM GERMANY

From Series 3

BBC Radio Four
Sunday 23 August 1978
Producer: David Winter

• • •

M ost of our popular hymn-tunes come from the Puritans (for
their metrical psalms), the Victorians (in the great wave of
hymn-writing of the nineteenth century) or the Germans (largely
through the close connection between the Lutherans and the
Church of England). And this week it is those German hymn-tunes
that we shall be considering.

Let's begin with a justly popular one. Nobody knows the name
of the composer but it first appeared in 1623 in one of those
German hymn collections with unpronounceable titles[1] that are
printed at the top of every other hymn in most of our books. The
tune is called 'Lasst uns Erfreuen' or 'Easter Song' and it's usually
sung to the canticle of St Francis of Assisi, 'All Creatures of Our
God and King'.

> ALL CREATURES OF OUR GOD AND KING,
> Lift up your voice and with us sing,
> O praise Him! Alleluia!
> Thou burning sun with golden beam,
> Thou silver moon with softer gleam!

[1] The *Ausserlesene Catholische Geistliche Kirchengesäng.*

O praise Him, O praise Him!
Alleluia, Alleluia, Alleluia!

Thou rushing wind that art so strong,
Ye clouds that sail in Heaven along,
O praise Him! Alleluia!
Thou rising moon, in praise rejoice,
Ye lights of evening, find a voice!
 Chorus

Thou flowing water, pure and clear,
Make music for thy Lord to hear,
O praise Him! Alleluia!
Thou fire so masterful and bright,
That givest man both warmth and light.
 Chorus

Dear mother earth, who day by day
Unfoldest blessings on our way,
O praise Him! Alleluia!
The flowers and fruits that in thee grow,
Let them His glory also show.
 Chorus

And all ye men of tender heart,
Forgiving others, take your part,
O sing ye! Alleluia!
Ye who long pain and sorrow bear,
Praise God and on Him cast your care!
 Chorus

And thou most kind and gentle Death,
Waiting to hush our latest breath,
O praise Him! Alleluia!
Thou leadest home the child of God
And Christ our Lord the way hath trod.
 Chorus

Let all things their Creator bless,
And worship Him in humbleness,
O praise Him! Alleluia!
Praise, praise the Father, praise the Son,
And praise the Spirit, Three in One!
        Chorus

Most of the German tunes we use are anonymous, but one
composer who is known is Joachim Neander, a seventeenth-
century scholar who wrote both words and hymn tunes. He lived
in Bremen and died at the age of thirty. One of his best and best-
known tunes is put to words by Job Hupton and J. M. Neale,
'Come Ye Faithful, Raise the Anthem'.

COME, YE FAITHFUL, RAISE THE ANTHEM,
Cleave the skies with shouts of praise;
Sing to him who found the ransom,
Ancient of eternal days.
God of God, the Word incarnate,
Whom the heaven of heaven obeys.

Ere He raised the lofty mountains,
Formed the seas or built the sky,
Love eternal, free and boundless,
Moved the Lord of Life to die,
Foreordained the Prince of princes
For the throne of Calvary.

There, for us and our redemption,
See Him all His life-blood pour!
There He wins our full salvation,
Dies that we may die no more;
Then, arising, lives forever,
Reigning where He was before.

High on yon celestial mountains
Stands His sapphire throne, all bright,

Midst unending alleluias
Bursting from the sons of light;
Sion's people tell His praises,
Victor after hard-won fight.

Bring your harps and bring your incense,
Sweep the string and pour the lay;
Let the earth proclaim His wonders,
King of that celestial day;
He the Lamb once slain is worthy,
Who was dead and lives for ay.

Laud and honour to the Father,
Laud and honour to the Son,
Laud and honour to the Spirit,
Ever Thee and ever One:
Consubstantial, co-eternal,
While unending ages run.

We've already mentioned Percy Dearmer in an earlier programme. He was vicar of St Mary the Virgin, Primrose Hill, in London and was one of the editors of the *English Hymnal* and editor of *Songs of Praise*. There's quite a difference between the two books: one is rather high and liturgical; the other is rather broad and modernist; so it's all a bit confusing. Anyway, he wrote several hymns and probably the most popular of them is this one, 'Jesus Good above All Other', to a very old German tune, possibly dating back to the fourteenth century, called 'Quem Pastores Laudarere'.

JESUS, GOOD ABOVE ALL OTHER,
Gentle Child of gentle mother,
In a stable born our Brother,
Give us grace to persevere.

Jesus, cradled in a manger,
For us facing every danger,

Living as a homeless Stranger,
Make we Thee our King most dear.

Jesus, for Thy people dying,
Risen Master, death defying,
Lord in heav'n, Thy grace supplying,
Keep us to Thy presence near.

Jesus, who our sorrows bearest,
All our thoughts and hopes Thou sharest,
Thou to man the truth declarest;
Help us all Thy truth to hear.

Lord, in all our doings guide us;
Pride and hate shall ne'er divide us;
We'll go on with Thee beside us,
And with joy we'll persevere!

The name of Johann Sebastian Bach figures prominently in most hymn-books, often in connection with hymn-tunes taken from his great choral works. Very often the tune, in fact, was not his own but his harmonisations were completely new. One of his loveliest, 'Eisenach', is from the St John Passion. It was set to Benjamin Webb's translation (1854) of a fifteenth-century hymn ascribed to Thomas à Kempis, 'O Love How Deep, How Broad, How High'.

O LOVE, HOW DEEP, HOW BROAD, HOW HIGH,
It fills the heart with ecstasy,[2]
That God, the Son of God, should take
Our mortal form for mortals' sake!

He sent no angel to our race,
Of higher or of lower place,
But wore the robe of human frame
Himself, and to this lost world came.

[2] Or 'How passing thought and fantasy'.

For us baptised, for us He bore
His holy fast and hungered sore;
For us temptation sharp He knew;
For us the tempter overthrew.

For us He prayed; for us He taught;
For us His daily works He wrought;
By words and signs and actions thus
Still seeking not Himself, but us.

For us to wicked men betrayed,
Scourged, mocked, in purple robe arrayed,
He bore the shameful cross and death;
For us at length gave up His breath.

For us He rose from death again;
For us He went on high to reign;
For us He sent His Spirit here,
To guide, to strengthen and to cheer.

To Him whose boundless love has won
Salvation for us through His Son,
To God the Father, glory be
Both now and through eternity.

Before the days of electric light and Teasmades, waking up in the morning seems to have been a very traumatic affair. There are lots of hymns celebrating the departure of the shades of night and the shaking off of dull sloth and so on. It's presumably the other side of those sombre evening hymns about the perils and dangers of the night. One of the best of these morning hymns was written by Charles Wesley and is usually sung to a German tune, 'Ratisbon'. Its theme is the typical one, of course – the triumph of light over darkness. But as usual, Wesley clothes the idea in unpredictable imagery and says it all more urgently than most of the others, especially in the third verse, 'Visit then this soul of mine . . .'

CHRIST, WHOSE GLORY FILLS THE SKIES
Christ the true, the only light,
Sun of righteousness, arise!
Triumph o'er the shades of night:
Day-spring from on high, be near;
Day-star, in my heart appear.

Dark and cheerless is the morn
Unaccompanied by Thee;
Joyless is the day's return,
Till Thy mercy's beams I see,
Till they inward light impart,
Glad my eyes and warm my heart.

Visit then this soul of mine,
Pierce the gloom of sin and grief;
Fill me, radiancy divine;
Scatter all my unbelief;
More and more Thyself display,
Shining to the perfect day.

You don't get very many short tunes from Germany, perhaps because there aren't very many short words in their language. One of their rather long tunes is usually set in English to a hymn for All Saints Day, 'Who Are These Like Stars Appearing?' The tune is called 'All Saints', it's from the *Darmstadt Songbook*[3] of 1698 and the words are translated by Frances Cox from the German of H. T. Schenk. To be quite honest, in places they sound like it:

These who well the fight sustained,
Triumph by the Lamb have gained

or

Still untouched by time's rude hand,
Whence come all this glorious band?

[3] The *Darmstadt Gesangbuch*.

295

Here is the hymn in full:

WHO ARE THESE LIKE STARS APPEARING,
These before God's throne who stand?
Each a golden crown is wearing;
Who are all this glorious band?
Alleluia! Hark, they sing,
Praising loud their heavenly King.

Who are these of dazzling brightness,
These in God's own truth arrayed?
Clad in robes of purest whiteness,
Robes whose lustre ne'er shall fade,
Still untouched by time's rude hand:
Whence come all this glorious band?

These are they who have contended
For their Saviour's honour long,
Wrestling on 'til life was ended,
Following not the sinful throng;
These who well the fight sustained,
Triumph by the Lamb have gained.

These are they whose hearts were riven,
Sore with woe and anguish tried,
Who in prayer full oft have striven
With the God they glorified;
Now, their painful conflict o'er,
God has bid them weep no more.

These, like priests, have watched and waited,
Offering up to Christ their will;
Soul and body consecrated,
Day and night to serve Him still:
Now in God's most holy place
Blest they stand before His face.

Many of the German hymns, like that one, have come to us complete: words and music. We're ending this week's programme with probably the best known of all such hymns, 'Now Thank We All Our God'. The tune, 'Nun Danket', was written by Johann Conger who was for forty years Precentor of St Nicholas Church, Berlin, in the seventeenth century. The words are by his contemporary, Martin Rinkart, who was Pastor in the walled town of Eilenberg during the Thirty Years' War. It became a centre for refugees and they are said to have brought disease and pestilence with them. Rinkart himself buried over four thousand people. Peace came in 1648 but he died the following year.

'Now Thank We All Our God' became a kind of German 'Te Deum', sung on special national occasions, and its English translation has been used similarly, notably at the service of Thanksgiving in St Paul's at the end of the Boer War. The translator, Catherine Winkworth, has kept close to the original but has yet managed to produce a very fine English hymn:

> NOW THANK WE ALL OUR GOD,
> With heart and hands and voices,
> Who wondrous things hath done,
> In whom His world rejoices;
> Who from our mother's arms
> Hath blessed us on our way
> With countless gifts of love
> And still is ours today.
>
> O may this bounteous God
> Through all our life be near us,
> With ever-joyful hearts
> And blessèd peace to cheer us;
> And keep us in His grace,
> And guide us when perplexed,
> And free us from all ills
> In this world and the next.

All praise and thanks to God
The Father now be given,
The Son and Holy Ghost,
Supreme in highest heaven,
The one eternal God,
Whom earth and heaven adore;
For thus it was, is now
And shall be evermore.

FROM THE REV. J. B. DYKES

From Series 3

BBC Radio Four
Sunday 30 August 1978
Producer: David Winter

• • •

It would be quite impossible to do a series of programmes about hymn-tunes and not mention the most prolific and popular of all English hymn-writers, John Bacchus Dykes. Despite the odium of scholars his tunes survive and flourish, presumably because they are good tunes with strong melodies and good passages. One of his strongest tunes was composed for John Henry Newman's words, 'Praise to the Holiest in the Height'.

> PRAISE TO THE HOLIEST IN THE HEIGHT,
> And in the depth be praise;
> In all His words most wonderful,
> Most sure in all His ways.
>
> O loving wisdom of our God!
> When all was sin and shame,
> A second Adam to the fight
> And to the rescue came.
>
> O wisest love! that flesh and blood,
> Which did in Adam fail,
> Should strive afresh against the foe,
> Should strive and should prevail;

And that the highest gift of grace[1]
Should flesh and blood refine;
God's presence and His very self,
And essence all divine.

O generous love! that He, who smote,
In Man for man the foe,
The double agony in Man
For man should undergo.

And in the garden secretly,
And on the cross on high,
Should teach His brethren, and inspire
To suffer and to die.

Praise to the Holiest in the height,
And in the depth be praise;
In all His words most wonderful,
Most sure in all His ways.

Dykes was a Yorkshireman and spent almost all his life in the North-East, much of it as Vicar of St Oswald's, Durham. He was a great contributor to *Hymns Ancient and Modern* and even the 1950 edition retains thirty-one of his tunes. Sometimes hymn-book compilers demote compositions to 'second tune' status, presumably to persuade organists to try something allegedly 'better'. That's what happened in the case of 'Beatitudo' which was set to Isaac Watts's words 'How Bright These Glorious Spirits Shine' and I suppose one has to admit that it's just a tiny bit sentimental. But who's to say that's a fault?

HOW BRIGHT THESE GLORIOUS SPIRITS SHINE!
Whence all their white array?
How came they to the blissful seats
Of everlasting day?

[1] Or 'And that a higher gift than grace'.

Lo! these are they from sufferings great
Who came to realms of light,
And in the blood of Christ have washed
Those robes which shine so bright.

Now with triumphal palms they stand
Before the throne on high,
And serve the God they love amidst
The glories of the sky.

His presence fills each heart with joy,
Tunes every mouth to sing:
By day, by night, the sacred courts
With glad Hosannas ring.

Hunger and thirst are felt no more,
Nor suns with scorching ray;
God is their sun, whose cheering beams
Diffuse eternal day.

The Lamb who dwells amidst the throne
Shall o'er them still preside,
Feed them with nourishment divine,
And all their footsteps guide.

Midst pastures green He'll lead His flock
Where living streams appear;
And God the Lord from every eye
Shall wipe off every tear.

To Father, Son and Holy Ghost,
The God whom we adore,
Be glory, as it was, is now
And shall be evermore.

Another tune of Dykes's relegated by the compilers of several
hymn-books to 'reserve' status is 'St Oswald', set to the words
'Through the Night of Doubt and Sorrow'; but like 'Beatitudo' it

obstinately refuses to slip into oblivion. The words are Baring-Gould's translation of a Danish hymn by H. S. Ingemann.

THROUGH THE NIGHT OF DOUBT AND SORROW,
Onward goes the pilgrim band,
Singing songs of expectation,
Marching to the Promised Land.
Clear before us through the darkness
Gleams and burns the guiding light:
Trusting God we march together[2]
Stepping fearless through the night.

One the light of God's own presence,
O'er His ransomed people shed,
Chasing far the gloom and terror,
Brightening all the path we tread:
One the object of our journey,
One the Faith which never tires,
One the earnest looking forward,
One the hope our God inspires.

One the strain that lips of thousands
Lift as from the heart of one;
One the conflict, one the peril
One the march in God begun:
One the gladness of rejoicing
On the far eternal shore,
Where the one almighty Father
Reigns in love for evermore.

Onward, therefore, pilgrim brothers,
Onward, with the cross our aid!
Bear its shame and fight its battle,
Till we rest beneath its shade.
Soon shall come the great awaking,
Soon the rending of the tomb;

[2] Or 'Brother clasps the hand of brother'.

Then the scattering of all shadows,
And the end of toil and gloom.

One tune of Dykes's has however been ousted in popular usage. He wrote a tune for Charles Wesley's 'Jesus, Lover of My Soul' and called it 'Hollingside', the name of his cottage outside Durham. His sister was staying with him at the time and recalled hearing him composing it on the piano while she sat on the verandah 'in the deepening twilight of a calm Sunday evening'. Recently the Welsh tune 'Aberystwyth', a rather sombre tune in a minor key, has increasingly been preferred but those of us of an older generation, at least, still enjoy hearing 'Hollingside' when it is sung.

JESU, LOVER OF MY SOUL,
Let me to Thy bosom fly,
While the nearer waters roll,
While the tempest still is high:
Hide me, O my Saviour, hide,
Till the storm of life be past!
Safe into the haven guide,
Oh, receive my soul at last!

Other refuge have I none,
Hangs my helpless soul on Thee;
Leave, ah! leave me not alone,
Still support and comfort me:
All my trust on Thee is stayed,
All my help from Thee I bring;
Cover my defenceless head
With the shadow of Thy wing.

Thou, O Christ, art all I want
More than all in Thee I find!
Raise the fallen, cheer the faint,
Heal the sick and lead the blind;
Just and holy is Thy name,
I am all unrighteousness;

> False and full of sin I am,
> Thou art full of truth and grace.
>
> Plenteous grace with Thee is found,
> Grace to cover all my sin,
> Let the healing streams abound;
> Make and keep me pure within:
> Thou of life the fountain art,
> Freely let me take of Thee,
> Spring Thou up within my heart,
> Rise to all eternity.

'Hollingside' and 'Beatitudo' are exceptions, of course. Most of Dykes's tunes are wedded indissolubly to the words for which he wrote them. Our next hymn, for instance, 'Fierce Raged the Tempest o'er the Deep': it would be unthinkable to sing it to any tune but 'St Aelred' with its bass line so beloved of the stout gentlemen of the choir, giving a passable imitation of a storm at sea. The words are by Canon Thring and they tell the story of the calming of the storm and apply the moral with a wonderful economy of words:

> FIERCE RAGED THE TEMPEST O'ER THE DEEP,
> Watch did Thine anxious servants keep,
> But Thou wast wrapped in guileless sleep,
> Calm and still.
>
> 'Save, Lord, we perish,' was their cry,
> 'O save us in our agony!'
> Thy Word above the storm rose high,
> 'Peace, be still.'
>
> The wild winds hushed; the angry deep
> Sank, like a little child, to sleep;
> The sullen billows ceased to leap,
> At Thy will.

So when our life is clouded o'er,
And storm-winds drift us from the shore,
Say, lest we sink to rise no more,
'Peace, be still.'

John Dykes became assistant organist at a church in Wakefield when he was eighteen but then went to Cambridge and took holy orders. His most prolific period of hymn-writing was his time at St Oswald, Durham and he named most of his tunes after northern saints or places in the locality. One of these tunes, 'St Cuthbert', was written for Harriet Auber's Whitsuntide hymn 'Our Blest Redeemer, ere He Breathed His Tender Last Farewell'.

OUR BLEST REDEEMER, ERE HE BREATHED
His tender last farewell,
A Guide, a Comforter, bequeathed
With us to dwell.

He came in semblance of a dove,
With sheltering wings outspread,
The holy balm of peace and love
On earth to shed.

He came in tongues of living flame
To teach, convince, subdue;
All powerful as the wind He came,
As viewless too.

He came sweet influence to impart,
A gracious, willing Guest,
While He can find one humble heart
Wherein to rest.

And His that gentle voice we hear,
Soft as the breath of even,
That checks each fault, that calms each fear
And speaks of heav'n.

And every virtue we possess,
And every conquest won,
And every thought of holiness,
Are His alone.

Spirit of purity and grace,
Our weakness, pitying, see:
O make our hearts Thy dwelling place
And worthier Thee.

We're going to end this programme with one of Dykes's most popular tunes, 'Horbury', set to Mrs S. F. Adams's words, 'Nearer, My God, to Thee'. Both words and tune are undoubtedly sentimental and have been known to make people cry – which means, of course, that they are very, very bad and should be banned. Horbury is a village near Wakefield and Dykes wrote this tune after he had preached there. The words are based on the story in the book of Genesis about Jacob's dream.

NEARER, MY GOD, TO THEE,
Nearer, to Thee!
E'en though it be a cross
That raiseth me;
Still all my song shall be,
    Nearer, my God, to Thee,
    Nearer, my God, to Thee,
    Nearer to Thee.

Though like the wanderer,
The sun gone down,
Darkness be over me,
My rest a stone.
Yet in my dreams I'd be
    Chorus

There let the way appear,
Steps unto heaven;

All that Thou sendest me,
In mercy given;
Angels to beckon me
    Chorus

Then, with my waking thoughts
Bright with Thy praise,
Out of my stony griefs
Bethel I'll raise;
So by my woes to be
    Chorus

Or, if on joyful wing
Cleaving the sky,
Sun, moon, and stars forgot,
Upward I'll fly,
Still all my song shall be,
    Chorus

There in my Father's home,
Safe and at rest,
There in my Saviour's love,
Perfectly blest;
Age after age to be,
    Chorus

ENGLISH TRADITIONAL MELODIES

From Series 3

BBC Radio Four
Sunday 6 September 1978
Producer: David Winter

. . .

Many hymn-tunes, as we remarked in the first of these programmes, have been applied to secular use – sometimes ribald use in parody. But it's not a one-way traffic. Quite a lot of folk tunes and traditional melodies that originally celebrated such things as feasting and fertility have been adapted to use for hymns. And we'll be listening to some of them in this, our last programme in the present series.[1]

Let's start with one called 'Sussex', which is said to have been a favourite of the famous Horsham bell-ringer and folk-singer Henry Burstow. It was set to Mrs L. M. Willis's words, 'Father, Hear the Prayer We Offer'. I always feel this hymn is the epitome of Victorian public school religion because it says, more or less, 'Don't let me be comfortable: make life difficult because a bit of privation can do wonders for your soul.' I wonder!

> FATHER, HEAR THE PRAYER WE OFFER:
> Not for ease that prayer shall be,

[1] Betjeman's words suggest that a fourth series of *Sweet Songs of Zion* was under consideration.

But for strength, that we may ever
Live our lives courageously.

Not forever in green pastures
Do we ask our way to be,
But the steep and rugged pathway
May we tread rejoicingly.

Not forever by still waters
Would we idly rest and stay,
But would smite the living fountains
From the rocks along our way.

Be our strength in hours of weakness,
In our wanderings be our Guide;
Through endeavour, failure, danger,
Saviour, be Thou at our side.

Dr Ralph Vaughan Williams was one of the most assiduous collectors of English folk tunes which he then adapted as hymns. You can see the results of his work in the *English Hymnal*, of which he was musical editor. In 1903, while visiting Forest Green, in Surrey, he noted an old tune, 'The Ploughboy's Dream'. It was suitably tidied up and married to some words of Bishop Philip Brookes – one of our most popular Christmas carols: 'O Little Town of Bethlehem'.

O LITTLE TOWN OF BETHLEHEM,
How still we see thee lie!
Above thy deep and dreamless sleep
The silent stars go by.
Yet in thy dark streets shineth
The everlasting Light;
The hopes and fears of all the years
Are met in thee tonight.

For Christ is born of Mary,
And gathered all above,

While mortals sleep, the angels keep
Their watch of wondering love.
O morning stars together,
Proclaim the holy birth,
And praises sing to God the King,
And peace to men on earth!

How silently, how silently,
The wondrous Gift is giv'n;
So God imparts to human hearts
The blessings of His heav'n.
No ear may hear His coming
But in this world of sin,
Where meek souls will receive Him still,
The dear Christ enters in.

Where children pure and happy
Pray to the blessèd Child;
Where misery cries out to Thee,
Son of the mother mild;
Where charity stands watching
And faith holds wide the door,
The dark night wakes, the glory breaks,
And Christmas comes once more.

O holy Child of Bethlehem,
Descend to us, we pray;
Cast out our sin and enter in,
Be born in us today.
We hear the Christmas angels
The great glad tidings tell;
O come to us, abide with us,
Our Lord Emmanuel!

Another great student of English folk song was Geoffrey Shaw, younger brother of Martin Shaw. Their father, James, was Organist of Hampstead parish church. 'England's Lane' was Geoffrey Shaw's title for a lovely melody he found and adapted to

F. S. Pierpoint's words, 'For the Beauty of the Earth':

> FOR THE BEAUTY OF THE EARTH,
> For the beauty of the skies,
> For the love which from our birth
> Over and around us lies,
> *Lord of all, to Thee we raise*
> *This our grateful song of praise.*[2]
>
> For the beauty of each hour
> Of the day and of the night,
> Hill and vale, and tree and flower,
> Sun and moon, and stars of light,
> *Chorus*
>
> For the joy of ear and eye,
> For the heart and brain's delight,
> For the mystic harmony
> Linking sense to sound and sight,
> *Chorus*
>
> For the joy of human love,
> Brother, sister, parent, child,
> Friends on earth and friends above,
> For all gentle thoughts and mild,
> *Chorus*
>
> For each perfect gift of Thine
> To our race so freely given,
> Graces human and divine,
> Flowers of earth and buds of heaven,
> *Chorus*
>
> For Thy Bride that evermore
> Lifteth holy hands above,

[2] More commonly 'This our grateful hymn of praise' or 'This our hymn of grateful praise'.

Offering up on every shore
This pure sacrifice of love,
    Chorus

For the martyrs' crown of light,
For Thy prophets' eagle eye,
For thy bold confessors' might,
For the lips of infancy,
    Chorus

For Thy virgins' robes of snow,
For Thy maiden Mother mild,
For Thyself, with hearts aglow,
Jesus, Victim undefiled,
    Chorus

A third great student of traditional English music was Cecil Sharpe, perhaps the greatest of all enthusiasts for folk song. He didn't contribute a lot as hymns but he did adapt a couple of lovely Somerset folk-songs as hymn-tunes, one of them called 'Mendip' after the Mendip Hills. It works well with Isaac Watts's verses, 'There Is a Land of Pure Delight', especially the last verse about climbing where Moses stood.

THERE IS A LAND OF PURE DELIGHT
Where saints immortal reign;
Infinite day excludes the night
And pleasures banish pain.

There everlasting spring abides
And never-withering flowers:
Death, like a narrow sea, divides
This heavenly land from ours.

Sweet fields beyond the swelling flood
Stand dressed in living green:
So to the Jews old Canaan stood
While Jordan rolled between.

But timorous mortals start and shrink
To cross this narrow sea;
And linger, shivering on the brink,
And fear to launch away.

O could we make our doubts remove
Those gloomy thoughts that rise
And see the Canaan that we love
With unbeclouded eyes!

Could we but climb where Moses stood
And view the landscape o'er,
Not Jordan's stream, nor death's cold flood
Should fright us from the shore.

The other Somerset folk tune discovered and adapted by Cecil Sharpe was originally known as 'Tarry Trousers' but as a hymn-tune it has the rather more respectable title of 'Shepton Beauchamp'. 'Tarry Trousers' wouldn't have looked very nice at the head of a page in *Hymns Ancient and Modern*, would it? You probably know it because of its setting to Monsell's[3] famous hymn 'Fight the Good Fight':

FIGHT THE GOOD FIGHT WITH ALL THY MIGHT:
Christ is thy Strength and Christ thy Right;
Lay hold on life and it shall be
Thy joy and crown eternally.

Run the straight race through God's good grace:
Lift up thine eyes and seek His face;
Life with its way before us lies,
Christ is the path and Christ the prize.

Cast care aside; upon thy Guide,
Lean, and His mercy will provide;

[3] See p. 216.

Lean, and the trusting soul shall prove
Christ is its Life and Christ its Love.

Faint not nor fear, His arms are near;
He changeth not and thou art dear;
Only believe and thou shalt see
That Christ is all in all to thee.

There was an old Warwickshire song, 'Don't you see my Billy coming?' It's the lament of a girl for her young man who had been killed on the battlefield: she could see him surrounded by angels. It's a rather pretty tune and it goes very pleasantly with Mary Duncan's children's hymn, 'Jesus Tender Shepherd'.

JESUS, TENDER SHEPHERD, HEAR ME,
Bless Thy little lamb tonight;
Through the darkness be Thou near me,
Keep me safe 'til morning light.

All this day Thy hand has led me,
And I thank Thee for Thy care;
Thou hast clothed me, warmed and fed me,
Listen to my evening prayer.

Let my sins be all forgiven;
Bless the friends I love so well;
Take me, when I die, to heaven,
Happy there with Thee to dwell.

Our last hymn is often sung to a traditional melody. The melody is old but nobody knows how old. It appeared in a collection of *English Country Songs* compiled by Miss L. Broadwood in 1893 but apparently it had been first noted in Westminster by A. J. Hopkins some years before. So perhaps it's a city rather than a country tune. It's often sung to Horatio Bonar's hymn, 'I Heard the Voice of Jesus Say', which requires a tune that 'lifts' for the more optimistic second half of each stanza. The hymn itself is not as popular as it

once was, perhaps, because it's rather too personal and subjective
for modern taste, at any rate where religion is concerned:

> I HEARD THE VOICE OF JESUS SAY,
> 'Come unto Me and rest;
> Lay down, thou weary one, lay down
> Thy head upon My breast.'
> I came to Jesus as I was,
> Weary and worn and sad;
> I found in Him a resting place
> And He has made me glad.
>
> I heard the voice of Jesus say,
> 'Behold, I freely give
> The living water; thirsty one,
> Stoop down and drink and live.'
> I came to Jesus and I drank
> Of that life-giving stream;
> My thirst was quenched, my soul revived
> And now I live in Him.
>
> I heard the voice of Jesus say,
> 'I am this dark world's light;
> Look unto Me, thy morn shall rise,
> And all thy day be bright.'
> I looked to Jesus and I found
> In Him my Star, my Sun;
> And in that light of life I'll walk,
> Till travelling days are done.

INDEX OF HYMNS

ALL THINGS BRIGHT AND BEAUTIFUL 102
ABIDE WITH ME; FAST FALLS THE EVENTIDE 133
ALL CREATURES OF OUR GOD AND KING 189, 289
ALL GLORY, LAUD AND HONOUR 118
ALL HAIL THE POWER OF JESUS' NAME! 205
ALL MY HOPE ON GOD IS FOUNDED 167
ALL PEOPLE THAT ON EARTH DO DWELL 258
AND CAN IT BE THAT I SHOULD GAIN 53
ANGEL VOICES, EVER SINGING 277
ART THOU WEARY, ART THOU LANGUID 117
AS PANTS THE HART FOR COOLING STREAMS 162
AT EVEN, ERE THE SUN WAS SET 146
AT THE NAME OF JESUS, EVERY KNEE SHALL BOW 109
BLESSED ASSURANCE, JESUS IS MINE! 67
BLEST ARE THE PURE IN HEART 116
BREAD OF THE WORLD IN MERCY BROKEN 60
BRIGHTEST AND BEST OF THE SONS OF THE MORNING 60
BY COOL SILOAM'S SHADY RILL 59
CHILDREN OF THE HEAVENLY KING 205
CHRIST THE LORD IS RISEN AGAIN 195
CHRIST, WHOSE GLORY FILLS THE SKIES 49, 295
CHRISTIAN, DOST THOU SEE THEM 119, 193
COME DOWN, O LOVE DIVINE 197
COME IN, O COME! THE DOOR STANDS OPEN NOW 235
COME YE SINNERS, POOR AND NEEDY 80
COME, LET US JOIN OUR CHEERFUL SONGS 22
COME, MY SOUL, THY SUIT PREPARE 213
COME, THOU FOUNT OF EVERY BLESSING 255
COME, YE FAITHFUL, RAISE THE ANTHEM 291
COME, YE THANKFUL PEOPLE, COME 242
CREATOR SPIRIT, BY WHOSE AID 163
CROWN HIM WITH MANY CROWNS 283
DEAR LORD AND FATHER OF MANKIND 182
ERE I SLEEP, FOR EV'RY FAVOUR 209
ETERNAL LIGHT, ETERNAL LIGHT! 249

ETERNAL RULER OF THE CEASELESS ROUND   259
FACING A TASK UNFINISHED   236
FATHER OF HEAVEN, WHOSE LOVE PROFOUND   214
FATHER OF MERCIES, IN THY WORD   106
FATHER, HEAR THE PRAYER WE OFFER   309
FATHER, WHATE'ER OF EARTHLY BLISS   106
FIERCE RAGED THE TEMPEST O'ER THE DEEP   141, 304
FIGHT THE GOOD FIGHT WITH ALL THY MIGHT   139, 216, 314
FILL THOU MY LIFE, O LORD MY GOD   131, 225
FOR ALL THE SAINTS, WHO FROM THEIR LABOURS REST   124
FOR THE BEAUTY OF THE EARTH   312
FORTH IN THY NAME, O LORD, I GO   260
FROM GREENLAND'S ICY MOUNTAINS   58
GLORIOUS THINGS OF THEE ARE SPOKEN   208
GLORY TO THEE, MY GOD, THIS NIGHT   158
GO, LABOUR ON: SPEND, AND BE SPENT   227
GOD BE IN MY HEAD   275
GOD MOVES IN A MYSTERIOUS WAY   33
GOD OF MERCY, GOD OF GRACE   279
GOD, THAT MADEST EARTH AND HEAVEN   62
GRACIOUS SPIRIT, HOLY GHOST   229, 274
GUIDE ME, O THOU GREAT JEHOVAH   77
HAIL THE DAY THAT SEES HIM RISE, HALLELUJAH!   50
HAPPY ARE THEY, THEY THAT LOVE GOD   166
HARK MY SOUL! IT IS THE LORD;   32
HARK THE GLAD SOUND! THE SAVIOUR COMES   200
HARK! THE SOUND OF HOLY VOICES, CHANTING AT
    THE CRYSTAL SEA   231
HE THAT IS DOWN NEEDS FEAR NO FALL   157
HE WHO WOULD VALIANT BE   156FN
HILLS OF THE NORTH, REJOICE   270
HO, MY COMRADES! SEE THE SIGNAL   188
HOLY, HOLY, HOLY, LORD GOD ALMIGHTY!   63
HOW BRIGHT THESE GLORIOUS SPIRITS SHINE!   300
HOW SWEET THE NAME OF JESUS SOUNDS   211
HUSHED WAS THE EVENING HYMN   139, 219
I CANNOT TELL WHY HE, WHEN ANGELS WORSHIP   254
I HEARD THE VOICE OF JESUS SAY   130, 228, 316
I HUNGER AND I THIRST   217
I WILL SING THE WONDROUS STORY   83
I'LL PRAISE MY MAKER WHILE I'VE BREATH,   28
I'M NOT ASHAMED TO OWN MY LORD,   25

IMMORTAL LOVE, FOREVER FULL	184
IMMORTAL, INVISIBLE, GOD ONLY WISE	84, 222
IN HEAVENLY LOVE ABIDING	86
IN THE BLEAK MIDWINTER	269
IT IS A THING MOST WONDERFUL	234
JERUSALEM THE GOLDEN, WITH MILK AND HONEY BLEST	87
JESU, LOVER OF MY SOUL	79, 303
JESUS CALLS US O'ER THE TUMULT	105
JESUS LIVES! THY TERRORS NOW	282
JESUS SHALL REIGN WHERE'ER THE SUN	23
JESUS THE VERY THOUGHT OF THEE	94
JESUS, GOOD ABOVE ALL OTHER	292
JESUS, PRICELESS TREASURE	196
JESUS, TENDER SHEPHERD, HEAR ME	315
JESUS, THOU JOY OF LOVING HEARTS!	144
JESUS, THY BLOOD AND RIGHTEOUSNESS	47
JESUS, WHERE'ER THY PEOPLE MEET	39
JUDGE ETERNAL, THRONED IN SPLENDOUR	85
JUST AS I AM, WITHOUT ONE PLEA	108
KING OF GLORY, KING OF PEACE	152
LEAD, KINDLY LIGHT, AMID THE ENCIRCLING GLOOM	122
LET ALL THE WORLD IN EVERY CORNER SING	153
LET US, WITH A GLADSOME MIND	149
LIFT UP YOUR HEADS, YE MIGHTY GATES	111
LO! HE COMETH, COUNTLESS TRUMPETS	207
LO, GOD IS HERE: LET US ADORE	261
LOOK, YE SAINTS! THE SIGHT IS GLORIOUS	253
LORD OF ALL BEING, THRONED AFAR	180
LORD, DISMISS US WITH THY BLESSING	250
LORD, SPEAK TO ME, THAT I MAY SPEAK	141
LOVE DIVINE, ALL LOVES EXCELLING,	43
LOVE OF LOVE, AND LIGHT OF LIGHT	172
LOVE OF THE FATHER, LOVE OF GOD THE SON	174
MAN OF SORROWS! WHAT A NAME	73
MY GOD, HOW WONDERFUL THOU ART	93
MY GOD, I THANK THEE, WHO HAST MADE	137
MY LORD, MY LIFE, MY LOVE	176
MY SONG IS LOVE UNKNOWN	154
NEARER, MY GOD, TO THEE	306
NEW EVERY MORNING IS THE LOVE	114
NOW THANK WE ALL OUR GOD	297
O BROTHER MAN, FOLD TO THY HEART THY BROTHER!	183

O come, O come, Emmanuel 91
O for a closer walk with God, 34
O for a thousand tongues to sing 45
O gladsome light, O grace 178
O God of Bethel, by whose hand 199
O God, our help in ages past, 26
O happy band of pilgrims 90
O help us Lord, each hour of need 240
O Jesus, let Thy spirit bless 81
O little town of Bethlehem 310
O Lord of Heav'n and earth and sea 232
O Love that wilt not let me go 143
O love, how deep, how broad, how high 293
O perfect Love, all human thought transcending 275
O praise ye the Lord! 267
O Sacred Head, sore wounded 173
O Spirit of the living God 65
O strength and stay upholding all creation 198
O Thou Who camest from above 54
O what their joy and their glory must be 191
O worship the King, all glorious above 264
O worship the Lord in the beauty of holiness! 218
O! Jesu mawr, rho d'anian bur 81
Once in royal David's city 103
Once to every man and nation 186
Onward Christian soldiers 127
Our blest Redeemer, ere He breathed 144, 305
Peace, perfect peace, in this dark world of sin? 233, 263
Praise to the Holiest in the height 96, 121, 299
Praise to the Lord 147
Praise, my soul, the King of heaven 132, 285
Rejoice, O land, in God thy might 168
Rescue the perishing, care for the dying 68
Ride on, ride on in majesty! 239
Rock of Ages, cleft for me, 41
Saviour, again to Thy dear name we raise 286
Softly and tenderly Jesus is calling 76
Soldiers of Christ, arise, and put your armour on
(long version) 51
Soldiers of Christ, arise (short version) 126
Sometimes a light surprises 35
Standing on the promises of Christ my King 71

STRONG SON OF GOD, IMMORTAL LOVE — 164
SUN OF MY SOUL, THOU SAVIOUR DEAR — 115
SUNSET AND EVENING STAR — 165
TEACH ME, MY GOD AND KING — 151
TELL ME NOT, IN MOURNFUL NUMBERS — 181
TELL ME THE OLD, OLD STORY OF UNSEEN THINGS ABOVE — 74
TELL OUT, MY SOUL, THE GREATNESS OF THE LORD! — 247
TEN THOUSAND TIMES TEN THOUSAND — 241
THE CHURCH'S ONE FOUNDATION — 98
THE DAY IS PAST AND OVER — 192
THE DAY THOU GAVEST, LORD, IS ENDED — 134
THE DUTEOUS DAY NOW CLOSETH — 177
THE GOD OF ABRAHAM PRAISE — 201
THE HEAD THAT ONCE WAS CROWNED WITH THORNS — 252
THE KING OF LOVE MY SHEPHERD IS — 123
THE LORD IS COME! ON SYRIAN SOIL — 244
THE SANDS OF TIME ARE SINKING — 223
THE SON OF GOD GOES FORTH TO WAR — 61, 262
THERE IS A FOUNTAIN FILLED WITH BLOOD — 37
THERE IS A GREEN HILL FAR AWAY — 104
THERE IS A LAND OF PURE DELIGHT — 30, 313
THERE WERE NINETY AND NINE THAT SAFELY LAY — 69
THINE ARM, O LORD, IN DAYS OF OLD — 245
THOU WHO WAST RICH BEYOND ALL SPLENDOUR — 237
THOU, WHOSE ALMIGHTY WORD — 215
THROUGH ALL THE CHANGING SCENES OF LIFE — 160
THROUGH THE NIGHT OF DOUBT AND SORROW — 129, 302
THY HAND, O GOD, HAS GUIDED — 246, 280
THY WAY, NOT MINE, O LORD — 224
TO GOD BE THE GLORY, GREAT THINGS HE HATH DONE — 75
WE SING THE PRAISE OF HIM WHO DIED — 251
WHAT A FRIEND WE HAVE IN JESUS — 82
WHEN ALL MY LABOURS AND TRIALS ARE O'ER — 187
WHEN ALL THY MERCIES, O MY GOD — 271
WHEN I SURVEY THE WONDROUS CROSS — 27
WHEN MORNING GILDS THE SKIES — 169
WHEN THIS PASSING WORLD IS DONE — 221
WHO ARE THESE LIKE STARS APPEARING — 296
WHO IS ON THE LORD'S SIDE? WHO WILL SERVE THE KING? — 72
WHO WOULD TRUE VALOUR SEE — 156
YE SERVANTS OF GOD, YOUR MASTER PROCLAIM — 55

INDEX OF HYMN-WRITERS

à Kempis, Thomas 293
Abelard, Peter 191
Adams, Mrs S. F. 306
Addison, Joseph 271
Alexander, Mrs Cecil Frances
  16, 101–105, 107, 109
Alford, Henry (Dean) 241–242
Ambrose, Saint 198
Anatolius Saint 192
Andrew, Saint of Crete 119
Auber, Harriet 144, 305
Baker, Henry Williams (Sir)
  123, 267
Baring-Gould, Sabine 13, 17,
  127–129, 302
Bernard of Cluny 87
Bickersteth, Edward H. (Bishop)
  233, 263
Binney, Marcus 249
Bliss, P. P. 73–74
Bonar, Horatius (*also* Horatio)
  130–131, 224-228, 315
Borthwick, Jane 109
Bowles, William Lisle 7
Brady, Nicholas 159–162
Bridges, Matthew 283
Bridges, Robert 166–168, 169–177
Brookes, Philip (Bishop) 310
Bunyan, John 155–156
Burns, J. D. 139
Burns, James Drummond 219
Carter, Russell Kelso 71
Caswell, Edward 94–96, 169
Cennick, John 205–207, 209
Chadwick, J. N. 259
Chalmers Smith, W. 84
Clephane, Elizabeth 69, 109

Cooper, Edward 214–216
Cosin, John 162
Cotterill, Thomas 65
Cousin, Anne Ross 223
Cowper, William 16, 18, 31–39,
  57, 211, 214
Cox, Frances 295
Crosby, Fanny 68
Crossman, Samuel (Dean) 153
di Siena, Bianco 197
Doane, W. H. 74
Doddridge, Philip 199–200
Donne, John 149, 151
Draper, William 189
Dryden, John 162
Dudley-Smith, Timothy
(Archdeacon) 247
Duncan, Mary 315
Ellerton, John 134, 198, 286
Elliot, Charlotte 108, 109
Faber, F. W. 87, 93–96
Fawcett, John 250
Francis, Saint of Assisi 4, 189, 289
Franck, Johann 196
Fullerton, William Young 254
Gabriel, Charles 187
Gerhardt, Paulus 173–174, 176
Gurney, Dorothy F. 275
Hankey, Arabella 74
Havergal, Frances Ridley
  72–73, 109, 141
Heber, Reginald (Bishop) 18, 57–64,
  113, 262–263
Herbert, John 150–152
Holland, H. Scott 85
Holmes, Oliver Wendell 179–180
Hort, Fenton John Anthony 198

Houghton, Frank (Bishop) 236–237
How, William Walsham (Bishop) 124–126, 234–235
Humphreys, Miss C. F., (*see Alexander, Mrs Cecil Frances*)
Ingemann, H. S. 302
James, Saint 183
Joseph the Hymnographer 89
Keble, John 113–116, 177
Kelly, Thomas 251–253
Ken, Thomas (Bishop) 157
Kethe, William 264
King James translators 217
Littledale, Richard Frederick 197
Longfellow, Henry Wadsworth 180
Lowell, James Russell 185
Lyte, H. F. 132–133, 279, 285
Madan, Martin 206
Marriott, John 215
Matheson, George 142–143
McCheyne, Robert Murray 220
Milman, Henry Hart (Dean) 239–240
Milton, John 149
Monsell, John Samuel Bewley 216–217, 314
Montgomery, James 18, 64
Moody, Dwight L. 15, 70, 74, 187
Moule, Handley Carr Glyn (Bishop) 235
Neale, John Mason 87–91, 117–119, 191–193, 291
Neander, Joachim (*see also under Composers*) 147–149, 166
Newman, John Henry (Cardinal) 87, 96, 120–122, 299
Newton, John 33, 57, 72, 208, 211–213
Noel, Caroline 109
Olivers, Thomas 201
Palmer, Ray 144
Pantycelin, William Williams 77–78
Perronet, Edward 202–203
Pierpoint, F. S. 312

Plumtre, Edward Hayes (Dean) 246, 279
Pott, Francis 277
Proctor, Adelaide 137
Rinkart, Martin 297
Rippon, Dr 204
Robinson, Robert 255
Rossetti, Christina 268
Rowley, F. H. 83
Sankey, Ira D. 15, 70, 73, 74, 187
Schenk, H. T. 295
Scriven, J. M. 82
Smith, Walter Chalmers 222
Stanley, Arthur Penrhyn (Dean) 243–244
Steele, Anne 106–107, 109
Stone, S. J. 97
Tate, Nahum 159–162
Tennyson, Alfred (Lord) 163–165
Tersteegen, Gerhard 261
Theodulph, Saint of Orleans 118
Thring, Godfrey 140
Thring, Godfrey (Canon) 304
Toplady, Augustus Montague 18, 40
Twells, Henry (Canon) 145
Upton, Job 291
Waring, Anna Laetitia 85–86
Watts, Isaac 2, 18, 21–29, 72, 175, 300, 313
Webb, Benjamin 293
Weisse, M. 194
Weissel, Georg 110
Wesley, Charles 16, 18, 43–55, 72, 78, 113, 175, 194, 199, 202, 205–206, 255, 260–261, 294, 303
Wesley, John 16, 18, 39, 43–49, 72, 113, 194, 199, 201, 202, 255, 261
Whittier, John Greenleaf 182–184
Williams, P. 77
Williams, William, see Pantycelin, William Williams
Willis, Mrs L. M. 309
Winkworth, Catherine 110, 147, 194–195, 297

Wither, George (*see also under*
   Collections)   260
Wordsworth, Christopher

(Bishop)   229–232, 273
Zinzendorf, Count   47

INDEX OF COMPOSERS

Bach, Johann Sebastian   196, 293
Barnby, Joseph (Sir)   275
ben Judah, Meir, *see Leoni,*
   Michael Bourgeois, Louis   259
Conger, Johann   297
Davies, Henry Walford (Sir)   275
de Giardini, Felice   216
Dearmer, Percy (*see also*
   under Collections)   292
Dykes, John Bacchus   13, 32,
      63, 179, 214, 228, 275, 299–307
Elvey, George (Sir)   282
Gauntlett, Henry   281
Gibbons, Orlando   174, 260, 263
Gore-Ousley, Frederick (Sir)
                                271–273
Goss, John (Sir)   285
Harwood, Basil   280
Holst, Gustav   268
Hopkins, A. J.   315
Hopkins, Edward   286
Jenkins, David   86

Knapp, Mrs J. F.   68
Leoni, Michael (Myer/Meir),
   (Cantor)   201
Monk, E. G.   277–278
Neander, Joachim   291
Oakley, Charles E.   270
Parry, Charles (Sir)   267–268
Parry, Joseph   78
Prichard, R. H.   83
Rowlands, William P.   82
Sharpe, Cecil   313–314
Shaw, Geoffrey   311
Shaw, Martin   270
Shrubsole, William   202
Stainer, John   273
Stuart, Henry Thomas   278
Vaughan Williams, Ralph   124,
                                270, 310

INDEX OF COLLECTIONS

Ancient and Modern, *see* Hymns Ancient and Modern
Ausserlesene Catholische Geistliche Kirchengesäng   289
Bridges, Robert, see Yattendon Hymnal, The
Darmstadt Songbook   295
Day, John, see Day's Psalter
Day's Psalter (1562)   257–259, 261, 264
Dearmer, Percy, see English Hymnal, The; (see also under Composers)
Divine and Moral Songs for the Use of Children (Isaac Watts)   26
Elliot, Charlotte, see Hours of Sorrow Cheered and Comforted;
  Invalid's Hymn Book, The
English Country Songs (Miss L. Broadwood)   315
English Hymnal, The (Percy Dearmer)   270, 292, 310
Gospel Magazine   204
Hours of Sorrow Cheered and Comforted (Charlotte Elliot)   107
Hymns Ancient and Modern (John Ellerton)   14, 123, 134, 155,
                              230, 241, 273, 274, 300, 314
Hymns and Songs of the Church (George Wither)   258–260, 263
Hymns for Little Children (C. F. Alexander)   101
Invalid's Hymn Book, The (Charlotte Elliot)   107
Lichfield (Edward Cooper)   214
Lyra Catholica (Edward Caswell)   94
Lyra Germanica (Catherine Winkworth)   194
Methodist Hymn Book   162, 235
Metrical Psalter (Tate and Brady)   159–161
New English Hymnal   14
Olney Hymns   33, 57, 211–212
Pilgrim's Progress (John Bunyan)   155
Professor at the Breakfast Table, The (Oliver
  Wendell Holmes)   179–180
Psalms of David, Imitated in the Language of the New Testament,
  The (Isaac Watts)   25
Sacred Hymns for the Children of God in the Days of Their
  Pilgrimage (John Cennick)   205
Sacred Songs and Solos (Sankey and Moody)   74, 187
Sarum Primer   275
Selection of Psalms and Hymns (Cotterill and Montgomery)   65
Songs of Praise   270, 292

Songs of Zion to Cheer and Guide Pilgrims on Their Way to
  the New Jerusalem (Robert Murray McCheyne)   220
Sternhold and Hopkins, see Day's Psalter
Tate and Brady, see Metrical Psalter
The Christian Year (John Keble)   113–116
The Temple (George Herbert)   152
The Young Man's Meditation (Samuel Crossman)   153
Verses for the Sick and Lonely (Caroline Noel)   109
Wither, George, see Hymns and Songs of the Church
Yattendon Hymnal, The (Robert Bridges)   165–168, 169–178